The Many Faces of
School–University Collaboration

The Many Faces of School–University Collaboration

Characteristics of Successful Partnerships

Ruth Ravid
Marianne G. Handler

2001
Teacher Ideas Press
Libraries Unlimited
A Division of Greenwood Publishing Group, Inc.
Englewood, Colorado

TEACHER IDEAS PRESS
Libraries Unlimited
A Division of Greenwood Publishing Group, Inc.
P.O. Box 6633
Englewood, CO 80155-6633
1-800-237-6124
www.lu.com/tips

Library of Congress Cataloging-in-Publication Data

The many faces of school-university collaboration : characteristics of successful
    partnerships / [edited by] Ruth Ravid, Marianne G. Handler.
        p. cm.
    Includes bibliographical references and index.
    ISBN 1-56308-792-8 (pbk.)
    1. College school cooperation--Case studies. I. Ravid, Ruth. II. Handler, Marianne G.

LB2331.53 .M37 2001
378.1'03--dc21

                                                                            2001033304

To my parents,
Menachem and Devora Doron,
whose encouragement and support sustained
me on my life's journey
                                    —Ruth Ravid

This book is dedicated to the memory of my parents,
Sally and Irving Greenfield,
who taught me that learning was important
                                    —Marianne Handler

Contents

MODEL II: Consultation

MODEL III: One-to-One Collaborations

About the Contributors

Preface

School–university collaboration, in its many forms, has become an important part of the educational scene. Many recent requests for grant proposals have dictated that partnerships include some combination of stakeholders in the development of the grant. Frequently, these partnerships include K–12 schools and a college of education as partners. These partnerships have been in existence for some time, and there is a great deal of literature describing projects undertaken within this format. Although reports about these partnerships usually include a detailed description of the goals and settings of these projects, these individual and separate reports often lack analysis of the reasons for their success or failure. There clearly is a need for more information about what makes certain projects succeed while others fail, as well as information about the dynamics of collaboration. This book is intended to fill the gap and provide this needed information. Although the context itself certainly impacts the collaborative relationship, there are some common factors that emerge across projects and partnerships. The reader will find that the key elements emerging from the authors' stories provide guideposts for those just beginning the collaborative process. The book describes a range of models and options available to those contemplating school–university collaboration, a description that includes the advantages and disadvantages of each model. Perspectives of educators from the United States, Canada, and Australia are included in this book.

Background

The Many Faces of School–University Collaboration is designed to help educators entering into these collaborative relationships have a clearer picture of conditions that seem to drive successful partnerships. The audience we address includes students in educational leadership programs striving to become principals and superintendents, as well as individuals who are already in these roles. It is also intended to serve the needs of university partners who can consider the various models highlighted in the book as they enter their own upcoming partnerships. Those who sponsor and award grants for the increasing number of school–university collaborations also will find the book a rich source of information. Last but not least, the book is also geared toward classroom teachers who become partners in collaborative relationships and may find themselves in such a role for the first time.

As veteran teachers of K–12 students, as well as teachers of college students in preservice and in-service teacher education programs, we have realized that most practitioners are not likely to study their own practice if they have to do it on their own, without any additional encouragement and support. An overwhelming majority of practitioners, for obvious reasons, feel that their first responsibility is to teach children. Only a small number of practitioners in schools all over the world are undertaking a systematic approach to classroom inquiry. Only selected few individuals have the time, the desire, the support, and the knowledge necessary to carry out a research study in their own practice. We hope this book will help them as they move into these new leadership roles.

Navigating the Book

This book is divided into two sections. The first, "Introduction," includes three chapters that provide the framework for the remainder of the book. The first chapter, "Models of School–University Collaboration," provides a description of the models represented in the book with brief sketches of the projects under each model. The second chapter focuses on the process of collaboration. This chapter, "The Process of Change in School–University Collaboration," and the third chapter, "Dancing in the Dark? Learning More about What Makes Partnerships Work," present a comprehensive review of the literature on the topic of school–university collaboration.

The second section, "Collaboration Through the Eyes of the Partners," includes a discussion of the collaborative process as told by various partners. The chapters in this section were put together under the specific collaboration model that the partners embraced and used. Each model is discussed in at least one chapter, written collaboratively by school–university educators, each providing their own unique points of view. Finally, "About the Contributors" provides brief professional biographies about the editors and authors who wrote the chapters in this book.

Section I
Introduction

Chapter

Models of School–University Collaboration

Marianne Handler and Ruth Ravid

A variety of school–university collaboration models can be found in books, papers, articles, and conference presentations from the last 20 years. The collaborative relationship may be between institutions (i.e., a school and a university) or between individuals from schools and universities. The school–university collaboration models that emerge from the literature are the following:

1. **Collaboration between a university and professional development school (PDS)**—The main purpose of this model of collaboration is preservice teacher training, although the schools also can serve other purposes, such as providing a location for students' fieldwork and fellowship training. The relationship between the school and the university may be formal or informal.

2. **Consultation**—In the consultation model, one or several university faculty members work with one or several teachers. The faculty members, in the role of consultant, provide resources and expertise to the teachers. Other stakeholders may also join as collaborators. The main purpose of this partnership is improvement of instruction and teachers' professional development.

3. **One-to-one collaborations**—A university faculty member works as equal partner with a school-based practitioner in this model. Both partners plan and carry out the research project.

4. **Multiple collaboration project teams under one umbrella organization acting as the facilitator**—In this model, each project team is composed of university-based and school-based educators, as well as other possible stakeholders. Collaboration takes place within each team, and across teams.

Following is a brief description of each model. This description includes a discussion of how the collaboration is initiated, the factors that contribute to the continuation of collaboration, the roles of individuals in maintaining the relationships, relationships among and between collaborators, and some of the factors that contribute to success and failure of the collaborative relationships. Subsequent to the description we have included a short description of the book chapters that fall under the particular model described.

The PDS Model

The collaboration is between a university and PDS for the main purpose of pre-service teacher training, although the schools also can serve other purposes, such as providing a location for students' fieldwork and fellowship training. The relationship between the school and the university may be formal or informal.

In this model, a university works with one or more schools or districts. The schools become the site for preparing new teachers. A well-defined structure is created. Usually the student teachers are placed, for at least one semester, in the classroom of cooperating teachers, who are asked to mentor and then assign a grade to the student. Supervisors, usually university faculty, oversee the process and visit each student teacher several times during the term to observe and monitor. Cooperating teachers usually get vouchers to take free courses at the university, and their school benefits from the collaboration.

Individuals or administrators at each institution (school/district and university) may initiate the collaboration in this model. Each of the partners enters the partnership for different reasons, and naturally the gains and benefits obtained by each partner are different. For the schools that serve as PDS sites, the main benefits of participating in the collaboration are the professional-growth opportunities for the teachers and other staff members, the availability of "an extra pair of eyes and hands" in the classroom, the prestige of being associated with a university, and the possibility of getting funds from the state or other sources. Usually universities enter PDS relationships to create a site for their preservice students to participate in the practicum experience and in their student teaching. In addition, university faculty gain access to schools for the purpose of maintaining close contact with the day-to-day life and practice of education and schooling. Faculty members also can use PDS sites to carry out research projects.

A PDS relationship requires the interest and support of the administrators at both the school and university level. Nonetheless, a personal connection between individuals in both institutions also can contribute to initiating and maintaining these relationships.

Often, universities and schools or school districts work collaboratively to train student teachers, to mentor new teachers for a whole year, or as sites for fieldwork and internships. This relationship is less formal than the PDS relationship. For a variety of reasons, some universities and schools are unable or unwilling to enter into a formal

PDS relationship; nevertheless, student teachers are placed in these schools in classrooms of cooperating teachers. Because every preservice teacher-education program, at the graduate and undergraduate levels, needs to find sites for its students to do their student teaching, the two institutions can still work together, and the school can still serve as a site for student teachers when formal PDS relationships are not possible. In many parts of the country, schools or school districts have developed long-term relationships with a local university to provide a site for student fieldwork and to place and train that university's interns in programs (such as school psychology) that include an internship component. Other schools open their doors and welcome preservice and in-service students to conduct observations, carry out class projects, and collect data for research projects.

Schools and universities also work collaboratively to place and mentor graduates of preservice teacher education programs. For example, master teachers in collaborating schools can serve as mentors to new teachers as part of programs that are created and monitored by a partner university.

Overview

The first three chapters in this model (Chapters 4, 5, and 6) describe formal university–PDS collaborations created through a formalized relationship between the university and the school district. Chapters 7 and 8 describe collaborations that emphasize preservice training, but those collaborations were not formally negotiated between the university and the school district.

Chapter 4: Recipes for Professional Development Schools: A Metaphor for Collaboration (P. Gates-Duffield and C. Stark)

Gates-Duffield and Stark describe a multiyear collaborative relationship that began in an atmosphere of tension, mistrust, and resistance. This partnership between a faculty member and a principal resulted in a strong relationship with teachers. Their story has important implications for those involved in school–university partnerships.

Chapter 5: Learning Connections: Working toward a Shared Vision (R. Hasslen, N. Bacharach, J. Rotto, and J. Fribley)

The development of collaborative relationships between two elementary schools and a university unfolds in the chapter about the Learning Connections Lab. The authors, representing all three partner institutions, present their own perceptions and unique views as they describe the successes and challenges of establishing the partnerships, one of which was successful, while the other experienced difficulties.

Chapter 6: A Collaborative Journey: Study and Inquiry in a Professional Development Middle School (C. Rafferty and M. Leinenbach)

The journey of two educators, Rafferty and Leinenbach, representing a school of education and a local PDS, unfolds in this chapter. The collaboration, which started in a portfolio study group, has continued and evolved as the teacher partner pursued the National Board Certification and later joined the university as a "teacher in residence."

Chapter 7. Blending Voices, Blending Lives: The Story of a New-Age Collaboration with Literature and E-mail (S. Steffel and C. Steltenkamp)

The authors of this chapter are a university faculty, Steffel, and a high school teacher, Steltenkamp. They present their story of three-way "virtual collaboration," in which they corresponded via e-mail. The authors also describe similar collaboration between their respective students (students from a preservice teacher education program and from high school English classes) who used e-mail to correspond with each other about literature.

Chapter 8: Our "Stealth PDS": An Undetected Professional Development School Relationship (A. Sosin and A. Parham)

This chapter describes a long-standing collaboration between a school of education and a nearby inner-city public school. The authors, Sosin and Parham, who have worked together for more than 10 years, relate how varying personalities, pressures, and opportunities, have influenced the quality and intensity of the partnership of the two institutions and of the authors.

The Consultation Model

In the consultation model, one or several university faculty members work with one or several teachers. The faculty members, in the role of consultant, provide resources and expertise to the teachers. Other stakeholders may also join as collaborators. The main purpose is improvement of instruction and teachers' professional development.

In this model, one faculty member works with one or several teachers or other practitioners. This is an example of an expert model, whereby the university researcher is considered to have expertise in a certain area or subject and is helping the teacher (or a group of teachers) gain and learn new skills or knowledge. For example, the university faculty may advise teachers or the school media coordinator on how to integrate technology into their teaching. Or, the university faculty may guide teachers and introduce them to innovative ways to address and resolve various issues related to inclusion. Other reasons for engaging a university professor to consult with a school may be to offer a professional development workshop or series of workshops on a given topic, such as the implications of current brain research on classroom instruction. All these examples share a common characteristic: The university representative is viewed as the expert, and the school staff's role is to learn something new to improve their practice. The knowledge flows in one direction, "top down," from the university professor, who has the knowledge, to the school practitioner, who is there to learn, grow, and benefit from the experience and expertise of the professor. The relationship sometimes levels out as the collaboration grows.

Another type of school–university interaction may occur when a university faculty member is interested in piloting a new curriculum or a new test in a school. The schoolteachers may modify their teaching to pilot the new curriculum, for example, and may be consulted and asked for their feedback. This model of collaboration may be better defined as "cooperation," rather than as true collaborative partnership. The power hierarchy is quite clear to all participants.

Occasionally, schools or school districts seek a partnership with a local university as a result of a mandate issued by a school district or the state administration. For example, a school on academic probation may be asked to collaborate with a local university to design and carry out a plan for improving students' performance. Administrators in the two institutions (school and university) may be involved in assigning faculty and staff to the collaborative project and may be further involved in planning and carrying out the project. Quite often, however, the involvement of the university administrator(s) is limited to assigning faculty members at the initial stages when the collaboration is planned. In contrast, the school administrators are likely to remain more actively involved throughout the collaboration. These types of collaborations, which are initiated in response to a mandate or external funding, usually are monitored more closely and involve formal plans, periodic progress reports, and detailed documentation of the collaborative process.

Overview

Four chapters fall under this model, each telling a different and unique story about the consultation model.

Chapter 9: Sailing the Ship: A Collaborative Journey (J. A. Robb and D. Cronin)

This collaboration grew out of a vision shared by a university faculty member, who had been supervising student teachers, and a junior high school principal to use issues of reform-based education as a road to professional development in the area of math and science. Robb and Cronin tell a story of personal growth and change for all the participants in the project.

Chapter 10: Developing School–University Intellectual Partnerships: The National Humanities Center's Teacher Leadership for Professional Development Program (R. Schramm, W. E. Bickel, R. H. McNelis, and C. K. Pine)

An initiative by the National Humanities Center to test, refine, and disseminate an innovative approach to teachers' professional development is outlined in this chapter by Schramm, Bickel, McNelis, and Pine. Based on an eight-year evaluation, the authors describe this alternative model that was developed and the collaboration among teachers, university faculty, and the center's own staff.

Chapter 11: From Practicum Improvement to School Improvement: A Developing Partnership (C. Sinclair and L. Perre)

In Australia, as elsewhere, there is frequent misunderstanding between university-based and school-based educators of their shared role in the professional preparation of teacher candidates. Sinclair and Perre describe the development of a learning community in which the goal was to better prepare teachers and the struggle in developing the necessary collaborative relationships. Two models emerged from the project, one a policy development/innovation model and the other a model for developing partnerships.

> *Chapter 12: Finding Keys to Educational Improvement Through*
> *Collaborative Work (K. Wiburg and Y. Lozano)*

The Wiburg and Lozano chapter illustrates what happens in a collaborative relationship as it moves from its original goals, a focus on integrating technology into literacy teaching, to a new focus on systemic reform. The authors discuss the importance of collaborative leadership in a successful relationship. The chapter includes a helpful table that provides a frame for looking at the principles of restructured schools with value added by the principles of successful collaboration.

One-to-One Collaborations Model

In one-to-one collaborations, a university faculty member works as an equal partner with a school-based practitioner. Both partners plan and carry out the research project.

This model has the greatest potential for true collaboration between and among the partners. In this model, a university researcher, usually a faculty member, collaborates with a school-based practitioner, usually a teacher. Each of the partners is likely to have different reasons and expectations for undertaking this partnership. In most cases, the partners may start to work together because they know each other, or they may start their collaboration to achieve a specific purpose, such as trying a new teaching technique or pilot testing a new instrument developed by the university professor. Quite often, personal relationships and friendships develop as a result of working together, and these relationships contribute to, or even become the main reason for, the partners' continued work together over a long period of time. For the faculty member, this partnership affords access to a classroom, whereas the teacher partner sees this mostly as an opportunity for professional growth and fulfillment. The camaraderie that usually develops over time between the partners is the glue that holds them together through some potentially difficult times. This friendship is also likely to help them overcome conflicts, disagreements, and tension that may be caused by different personality styles, lack of time, and a host of other potential difficulties and pressures. In some cases, these one-to-one partnerships may start as the consultation model, but evolve, develop, and change over time. The school-based practitioners often assume more and more responsibility and may decide to take additional courses at the university or to complete an advanced degree. In many cases, the school partners gain confidence and skills by conducting research and writing reports. The faculty member is likely to play the role of a mentor and encourage the school partner to grow, develop, and gain new knowledge and skills.

Overview

The four chapters under this model describe multiyear partnerships. Although the stories differ, they all focus on the authors' collaborations and friendships.

> *Chapter 13: The Dialectic Nature of Research Collaborations: The*
> *Relational Literacy Curriculum (R. Freedman and D. Salmon)*

The six-year collaboration described in this chapter was between Freedman, a school-based practitioner, and Salmon, a university faculty member, each of whom had different areas of interest and expertise. Through a shared and equal partnership, the authors developed, implemented, and evaluated the Relational Literacy curriculum, which is designed to address both the individual and classroom social development needs of elementary school children.

Chapter 14: Working Together: A Successful One-to-One Collaboration (J. Kornfeld and G. Leyden)

This chapter describes a collaboration that grew out of parent helper–teacher relationship and moved into an informal one-to-one partnership. A shared interest in literacy, drama, and African American history and literature undergirded this evolving relationship. According to Kornfeld and Leyden, the attributes of a successful collaboration offer a framework for engaging in ongoing self-examination.

Chapter 15: The Angst, Ecstasy, and Opportunities of Collaborative Inquiry (C. Lafleur and J. MacFadden)

Lafleur and MacFadden share a unique collaboration, that between a school-district researcher and a classroom teacher. Lafleur, the school district researcher, served in a role similar to that of a university partner as described in other chapters. It is the authors' shared belief in action research as a road toward improving student learning that has maintained this fifteen-year collaboration. Their story shows us that the issues of their collaboration are similar to those that can be found in many other school–university collaborative relationships.

Chapter 16: A School–University Partnership: A Commitment to Collaboration and Professional Renewal (L. Vozzo and B. Bober)

The Vozzo and Bober chapter tells the story of collaboration that grew out of a principal's application for and awarding of an Innovative Links grant for professional development. In working toward developing best practices, the chapter illustrates how the teachers and the researchers formalized and articulated the process of action research—the teachers on their practice, the researchers on their developing collaboration.

The Umbrella Model

In this model, one umbrella organization acts as facilitator to each of the project teams, which are composed of university-based and school-based educators, as well as other possible stakeholders. Collaboration takes place within each team and across teams.

This variation of the one-to-one model can be seen in some places, usually school districts, where several school–university one-to-one partnerships are brought together under one roof or center. The center's directors recruit and provide support to the collaborators. Several collaborative projects are conducted simultaneously under the auspices of the center. As in one-to-one collaboration, the agreed-on agenda, or topics to be investigated, may be determined mutually by all partners or by any one of the partners. Similarly, the partners plan and carry out all the activities connected with their research project; however, not all partners necessarily have to participate in all activities. The main difference between these two models is that in the umbrella model, there is another layer of support and collaboration. In addition to the collaboration between the school–university partners on each team, the multiple teams of partners also help and support each other. This can add motivation, as well as provide advice and collegial support, which are extended to each team from the other teams of educators.

Many school districts today have multiple relationships, formal and informal, with colleges of education. Those districts also may work with other partner agencies. Someone in each of these districts (or perhaps several people) must have oversight responsibility for all the ongoing projects, which include maintaining the records and paperwork, providing support, solving relationship problems as they occur, and making sure all connections are maintained. These oversight responsibilities are similar to those that center directors undertake.

Overview

This chapter, written by the book's coeditors, describes their experience in co-directing an umbrella organization.

Chapter 17: The Center for Collaborative Research at National-Louis University (M. Handler and R. Ravid)

Handler and Ravid describe their five-year experience as co-directors of the Center for Collaborative Research (CeCoR), which has brought together school-based practitioners and university faculty to design and carry out research projects on topics mutually selected by the partners. The center functioned as an umbrella organization to support the work of its teams. Collaboration took place on several levels. The members of each team collaborated with each other while planning and carrying out the research project. Team members also supported and collaborated with other team members. Additionally, the center's two co-directors collaborated with all team members and with each other.

Chapter 2

The Process of Change in School–University Collaboration

Judith J. Slater

School–university collaboration is a process that occurs over time. It is the culmination of sustained interactions between people who are representatives of their parent organization's structure and function. Collaboration, if it is successful, should create systemic change within each of the parent organizations so that all future interactions with those on the outside take on new qualities of mutuality and cooperation. In effect, this is a change effort that overcomes the limitations of *habitus,* or traditional ways of operation among people within a social structure. Real change has to include changes in people. This chapter discusses first how difficult such transitions are for organizations and the people in them. The chapter then explores the conditions necessary for successful collaborations.

Practices within schools and organizations can be understood clearly through the construct of habitus as defined by Bourdieu (1993). Habitus refers to the self-perpetuating dynamic that mediates between structure and praxis, making it difficult to bring about change both at the personal level and in large bureaucratic structures such as schools. Habitus imposes and inculcates an arbitrary set of power structures that is fully achieved through pedagogic work environments (Bourdieu & Passeron, 1977, p. 31). Symbolic interactions impose conditions through which the habitus is inculcated, like the transmission of cultural norms in traditional societies (p. 32). This analysis

11

questions why ventures such as collaboration and partnerships between schools and institutions of higher education falter, why people resist change, and what conditions are necessary in human systems to effect systematic planned change. Resistance to change results in cultural and social reproduction of the status quo and an ideology of acceptance that is embedded in the habitus of operation of the organization.

Using qualitative participant observational criticism and critique methodology (Bourdieu, 1984; Eisner, 1994) as a frame of reference, this analysis explores the idea that modification and transformation require personal revolutions of thought coupled with an atmosphere of belief and value change. Old notions of accommodation, adaptation, and assimilation of the new are no longer viable alternatives and remain a sedentary response to contemporary problems faced by schools and those who work in them. What I propose is a cognitively based construct of competence as exhibited by a sense of alignment between the environment, behaviors, and strategies that individuals use to mediate their world of work and those beliefs and values that they hold about their participation in that world. These factors lead to a clear sense of identity and accomplishment and, therefore, to a strong sense of self-efficacy that supports innovation and change.

Why must habitus be overcome? If we accept the notion of community, that organizations exist within a larger interconnected relationship, then habitus is a formidable impediment to movement that could make responsible future planning possible. Public schools and universities must be committed to working together to help solve societal problems by producing students who can make a difference in their world. The same old solutions for the same old problems arise again and again, as each old solution is reborn and the participants are bound by the habitus that limits their movement and imagination to create something new that is more responsive to identified needs.

Habitus in Organizations

I have spent several years working on a project that concerns the elements of collaboration, that of collaboration between a public school system and a university to design, create, and build a public elementary school on a university campus. The project is about change, personal change and change within organizations; in reality, it is about beliefs held by ordinary people concerning their daily lives, how they see themselves, and how they respond to the forces that push and tug at them. Some of these forces are planned. Others seem arbitrary and defy rationalization, but they nevertheless affect the everyday lives of the participants. What differs is each individual's interpretation and understanding of those forces that produces his or her behavior.

What I investigated were the conditions of work that may be antithetical to participants' sense of who they are (their identity, beliefs, and values) and what their competencies (strategies and skills) are. There is a similarity of participant responses to the overwhelming milieu of the habitus of the work environment and ethic in which they operate. Bourdieu (1993) was interested in the socially constructed mental structures that generate practice. The habitus, or field, accounts for the creative, active, inventive capacities of people within an organizing structure (p. 5). There is no universal, unified mind; it is different for each individual. Adaptation and practice that keep people in line with the commonplace modes of operation are not conscious; there is an unconscious compliance with engendered practices when one lives, works, and functions in a particular environment as evidenced by commonality of extant behavior. Slater (1996) argued, "This is not restrictive since there is a real process whereby newcomers to an organization learn to behave in ways that are congruent to the organizational goals. They come to establish beliefs about the organization and what is appropriate behavior within that organization wholeheartedly. The production and ultimate reproduction of these behaviors become the norms of operation" (p. 18).

The process of inculcation endows certain behaviors and certain knowledge as legitimate at the expense of other knowledge that may be transformative. Know-how becomes a duplication of what already exists, and the market allows for only the symbolic products that duplicate process. The levels of the habitus in organizations are layered: There is the center core of traditional bureaucratic structure, and around that core are the layers of symbolic and real dispositions and behaviors that perpetuate and protect that core. The more layers there are, the more irreversible is the disposition of the organization to perpetuate the status quo and the harder it is to get to the core to make fundamental structural changes in the modes of operation; it is harder still to change the core beliefs.

Thus, the bureaucratic responses are but one part of the habitus enacted. The other is the personal responses of the players in that structure who lose their own identity, giving it over to the expectations of a nonhuman entity called the "organization." This clouds both the intrapersonal response and the circumstantial interpersonal response by creating an environment, an expected environment, that is characterized by acceptance of the social order. Learning for a newcomer becomes irreversible as the layers are penetrated and the media message of the organization is transmitted loudly and clearly to the initiate. Habitus creates the receptivity and the assimilation of the messages of the total institution at each layer, thus aiding the deculturation and reculturation of participants, leading to the reproduction of the preexisting habitus (Bourdieu & Passeron, 1977, pp. 43–44). It is the active quest to understand the code of the primary habitus that speeds up the transmission process itself. Instead of looking with an eye toward improvement, the participants look with an eye toward conformity and personal acceptance into the milieu.

In essence, this analysis talks to the fundamental and systemic qualities of change and the overcoming of organizational habitus. I accomplish this by discussing generally the necessary requirements for overcoming the habitus that impedes movement toward change and makes people settle into their current state, thus consecrating (Bourdieu's term) it with the acceptable social order. Similarly, analyzing a college of education and public school collaboration necessitates a description of those factors that serve to impede understanding between and among the participants. These factors are manifestations of the construct of habitus.

Consequences of Habitus

The question of change becomes that of overcoming the power embedded in the legitimacy of the organizational habitus. How to evolve a new mode of operation that transcends the traditional is the task. For the individual, this requires cognitive efforts to align the environment, behaviors, and strategies used to mediate the world of work with personal identity, beliefs, and values held about participation in a particular world. Perpetuation of the past is controlled by the organizing structures that form the familiarity of response. This constant exertion provides continuity and regularity in social practice or in the responses of members of organizations or in the work environment. The structures regulate and transform behavior so that it fits in with the objectivist world. Bourdieu and Passeron (1977) found that "every power which manages to impose meanings and to impose them as legitimate by concealing the power relations which are the basis of its force, adds its own specifically symbolic force to those power relations" (p. vi). Those ruling ideas are generated by the ruling class and are culturally arbitrary and based on power. Power of the market is maintained by positive and negative sanctions, performance evaluations, reinforcing what is deemed acceptable behavior, discouraging unacceptable behavior, and conferring valuelessness on behaviors that are out of the realm of acceptability (Bourdieu, 1984). It is power that causes the reproduction of the culture because culture in itself is made up of arbitrary choices conferred upon by leaders through abeyance by followers that reproduces the power relationships. This power is not just political but instead is about control; that control can be on a personal level or on a cultural level in the larger society.

The power of the organizing structures is seen in the psychological construct of competence. The regard one holds for oneself as a person, or the competence ascribed by the individual to him or herself, is a product of complex judgments resulting from repeated interactions with the environment. Internal and external factors combine into a degree of competence (Harter, 1990, p. 70). How people are judged is an important factor in how they perform and how they feel about their own capabilities. To overcome low feelings of competence, self-efficacy, or self-worth, cognitive strategies tend toward self-created "patterns of appraisal, retrospection, and effort that translate into one's goals and beliefs and actions" (Sternberg & Kolligan, 1990, p. xiii). Often capabilities are impeded by a lower personal sense of competence that builds up over time. If conflict arises between behaviors, beliefs, and capabilities, people tend to retain their beliefs at all costs to legitimize their own lives (Bandura, 1990). This is the way people gain control; it accounts for the way they explain the world to themselves and others and justifies their actions in particular environments. It cements the habitus and prevents a questioning of those configuring structures that produced it in the first place.

The habitus of the educational system is bound in its structure and function to produce and self-reproduce institutional conditions necessary to inculcate workers and their charges into the arbitrary cultural milieu (Bourdieu & Passeron, 1977, p. 54). This also can be seen in universities. For a collaboration to occur between these two institutional types, a transorganizational structure needs to be established that transcends the habitus of the organizations. Collaborations exist at the end of a continuum of interorganizational arrangements, and their sustainability over time requires an evolution to a new understanding of the limitations of the habitus of each parent organization. (For a full description of the process, see Slater, 1996.)

How can the above habitus be broken? Can the collective consciousness of an organization be changed to identify with new symbols and signs, values, and beliefs? Can persons be enabled to see and hear in ways that formulate questions of self, of identity, of purpose and actions and behaviors that are appropriate for the future of the organization? What are the authentic actions that help align these people and their organizations to the work that lies ahead, so that they do not continue to look back? The focus should be on the individuals who have shifting, multiple, and overlapping connections to each other. People give themselves, their essence, over to the habitus of the organization, often to the illusion that the institution is responsive and interdependent with the people who work there. There is much evidence to support this.

To operationalize the transition from individual organizations working in parallel with their own habitus to organizations that learn to integrate operations and transform their life of work into community-oriented collaborations, I have hypothesized three Zones of Organizational Involvement (see Figure 2.1).

Figure 2.1. Zones of organizational involvement.

ZONE I: Separate Operating Structures of Parent Organizations

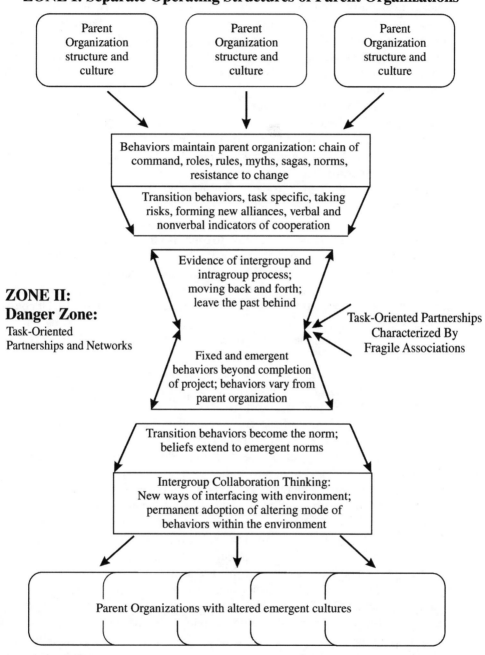

Parent Organization structure and culture	Parent Organization structure and culture	Parent Organization structure and culture

Behaviors maintain parent organization: chain of command, roles, rules, myths, sagas, norms, resistance to change

Transition behaviors, task specific, taking risks, forming new alliances, verbal and nonverbal indicators of cooperation

ZONE II:
Danger Zone:
Task-Oriented
Partnerships and Networks

Evidence of intergroup and intragroup process; moving back and forth; leave the past behind

Task-Oriented Partnerships Characterized By Fragile Associations

Fixed and emergent behaviors beyond completion of project; behaviors vary from parent organization

Transition behaviors become the norm; beliefs extend to emergent norms

Intergroup Collaboration Thinking: New ways of interfacing with environment; permanent adoption of altering mode of behaviors within the environment

Parent Organizations with altered emergent cultures

ZONE III: Collaboration
Integrated Emergent
Learning Organizations

Optimal movement and direction of collaborative; integrated operations; thinking like a community; problem solving; future-oriented learning organizations

Zone I depicts the "separate structures" of each organization, each with its own tasks, charges, concerns and way of operating. At the first level of interacting, each sends representatives to work together on a project. The underlying habitus is that individuals maintain the parent organization's behaviors that are characteristic of their understanding of work. Cultural maintenance is primary and resistance to change and adherence to cultural norms is maintained. If this interaction persists, over time a second level of interaction occurs, and there appears to be transition behaviors that are task specific but require interactions that diverge from that of the parent organization. These come into play to get the task or job done. Here, participants take risks, form new alliances with persons from other parent organizations, and make formal and informal connections that indicate movement toward the transorganizational behaviors.

Zone II is the "danger zone" in which task orientation is toward completion of the project. Here, intergroup and intragroup processes emerge in ways that clearly depart operationally from the parent organization. Above the "danger zone" is an area where individuals move back and forth between their traditional way of working and thinking and the emergent mixture of new ways to work together. Below the "danger zone" are the partnerships and networks that begin to establish their own legitimacy of emergent behaviors to be responsive to each new task. This is a virtual structure at this point because it is not perceived by the outside world as fully formed. Each parent organization still has expectations for their workers, but tradition is altered by successful new ways of working that are impacting on the beliefs of the individuals involved. Of course, this is always in motion, forward toward Zone III and backward toward Zone I. It is a state of flux, not firmly part of the identity of the culture that is characteristic of the collaborative it could become.

Zone III is the "collaboration" area. It has two stages. The first is the transition stage where the behaviors emerging in the "danger zone" become the norm when participants have a task or project on which to work. Beliefs are embedded, and behaviors reflect the emergent norms of the group more than those of the parent organization. The second stage under Zone III is characterized by new ways of interfacing with the larger community by adoption of a permanent mode of behavior with the environment that is collaborative. The group now thinks collaboratively, and true intergroup problem solving is the norm. Behaviors in Zone III alter the operations of the parent organization by causing them to think collaboratively. Their boundaries are no longer separate entities but overlapping structures that deal with the world synergistically. These become true learning organizations that think as a community, problem solve together, are future oriented, and integrate operations (Slater, 1996, pp. 133–136).

Change as a process has become the new social order. Happily, when this change enables a belief, a collective consciousness that is optimistic, it creates a language of optimism (Botstein, 1997, p. 72). Habitus breaking requires a discourse to make public and explicit the illegitimacy of the old dialogue. The logic of the old must be found faulty and exposed, otherwise it will remain as basic principles on which the habitus of the institution rests. With this comes a vicarious authority to reproduce the artifacts, even if they are no longer legitimate. This language can be one of limitation of choices (by not allowing certain discourse to occur by not legitimizing it), or it can be one that is democratic and open. The prior language consecrates the way people act, their positions, and their authority. It proves that the authorities are truly masters of their realm.

Followers are left without participation in the discourse, only to be "good soldiers," to follow the duty they have been assigned but for which they have not had the opportunity to participate in the forming or revising. Public school systems and universities are full of transposable, durable dispositions that support the status quo. The system itself creates connections that unite structures and practices through habitus that define the validity of actions and policies that in turn define the organization and perpetuate it over time. The longer this goes on, the stronger those very structures already in place become, limiting the chances for participants to change themselves, let alone the organization. The artifacts of such a system have been studied by the critical theorists and the reconceptualists (e.g., Michael Apple, William Pinar, Joe Kincheloe). Why hasn't the exposure to truths been successful in making change? Perhaps the truth is not fully revealed: By studying the textbooks, the selection process, and the stories of the individual, we have glossed over the structural impediments to change that are so powerful, they can sustain against the criticism. Curatives do not work because they do not create systemic change. What is needed is a durable mass of people who are convinced, as the disinherited class, that they can change their education and their future, and then they may be able to participate in a democratic interchange of authentic dialogue (Freire, 1970).

Knowing when the durable mass reaches a critical size is important as an indication to others that the time has come to participate, question, and dialogue. This "feel for the game" is the practical sense that makes people act and react in certain ways in specific situations that cannot always be calculated and are more than mere responses to the observance of rules. The durable mass must overcome this internalized set of dispositions, which generates practices and perceptions that require a process of inculcation, often beginning in childhood, and become second nature as they elicit unconscious responses to the demands and changing field of everyday life. There is much to overcome.

The agent of cultural reproduction—the determiner of taste, of appropriate behavior, of the dispositions throughout life that are transposable to situations removed from the learning environment—is the result of the acculturation process. Everyone attends school. We understand the norms of behavior and the expectations of school. The overt teachings—and more important, the covert teachings—become internalized into our beliefs and dispositions, and they are tied to what appears to be effective practice. Why are schools so resistant to change? The very thing we are trying to reform is the structure that produced our dispositions and generated our practices in the first place. School is the configuring structure and education is the social situation in which the habitus is formed. It creates the rules, regulations, and laws by which we function in society, and changes in that structure are often superficial or resisted (Slater, 1996, pp. 18–19).

These durable predispositions last throughout a lifetime, are transposable across situations, and form the configuring structures of different occupations as well as the unique responses men and women have to similar situations. They provide the blueprint for generative practices that the individual uses to adjust to specific situations.

The Breaking of Habitus

I have an interest in why people persist in the habitus of everyday life, in the habitus of work environments, and in the beliefs they hold about best practice. Pertinent to this is the concept of opacity. An example of this phenomenon exists in Israel concerning nuclear weapons. The nuclear capabilities of Israel are not to be discussed in the open by its citizenry, even though there is a tacit understanding that the capability exists to deter attacks and maintain a position of power in the Middle East. This is a cultural and normative phenomenon aided by a pact of silence about its existence. Since the 1950s and 1960s "opacity has become embedded in Israel's national security culture—in the values, attitudes, and norms passed on to those who are initiated into the culture" (Cohen, 1998, p. 343). Absence from the public agenda causes a shift in the focus of dialogue from the real issues to those of peripheral or tangential themes. This also results in a lack of democratic debate about issues; democratic dialogue persists about standards and failures, but there is none about the central opaque theme or whether the policy itself or the practice—the habitus—needs to be changed.

What are the consequences of breaking such codes of silence, such habitus, in schools and universities? First, there must be a platform for the disclosure. This comes with great risks. Second, there are jobs at stake, and there is tremendous effort to change the way people operate, let alone think. Opacity allows the delaying of decision making about identity, and thus it limits personal action by allowing the perpetuation of personal beliefs that have long outlived their usefulness. Hence, progress is deterred. Opacity makes us impervious to the facts, traumatizing the ability to plan long term. Habitus becomes a way of life in a society that is not transparent. The culture of belief becomes ingrained and accepted, and this is too difficult to change because it goes to the core of one's being, to the core values that define who each person is in work and in life.

Individual responses to situations are structured by relationships between positions of people in the particular field. For example, when a principal in one school changes, the field becomes confused until the new individual adapts his or her field to the created social situation; when a new superintendent comes or a new program is initiated, the response is still relational to the old. Evolution is extremely slow; associations consecrate responses because these serve primarily as maintenance of a social system that functions for the reproduction of the structural culture that makes each school system look like and act like all others (Slater, 1996).

There is always competition in the field for control, for position, for resources, or for personal or special interest. Position and responsibility, power and control were the impetus to participate fully for some of the people I interviewed in schools and universities as part of the data gathering for an analysis of a collaboration project. The competition is not always for material things; competition exists also for recognition, consecration from the system, or for prestige in one's field. Symbolic power (Bourdieu 1993, p. 7) is marked by competition for accumulated prestige, celebrity, or honor, whereas academic power derives from formal education measured by degrees and diplomas. The project had participants enter the game with conflicting habitus originating from each parent organization. Status and power were assumed to follow the rules defined by the parent organization. So, to enable change, a transfer of concepts had to be undertaken from one field to the other requiring analogy, metaphor building, and myth creation. In this manner, participants of one organization could understand participants of the other. The effort was to try to place oneself in the other's shoes by creating awareness of the limitations of personal habitus conscious. Renewal for a field, and for effective change, requires that there be a collective consciousness because it is the parameters of the structures themselves that stop innovation and reform (Slater, 1996).

In addition, there are prerequisites to the "playing of the game" of innovation and reform for anyone wishing access. First, there must be a desire to play this game rather than another. Knowledge, skill, and talent may be enough for a person to make the decision to play. Investment must be made to maximize the potential of one's participation. People have to enter to win, and they have to make an investment, using Bourdieu's economic metaphor, in themselves and in the operation of the organization into which they want an entrée. Here is where strategies come in. Strategies, or reflections of competence, are based on unconscious dispositions toward practice. They are based on the position that people occupy in the field and on the issues or questions by which they choose to be engaged.

There is a lot at stake in the symbolic struggle for the cultural field. The challenge to the person who is part of the field is to understand and be aware of the changes in the field, the relationships of power, and the struggles for the transformation of the hierarchy of legitimacy resulting from change efforts. The individual must therefore learn to see, to be the voyeur who gazes purely at the operation while looking and appreciating the value-driven enterprise. External sanctions and demands may limit this opportunity to see. Conditions for minimizing the obscuration of the field then must occur; this may be as simple as having the time to "see the forest for the trees," or the opportunity to provide a place to view from the outside.

What is the effect of a rejection of the norms of the culture? There is scandal, heresy, finger pointing at antinormative behavior, rumors, and rejection as the rules are perceived to have been violated. Punishment or exclusions, even from the profession or from its full participation, are not uncommon. Schooling and education at all levels reinforce similar social dispositions rather than democratizing and opening up possibilities. This is as true for public schools as it is for higher education. Similarity of disposition is touted as the ideal because the conditions of acquisition of position and status come with the reinforcement of the cultural milieu. Education transforms social hierarchies into academic hierarchies and academic hierarchies into hierarchies of merit (Bourdieu, 1993, p. 22). Virtue and status are legitimated by virtue of the collective belief that confers status upon the work.

Education also generalizes and legitimates modes of consumption. This has been discussed regarding textbooks and materials used in schools that discourage the introduction of new forms and new materials. This is true in science, which values the process of scientific discovery and the reconfirmation of theories over the controversial and often risky business of creating something new. The loss is of the commentary about what is being worked on rather than simply on how it is done. Instead of being praised for their inventiveness, new ideas are criticized because they do not follow the rules of the game.

Often, change falls to those newest members who are somewhat resistant to the inculcation of the field. Because they also are the least endowed with capital and status, they must be assertive and thrust themselves into the forefront to impose new modes of operation. They are usually perceived as out of sync with current patterns, a fact that is disconcerting to the orthodoxy (Bourdieu, 1993, p. 58). In addition, they are also out of sync with the reward structure that has been set up to support the old way of doing things. The thinking person requires an institution that is free from the bureaucracy, institutional habitus, and popular trends that may inhibit innovation. This is true of innovations in schools and accounts for the criticism of vouchers, charter schools, and the like, or the "whole language approach." Often, these innovations are not given the time necessary for them to succeed, to "play out their game." The struggle for control, for a monopoly of a corner of power, and for the consecration of that power permeates the world of science, art, mathematics, and community. It is embedded in the belief in the value of yesterday's enterprises that were and are as good as, or better than, what is proposed. This limits the opportunity to make change in individuals and consequently in the institutions of which they are a part.

Every field and the participants in that field are at once contemporaries and out of phase (Bourdieu, 1993, p. 107). The current reality is a field where struggles take place, where the authors of the past are always part of the struggles of the present and the direction of the future. This is true of efforts to change the working relationship of public schools and universities. Anything new must push aside a whole set of producers, systems, products, and tastes of the past as the old symbols and systems are co-opted, sanctioned, or banished.

The education system consecrates works of the past and selects what is acceptable production for the new by conferring diplomas for certain kinds of knowledge over others. Changes are slow to occur because evolution must overcome the monopoly of reproduction. There is a disjunction between the outside world and the popular culture it creates and the "scholastic culture which is routinized and rationalized by inculcation" (Bourdieu, 1993, p. 123). Those who wear the spectacles of a culture like school never become the critic because they see only what they have been taught to see. Hence, they are devoid of the freedom of selecting or inventing possibilities. The ability to be the connoisseur is an artistic process; it is an art of thinking that cannot be entirely taught but must be refined over time along with experience and prolonged contact. Bourdieu (1993, p. 228) warned academics that rationalizations mint the habitus that is taught, making it more difficult to be open to analytic analysis and reasoned discourse. This perpetuates the status quo for institutions, for schools, and for the university when there is no reasoned criticism and critique, only consecration of the norm.

What is needed to break habitus is a new idea with its own concepts, its own tacit way of seeing things, and its own questions that allow new answers to be generated (Langer, 1951, p. 17). We need to create generative ideas, a new science, and new theories to explain phenomena that we take for granted because "this is the way it always has been." New signs and symbols need to be created so that they can lead to new conceptions of objects and events. Thus, we can transform the opacity into a transparency of speech, a transparency of ideas, and a transparency of action. The root of this change is in the vision of what can be. It is a future envisioned.

It is humanity that holds the true test of ideas; it is the collective understanding that grows from a changing future—a future of participation and responsiveness to the people. It only takes one person armed with imagination to see beyond rules and restrictions to guide oneself out of the confines of an established community that is no longer functioning as a moral or just arena representing the individual. The solution may lie in looking toward a participative future. It is possible to envision a place for ourselves in a future of our own making. This future is one in which the public discourse is at the heart of participatory decision making. Then the problems that are most relevant to the people can be mediated through authentic clarification of the issues.

Possibilities

Change efforts often require that a new culture or a variation of the cultural milieu be produced, often emerging as a new mode of operation from what existed previously. Bourdieu (1993) interpreted these efforts as cultural production, and the problem became one of a variety of dichotomies, such as the individual versus society, freedom versus necessity (p. 3). The interpretation of the experience that results for the individual is subjective, based on perceptions of the experience and individual perceptions and interpretations of meaning. Interpretation becomes a complex process of observation and perspective for the researcher who seeks to understand why some change efforts are resisted and why others are embraced by few, by many, or by no one at all. Objective methods of analysis explain the social world by focusing on individuals' experiences and their own interpretations of those experiences. Subjective methods focus on the conditions that structure practice independent of human motivation and conscious and unconscious choice. Subjective methods do not provide interpretation into the motives of the person or the reality of the situation as it is perceived. Objectivism fails to recognize the extent that individuals' interpretations of their social world impact their behavior.

The project with which I was involved, a collaborative effort between a university and a local school system, involves two separate organizations, each with its own habitus. Interpreting these two systems in accordance with Bourdieu's terminology, there appears to be a class war between the university and the school system. Each protects its own capital. The school system perpetuates its bureaucratic model of school. The college supports innovation, the production of knowledge, and research. Each is sure that its habitus is correct. To work together on a long-term project, each must understand the other's habitus; each must get into the mind and soul of the other. Because each operates from its own world view, the game played is different for them, as are the internalized sanctions for operating with any perspective that is not owned by the organization. Change is slow and artificial, competing with practices that are ingrained.

What is needed is a congruence between theories of action and theories in use (Argyris & Schon, 1974). Theories of action are those expectations and their accompanying language and dialogue that speak to change, improvement, standards, and success. Theories in use are those practices in place that are routinized and bureaucratically driven, unthoughtful behaviors that are the acceptable cultural everyday actions of participants in organizations. When these mesh and the theoretical espoused dialogue of change and innovation for improvement become transformed into practice, there can be a realistic movement from behaviors that perpetuate the status quo to those that engage the participants to create a new collective identity. Of course, that might mean that schools need to be redesigned structurally or systemically, or that universities need to operate in new ways. This congruence allows new beliefs and values to emerge from suppression and optimize individual capabilities in an environment that is conducive to imagination and possibilities.

Bourdieu (1993, p. 236) said that consecration of the social order enables the educated to believe that there are "barbarians at the gates" from whom they must hide behind social conditions that perpetuate the habitus of old. This consecration legitimizes the dominance of a particular view of culture as we create temples of institutions and people within them who arm the gate with inflexible visions of an older set of values, thoughts, and possessions. Sometimes, however, the gates are stormed by new ideas, by new ways to work together, and by new dialogue and opportunities to communicate. People within the temples begin to see that they are masters of their fate, masters of the universe, captains of their souls—that they are able to have new values and beliefs and that they can envision an environment where these are aligned with those with whom they identify. Hence, change occurs.

References

Argyris, C., & Schon, D. A. (1974). *Theory in practice: Increasing professional effectiveness.* San Francisco: Jossey-Bass.

Bandura, A. (1990). Conclusion: Reflections on nonability determinants of competence. In R. J. Sternberg & J. Kolligan (Eds.), *Competence considered* (pp. 315–362). New Haven, CT: Yale University Press.

Botstein, L. (1997). *Jefferson's children: Education and the promise of American culture.* New York: Doubleday.

Bourdieu, P. (1984). *Distinction: A social critique of the judgement of taste.* Cambridge, MA: Harvard University Press.

Bourdieu, P. (1993). *The field of cultural production.* New York: Columbia University Press.

Bourdieu, P., & Passeron, J. (1977). *Reproduction in education, society and culture.* London: Sage.

Cohen, A. (1998). *Israel and the bomb.* New York: Columbia University Press.

Eisner, E. (1994). *The educational imagination.* New York: MacMillan.

Freire, P. (1970). *Pedagogy of the oppressed.* New York: Seabury.

Harter, S. (1990). Causes, correlates, and the functional role of global self-worth: A life span perspective. In R. J. Sternberg & J. Kolligan (Eds.), *Competence considered* (pp. 67–97). New Haven, CT: Yale University Press.

Langer, S. K. (1951). *Philosophy in a new key.* New York: New American Library.

Slater, J. J. (1996). *Anatomy of a collaboration.* New York: Garland.

Sternberg, R. J., & Kolligan, J. (1990). *Competence considered.* New Haven, CT: Yale University Press.

Chapter

3

Dancing in the Dark? Learning More About What Makes Partnerships Work

Arlene C. Borthwick

Understanding Partnerships Means Understanding Process

In her book *When Giants Learn to Dance,* Rosabeth Moss Kanter (1989) described the need for, and process of, two organizations working together in a synergistic relationship. Her metaphor for "process"—*dancing*—makes me wonder if many of us involved in collaborative partnerships are dancing in the dark. Very often as we work together, we are focused on tasks and outcomes, forgetting to take time to examine our dance steps. This chapter provides a framework for examining, reflecting on, and perhaps rethinking partnerships, hopefully turning all partners into "better dancers."

Origins of School Partnerships:
Gearing up for Change

The interest of outside groups in public education is not new. Initial preparation of and lifelong learning by the workforce brings business and education into partnership. The articulation of school–university programs, as well as preservice and in-service teacher education, joins school and university. In addition, recent national educational goals encourage collaborative approaches to reform and restructuring. For example, federal legislation for Goals 2000 encouraged local groups to create " 'whole community' partnership[s] to improve teaching and learning" (U.S. Department of Education, 1994, p. 3). Grant funding also encourages proposals involving partners, for example, in the Teacher Quality Enhancement, Preparing Tomorrow's Teachers to Use Technology, and Comprehensive School Reform Development programs. Currently, the National Association of Partners in Education (NAPE) boasts members from 400,000 partnerships nationwide (NAPE, 2000).

Efforts at university–school collaboration increased in the late 1980s as ninety-six major research universities forming the Holmes Group sought to improve preservice and in-service teacher education through increased ties to colleges of arts and sciences and to school-based educators. As described by Clark (1999a), professional development schools (PDSs), designed as a part of the Holmes Group movement, "provide a clinical setting for preservice education, engage in professional development for practitioners, promote and conduct inquiry that advances knowledge of schooling, and provide an exemplary education for a segment of P–12 students" (p. 9). Evolving into The Holmes Partnership, this group now partners with seven national professional education associations including the National Board for Professional Teaching Standards, National Education Association, and the National Council for Accreditation of Teacher Education (NCATE), as well as seventy-four universities with local school partnerships (The Holmes Partnership, 2000).

Levine and Churins (1999) outlined NCATE's development of a set of standards for PDSs in response to the proliferation of PDSs "with little attention to definition and quality" (p. 3). Collaborative development of the standards included a two-year pilot test of both standards and methods of assessment involving eighteen PDS partnerships. Characteristics of PDSs are described in five standards and developmental guidelines addressing the following: learning community; accountability and quality assurance; collaboration; equity and diversity; and structures, resources, and roles (NCATE, 2001). Collaborative development of the standards included a two-year pilot test of both standards and methods of assessment involving eighteen PDS partnerships. Characteristics of PDSs are described in five standards and developmental guidelines addressing learning community; accountability and quality assurance; collaboration; equity and diversity; and structures, resources, and roles (NCATE, 2001). PDSs are seen as complex partnerships going "well beyond cooperation—it means the clustering and blending of financial and human resources of all the partners in order to carry out the PDS mission" (Levine & Churins, p. 7).

Other national networks also espouse the PDS model, including the National Center for Restructuring Education, Schools, and Teaching (NCREST) and the National Network for Education Renewal (NNER). Started in 1986 by John Goodlad, NNER focuses on promotion of school–university collaboration to assure exemplary performance of both institutions through simultaneous renewal. Currently, NNER lists sixteen collaboratives involving thirty-three college and universities, more than 100 school districts, and about 500 schools (NNER, 2000). In 1996, Goodlad described the attempt to bring the cultures of schools and colleges together as "an incredibly demanding enterprise" (p. 4). This concern is repeated in his 1999 reflection on how "even the concept of partnership roils the waters of each, especially those of higher education" (Goodlad, 1999, p. 86).

Partnerships come in many sizes (dyads to networks) and shapes (e.g., focusing on preservice and in-service education, teacher renewal, school restructuring, urban school reform, or integration of technology). Fullan (1993) reminded us that working together to make change happen denotes "complexity, dynamism, and unpredictability" (p. 20). Accepting these states as normal, Fullan shared the thoughts of one group he worked with "who defined change as 'likened to a planned journey into uncharted waters in a leaky boat with a mutinous crew' " (Fullan, 1993, p. 24).

The importance of examining partnerships rests on the seriousness and pervasiveness of social and educational problems to be solved through educational collaboration. Societal changes, including the increasing number of minority and disadvantaged students, movement from a manufacturing to a service economy, criticism of public school preparation of its graduates, criticism of college preparation of K–12 teachers, and the "growing gap . . . developing between our nation's educational achievement and that of other industrial countries" (Grobe, 1990, p. 3) are factors in a turbulent environment. As schools, businesses, communities, and universities find themselves facing this environment, the need for joint ventures increases. Establishing and maintaining effective partnerships requires effective process. We know *why* we need to work together. We need to know *how* to work together.

Theoretical Frameworks

Several theoretical frameworks offer a basis or lens for examining educational partnerships; these include organization theory and interorganization theory. In the former, we consider partnerships as organizations, whereas in the latter we focus on partnerships as relationships between organizations. Organization theory is relatively new. According to Bolman and Deal (1991), "Only in the last twenty-five years have social scientists devoted much time or attention to developing ideas about how organizations work (or why they often fail to work)" (p. 9).

Organization Theory

Of first consideration might be whether we can define a partnership as an organization. Almost four decades ago, Etzioni (1964) defined organizations as "social units (or human groupings) deliberately constructed and reconstructed to seek specific goals" (p. 3). In addition to members, structure, and goals, other elements of organizations include resources and output. Organizational processes include communication patterns, styles, and flows; goal setting; decision making, problem solving, and action planning; conflict resolution and management; managing interface relations; superior–subordinate relations; technological and engineering systems; and strategic management and long-range planning (French & Bell, 1984).

The value of organization theories is to enable the observation, analysis, understanding, and management of partnerships as organizations. Bolman and Deal (1991) described four major schools that provide the organization theory base. These include rational systems theories, human resource theories, political theories, and symbolic theories. Rational systems theories focus on development of structures to enable organizational purposes, taking into consideration the organization's environment. Human resource theories consider the interdependence of people and organizations. Political theories focus on the issues of power, conflict, and limited resources. Symbolic theories emphasize images and meaning in the management of organizations.

A rational model of organizations emphasizes efficiency and effectiveness of operation where decisions are made in an orderly, logical fashion within a structure of centralized power and control. On the other hand, as described by Daft (1989), a political model suggests the existence of struggle and conflict of "shifting coalitions and interest groups" (p. 418). The mixed model view, as described by Daft, describes organizations as operating under both the rational model and the political model at different times. In fact, "managers may strive to adopt rational processes, but it is an illusion to assume that an organization can be run without politics" (Daft, p. 418).

A view of organizations as open systems provides another way of thinking about organizational processes. Huse and Cummings (1985) explained that "*open systems . . . exchange information and resources with their environment. They cannot completely control their own behavior and are influenced in part by external forces*" [italics in original] (pp. 35–36). Attention to the environment becomes particularly important if that environment is unstable; the complexity of the environment is an additional factor. Daft (1989) described a contingency framework for assessing environmental uncertainty and appropriate organizational responses. A "low uncertainty environment is simple and stable.... The high uncertainty environment is both complex and unstable" (p. 62).

Appropriate organizational responses to a high-uncertainty environment include boundary spanning. According to Daft (1989), "Organizations can reduce vulnerability and uncertainty through formal linkages to other organizations" (p. 63). Individuals who provide information about changes in the environment, as well as providing favorable information to the environment about their home organization, are called boundary spanners (Daft, 1989). As explained by French and Bell (1984), development of relationships across departments, divisions, organizations, or a combination of these requires leadership from an individual who can promote and manage interface relations, assisting two separate groups to achieve "an objective but have separate accountability" (p. 73).

An open systems view of organizations suggests two roles for educational partnerships. First, such partnerships may be formed as an appropriate response to the environmental turbulence or uncertainty of member organizations. Second, if the partnership is conceived of as an organization, it, too, will need to be responsive to its environment, including, for example, potential users of services, demographics, availability of external resources, and federal programs.

Interorganization Theory

It can be somewhat difficult to determine where organization theory ends and interorganization theory begins. In determining the relevancy of interorganization theory to the study of partnership process, we will want to examine the definition of an interorganizational unit. Van de Ven, Emmett, and Koenig (1980) defined an interor-

ganizational collectivity as having two or more organizations as the primary participants who

> join together as an action system to attain a specific objective by
> performing a set or series of goal-directed behavioral acts.... As a
> social system, the actions of organizations or representatives
> thereof take on specialized roles and develop behavioral expecta-
> tions of each other regarding the rights and obligations of mem-
> bership in the collectivity. (pp. 26–27)

Such a definition might exclude some educational partnerships, for example, a
school–business partnership in which the business partner simply provides funding for
a specific activity.

The study of interorganizational relations (IOR) began in several disciplines,
each representing a different orientation. These included public administration, mar-
keting, economic, and sociological orientations (Whetten, 1981). Two of these most
applicable to the study of educational partnerships are public administration, with a focus on improved coordination of delivery of public services, and sociology, with a focus
on networks of community organizations.

Andrew Van de Ven (1976) developed a theory on the formation and maintenance of interagency relationships (IRs) when "knowledge of the inter-organizational
field [was] still at a primitive stage" (p. 25). Viewing the relationship as a social action
system, Van De Ven thought IR development was dependent on situational factors, including an organization's need for resources; its awareness of services and goals of
other agencies; its domain similarity; and its degree of commitment to and consensus
on problems, goals, solutions, or opportunities. Interorganizational relationships were
expected to grow incrementally as small successes were achieved beginning a cycle of
need, commitment, communications "to spread awareness and consensus" (p. 33), resource exchange, and structural adaptation. Termination of the IR was viewed as a
function of achieving "their self-interest objectives and no longer depend[ing] upon
other agency members for resources" (pp. 33–34).

Interorganizational linkages occur at multiple levels ranging from dyadic relationships (pairs) to joint ventures to networks. School districts may, in fact, be viewed
as part of a broad network of linkages that include many community and governmental
agencies. School–university connections for preservice and in-service education can
be viewed as joint ventures to meet the needs of both institutions.

An environment conducive to the establishment of an educational partnership includes such factors as seed money and organizational norms that reinforce participation in collaborative efforts (Intriligator, 1986). Additionally, agencies will be
motivated to participate in partnership efforts if their own environmental scanning (assessment of external constraints, pressures, and opportunities, e.g., of the economy, of
human resources) suggests that their home organization "can better respond to such
external pressures through collective action" (Intriligator, 1986, p. 6).

Descriptions for how organizations interrelate include the terminology of cooperation, coordination, and collaboration. Some authors use the terms interchangeably.
On the surface, distinguishing between these three terms may appear to be mere se-
mantics. Nonetheless, Hord (1986) argued that "collaboration and cooperation are distinctly different operational processes" (p. 22). Intriligator (1992) compared

coordination, cooperation, and collaboration based on the level of interdependence of organizations as evidenced in seven qualities or variables of the interagency unit: objective, policies, structure, personnel roles, resources, power and influence, and interagency relationships. Collaboration is viewed as the most difficult form of interaction to achieve. Furthermore, Hill (n.d.) outlined three forms of collaboration, suggesting that groups may be identified along a continuum from comfortable (informal sharing), to structured (bureaucratic), to critical collaboration. The latter form may enable members to generate new knowledge through critical reflection on schooling and the social, economic, or political context of that schooling.

Barbara Gray (1989) used resource exchange in her discussion of a theory of collaboration: "Collaborations can be thought of as negotiated orders created among stakeholders to control environmental turbulence by regulating the exchange relationships among them" (p. 228). Although individual organizations may have succeeded by acting alone in the past, environmental conditions require them to develop collaborative strategies to deal with problem areas. Fullan (1999) approached the need for school collaboration from a similar perspective, noting that

the combined effect of collaborative cultures serves to mobilize three powerful change forces. Moral purpose (the spiritual) gains ascendancy. Power (politics) is used to maximize pressure and support for positive action. Ideas and best practices (the intellectual) are continually being generated, tested, and selectively retained. In collaborative cultures these three forces feed on each other. They become fused. (p. 40)

Barbara Gray (1985) proposed three phases of the collaborative process: problem setting (identifying stakeholders and problem domain), direction setting (articulation of common goals and values), and structuring (managing interactions through agreement on goals, tasks, roles). Gray suggested that interorganization members negotiate and renegotiate their relationship. B. Gray (1989) suggested that "This conceptualization captures the imprecise, emergent, exploratory, developmental character of these interorganizational arrangements" (p. 230), which may later develop an institutionalized agreement. Based on previous research findings, Gray developed a series of propositions and corollaries for managing movement through the phases. For example,

Proposition 7. Collaboration will be enhanced when power is dispersed among several rather than among just a few stakeholders. An equal power distribution is not necessary and may prove undesirable since it can provoke stalemate and inaction. However, a sufficient distribution of power is necessary to insure that all stakeholders can influence direction-setting. (p. 927)

Gray concluded that "inability to achieve the appropriate conditions during each phase may be the best source of explanation . . . for why collaborative efforts fail" (p. 932).

Like B. Gray, Ring and Van de Ven (1994) offered a set of propositions to elucidate how a balance of formal and informal partner interactions are required to maintain IORs. For example, they suggested that "if personal relationships do not supplement formal role relationships over time, then the likelihood increases that conflicts will escalate between the role specialists of the organizational agents" (p. 10). This implies that beyond the need for trust, an element of friendship between the partner representatives may be key.

Many Facets: Key Elements of Educational Partnerships

My own interest in educational partnership process began when I was appointed as the project director of an OERI-funded partnership. Seven partners (four universities, two schools, one business) provided leadership to the partnership, while eleven organizations provided representatives for an advisory council. Partnership activities took place in five schools of an urban school district located about thirty-five miles from the university. Results of my own research activities (Borthwick, 1994, 1995) identified five major areas (domains) and thirteen key elements to consider in establishing and maintaining successful school–university partnerships (see Table 3.1). These elements include goals; context; outcomes; member characteristics; commitment; roles and responsibilities; funding and other material resources; connections, sharing, exchanges; communications; decision making and action planning; group dynamics; inquiry into partnership process; and stages. These items were tested using Q-Methodology (Borthwick, Stirling, Nauman, & Cook, 2000) and are also widely supported by both research and theory. In an effort to expose the inner workings, pitfalls, and "must-do's" of school–university partnerships, each element is discussed in the remainder of the chapter. Literature reviewed includes reviews of research (e.g., Clark, 1988, 1998; Su, 1990; Thorkildsen & Stein, 1996), multisite and longitudinal studies, and dissertation studies.

Table 3.1. Elements of the Partnership

Domain	Category
Focus	Goals
	Context
	Outcomes
Members	General characteristics
	Commitment
	Roles and responsibilities
Needs and resources	Funding and other material resources
	Connections, sharing, exchanges
Interactions	Communications
	Decision making and action planning
	Group dynamics
	Inquiry into partnership process
Stages	Stages

Goals

Members should establish common goals that address overlapping self and community interests. This creates a web of interdependence among partnership members (Zywine, 1991). Maeroff (1983) suggested that the ability to establish common goals is a predictor of "the potential for cooperation" (p. x) of the partnership members. Furthermore, the scope and complexity of the goals may suggest whether interagency efforts should take the form of cooperation, coordination, or collaboration (Intriligator, 1992) as well as desired members and support mechanisms (governance and funding) (Clark, 1999a). Clark found that member understanding of goals may be best accomplished through "extended conversation" as opposed to formal agreement (p. 3). Partners will need to consider the scope of goals they set—not so broad as to be immeasurable or unachievable (e.g., school reform; Fullan & Miles, 1992), yet not so specific that they limit or frustrate the group's potential (Trubowitz & Longo, 1997). Furthermore, as priorities change over time, goals may expand (Padak, Shaklee, Peck, Barton, & Johnson, 1994).

Context

In developing and implementing partnership projects, members should focus on the specific context or setting, taking into consideration local school district procedures and politics (Borthwick, 1994; Fullan, 1999), school climate (Trubowitz & Longo, 1997), and past successes and failures (Clark, 1999b). Trubowitz and Longo (1997) affirmed the importance of "understanding that each collaborative venture will present its own specific set of challenges" (p. 66). Although a partnership was expected to be more effective if operated in a stable and supportive school district and community (Borthwick, 1994), participants in ten partnerships in the Chicago Public Schools did not identify school or community stability as essential elements for successful partnerships (Borthwick et al., 2000). These members seemed to accept somewhat unstable communities and school populations as the norm. Levine (1997), however, expressed concern about establishing PDSs in challenging urban environments where "teacher shortages, inadequate facilities, large numbers of at-risk students, and high turnover among district leaders threaten the fragility of these partnerships" (p. 6).

Outcomes

Borthwick (1994) reported that members' reasons for staying involved in a partnership project included successfully meeting goals. Partners collected data to demonstrate success in achieving established goals as well as broader educational reform. Members looked for project impact on students, teachers, the school system, and wider community through in-person visits, performance measures, and other data gathered as part of an evaluation design. Likewise, Trubowitz and Longo (1997) shared the following: "For a collaboration to prosper over an extended period requires that participants believe important and useful purposes are being accomplished" (p. 7). Clark (1999b) put it even more strongly, stating that "a partnership that has as its purpose the creation of a partnership—rather than the accomplishment of some ultimate goal—is inevitably doomed to early failure" (p. 3). As far as PDS partnerships effecting change in schools and universities, some authors expressed disappointment primarily about impact on the university (Goodlad, 1999; Trubowitz & Longo, 1997). In some partnerships "the ethos was more that of universities in the traditional role of . . . bringing succor to the needful schools—than of equal partners in mutual assistance" (Goodlad, 1999, p. 86).

Member Characteristics and Leadership

Complementary diversity can be expected to add strength to a partnership in conceptual as well as practical matters (Padak et al., 1994). According to Intriligator (1986), members may need time "to learn about each other's cultures and structures" (p. 21). In some cases, partnership activities may even require alteration of member organizations' operational routines (Intriligator, 1992), perhaps an anticipated result in the case of simultaneous renewal in NNER partnerships. Members who are competent (Flowe, 1989/1990), stable (Smith, 1988/1989), and are part of or have access to top-level management (Grobe, 1990/1993; Intriligator, 1992) are desired. Necessary styles of leadership may vary over time, catalytic at first and later stabilizing (Havelock, Cox, Huberman, & Levinson, 1982). Those who serve in a leadership capacity may also vary (Padak et al., 1994; Tushnet 1993), helping to assure the partnership is not dependent on any one person (Goldman & Intriligator, 1990). Nonetheless, turnover in key participants is a strong possibility (Trubowitz & Longo, 1997), and Clark (1999b) recommended that resources be set aside for training new participants.

Commitment

Havelock et al. (1982) described commitment as member support "manifested in attitudes, behavior, and dollars" (p. xiv). Including various stakeholders right from the beginning enables the sense of ownership required to see the project through (Boyd et al., 1992; Tushnet, 1993). Furthermore, partnerships must establish commitment at both the personal and institutional level (Intriligator, 1986; Maeroff, 1983). To maintain commitment, partners should involve college, district, and school administrators (Clark, 1999b), particularly principals (Kersh & Masztal, 1998; Trubowitz & Longo, 1997); use recognition and awards (Maeroff, 1983; Smith, 1988/1989); and affirm perceptions of worthwhile goals (Borthwick 1994, 1995) and successful outcomes (D. Gray, 1989/1990; Grobe, 1990/1993). In addition, involving multiple members of participating organizations may enhance acceptance of collaboration as a value within the member organizations' cultures (Smith, 1988/1989). Finally, Tushnet (1993) recommended openness of members in sharing constraints on their participation. "Knowing about the constraints makes members more tolerant of others' limitations" (p. 33).

Roles and Responsibilities

As a partnership is formed, there is a need to clarify roles and responsibilities of the participants (Grobe, 1990/1993; Wangemann, 1988/1989). Partnerships may create new roles for both high-level decision makers and classroom teachers as they collaborate in a nonhierarchical setting (Tushnet, 1993). Although the principal should expect to share his or her leadership role, this may be easier said than done (Kersh & Masztal, 1998). As described by Simmons, Konecki, Crowell, and Gates-Duffield

(1999), members may become shape shifters serving in the roles of "leader, follower, director, facilitator, listener, speaker, researcher, information provider, challenger, protector, counselor, secretary, designer, cook, teacher, and learner" (p. 41). According to Grobe (1990), leaders' groups or planning teams serve as "idea generators, oversight providers, policy developers or strategic planners" (p. 32); however, participation of project implementers on such boards should also be considered (B. Gray, 1985; Tushnet, 1993). Taking a cautionary stance on forming additional new committees, Teitel (1997) noted that schools involved with restructuring "can be overwhelmed by a sense of too many groups, too many projects, too many committees" (p. 123).

Funding and Other Material Resources

Resources include money, time, space, and "professional guidance and expertise" (Harrington, 1989/1990, p. 78). Havelock et al. (1982) saw federal funding as an effective means to initiate collaborative arrangements, but Kersh and Masztal (1998) warned that grant-writing teams are usually small groups working under tight deadlines who may not exemplify collaborative planning. Havelock et al. (1982) reflected that partnership leaders may initially underestimate the level of resources required, and Fullan and Miles (1992) warned that "change is resource-hungry" (p. 750). Contributions from interagency members need not be equal, provided that partners agree on expectations at the onset (Intriligator, 1986). Other concerns related to funding include sharing of resources that became available to a partnership. Participants may compete or cooperate in obtaining resources from a common pool (Klohmann, 1987/1988; Lieberman, 1992). Tushnet (1993) recommended open discussion of expectations related to external funding, including participants' roles in obtaining funding, "how funds will affect work *within* each participating organization" [italics in original] (p. 9), and agreement on how to deal with any reduction in funds. Furthermore, Tushnet (1993) cautioned against reducing the funding of technical support to programmatic change.

Connections, Sharing, and Exchanges for Mutual Benefit

Members may be encouraged to think of partnership as an opportunity for resources to be exchanged, which in turn enhances the level of trust among members (Intriligator, 1986). Goodlad (1988) described partnerships as symbiotic relationships. According to Havelock et al., mutual benefits include an exchange of "items of perceived value and benefit" (1982, p. 265). Such an exchange of resources makes the interorganizational relationship a partnership instead of a "sponsorship" (DelPizzo, 1990/1991). Harrington (1989/1990) commented on the need for a balance of contributions and benefits, and Intriligator (1986) confirmed that members must see some benefit over the long term. "When such benefits are so small that members do not believe there is any exchange to be derived from their investment in the joint effort, they will withdraw from the IOR" (Intriligator, 1986, p. 22). Likewise, Borthwick (1994) found that "member participation was sustained primarily because of project focus and exchanges for mutual benefit" (p. 231). Tushnet (1993) addressed the issue of opportunism, which may represent a partner's reasons for participation. An opportunistic partner is not seen as harming the partnership if others are able to maintain the focus on implementation of project goals, for example, changes in curriculum and instruction (Tushnet, 1993).

Communications

Partnerships involve open, honest discussion (DelPizzo, 1990/1991) in which members share and understand each others' points of view (Caplan, 1987/1988). Although a project director may serve as the hub for communications, open lines of communication among all participants should be encouraged (Borthwick, 1994; Goodlad & Soder, 1992). Kersh and Masztal noted that "it is critical to gather perceptions constantly from all directions and ensure that all factions communicate, even if it is difficult" (1998, p. 3). Prepartnership conversations enable participants to match their expectations about roles and commitments, program content, and external funding (Tushnet, 1993). Institutionalization of partnerships requires continued communications with frequent exchanges of information (Flowe, 1989/1990; Padak et al., 1994) through personal contact, small group meetings, the provision of systematic written information, and contact via telecommunications (Borthwick, 1994). Changes in organizational representatives as well as school system personnel also require continued communication (Padak et al., 1994; Zywine, 1991). Partners may disseminate information about their project in a systematic fashion, expanding dissemination over time (Borthwick, 1994) within the school district (Smith, 1988/1989) and the community (Grobe, 1990/1993; Tushnet, 1993); however, partners carefully weigh the cost–benefit ratio of dissemination activities (Borthwick, 1994, 1995).

Decision Making and Action Planning

Shared decision making requires a sharing of authority where no partner dictates or dominates the decision-making process (Boyd et al., 1992; Harrington, 1989/1990). Kersh and Masztal (1998) warned that "unilaterial decisions can destroy the partnership" (p. 3). In describing the benefits of collaborative decision making, Trubowitz and Longo (1997) suggested that it can serve as a form of self-correction in which partners reject "bad or premature ideas" (p. 52). Voting may work for groups functioning under interagency coordination, whereas consensus is used by groups functioning under interagency collaboration (Intriligator, 1992). If partnership representatives need to seek authorization from top-level management of their organization, this could serve as a barrier to their full participation in the decision-making process (Smith, 1988/1989). Teitel (1997) conceptualized a ladder of decision making that is helpful in examining parity in partner decision making. Higher rungs on the ladder suggest decisions of greater impact and higher stakes; partners should consider whether high-stakes decisions impact the school partner, the university partner, or both. Action planning serves as a method for determining operational steps and for solving problems that can be expected to arise during the normal course of business (Borthwick, 1994; Trubowitz & Longo, 1997). Fullan (1999) eschewed consensus to obtain diverse perspectives for solving complex problems.

Group Dynamics

Successful partnerships couple hard work with attention to group dynamics. Borthwick's (1994) analysis found that multiple partners operating as peers expected to establish a working relationship that included attention to political considerations, workload, level of involvement, member input, affect (trust and comfort level), and the time required for functioning as a group. Partners' efforts to interact productively take time (Greene, 1985; Lieberman, 1992), and Tushnet (1993) encouraged members to "sacrifice 'efficiency' for building the partnership" (p. 43). Greene (1985) discussed the difficulty that interagency collaboratives have in establishing an identity when members do not share the same "built-in contextual and physical variables" (p. v) of a single organization, and Payzant (1992) discussed expectations for the uneven work load of the partners at specific junctures. Bringing together representatives of diverse cultures can create dissonance, conflict, and anxiety (Lieberman, 1992; Fullan & Miles, 1992). Fullan (1999) mentioned the importance of team building, and Fullan and Miles (1992) suggested that steering groups obtain assistance to learn to work together. Group dynamics may be more difficult in "forced" partnerships such as those required by a district for schools on probation where data collected by Borthwick et al. (2000) suggested that partnerships were born "in a climate of distrust or even fear [for their jobs], particularly on the part of teachers" (p. 16).

Stages

Padak et al. (1994) reported that "informants saw partnerships as dynamic, evolving entities" (p. 25); members anticipated changes throughout the partnership process, including modifications in goals, members, needs and resources, and interactions as they moved through stages of development, stabilization, and institutionalization (Borthwick, 1994). Several authors outlined a variety of stages (e.g., Trubowitz & Longo, 1997; Williams, 1996), with Wilson, Clark, and Heckman (1989) indicating that partnerships move through five "fairly predictable" (p. 15) stages: (a) getting organized, (b) early success, (c) waiting for results, (d) major success and expansions, and (e) mature partnership. Partners may invest considerable energy up front, underestimating the personnel, resources, and processes required to maintain the partnership (Trubowitz & Longo, 1997). Clark (1998) noted that, depending on conditions, over a period of time the partnership may slide back from later to earlier stages and that if partnerships "fail to maintain structure, support mechanisms, and purposes which are consistent with each other" (p. 77), they will likely dissolve. Furthermore, Clark (1998, 1999a) identified four types of partnerships—narrow, moderate, broad, and mixed—based on purpose, structure, and support mechanisms.

In addressing changes in PDS partner relationships over time, Teitel (1998) used metaphors, describing separations, divorces, and open marriages. For example, schools may choose to expand their relationship to accommodate field placements from another college or university, creating, in effect, an open marriage. Perhaps such changes may occur because of frustration on the part of the school or a transition in partnership representatives. Teitel noted a reluctance of members to withdraw from a state-sponsored network of partnerships, but he found that "each relationship that went through a divorce or a reconfiguration came out stronger and went on to continue and push further than it had with its original partner" (p. 94). D. Gray (1989/1990) concluded that application of an organization development model would enable collaborators "to address predictable series of critical concerns and key issues that will confront organizations in their development" (p. 3).

Inquiry, Research, and Evaluation

An ongoing system for research and evaluation was among elements contributing to the success of educational partnerships (Wangemann, 1988/1989). Such self-study provides formative evaluation of a partnership's structure, process, and agenda (Sirotnik, 1988) and enables adaptive planning (Tushnet, 1993). Padak et al. (1994) noted that examination of data by those involved in the partnership suggests that "meaning is socially constructed and context dependent" (pp. 29–30). Tushnet (1993) recommended that "feedback about the partnership itself should be either part of regular public meetings or be collected by a neutral party" (p. 37), and others suggested a critical friend or outsider help the members examine partnership activities (Teitel, 1999; Trubowitz & Longo, 1997). Whereas Clark (1998) recommended documentation of partnership work, Havelock et al. (1982) addressed the issue of funding the documentation of partnership arrangements, concluding that it is "rarely . . . done without federal or other third party assistance" (p. xv). Borthwick (1994, 1995) found that members evaluated their partnership across all areas, including goals, outcomes, members, needs and resources, interactions, and stages. Kersh and Masztal (1998), however, observed that "people reflect on university–school collaborations, but few study, or report the study of, the collaborative act" (p. 5). This suggests that partners may not wish to publicly share information about what may turn out to be unsuccessful relationships.

Accepting the Challenge: Dancing the Two-Step

Based on an in-depth case study (Borthwick, 1994, 1995) and the literature and research reviewed in this chapter, I propose the following general description (grounded theory) for how educational partnerships work.

 Educational partnership is a process that brings together members (e.g., institutions, organizations, and agencies) and resources to produce outcomes directed to the enhancement of education. Diverse members develop open lines of communication and working relationships to focus on long-term goals, identifying both needs to be met and resources to be tapped. Partners expect to operate as peers and seek consensus in determining priorities and project activities. Bringing different perspectives, members value discussion of issues and problems in the development of action plans to enable smooth implementation. Commitment from individual participants as well as their organizations is anticipated. Personal commitment is demonstrated by interest, support, ownership, and attendance. Organizational commitment is demonstrated by continuity of membership as well as resources to support partnership activity. Resources extend beyond funding to include other material resources and the sharing of information or technical expertise. Networking links partnership members to other individuals, groups, and organizations for mutual, project, and community benefit. Roles and responsibilities of specific members often relate to their strengths or expertise and may evolve over time. Member involvement is sustained primarily

because of project focus, including worthwhile goals and the perception of successful outcomes as well as exchanges for mutual
benefit. Commitment also may be maintained through recognition of contribution and other tangible or intangible rewards. Examination of data gathered about project outcomes (impact on
students, teachers, the school system, and wider community) as
well as partnership process provides members with feedback of a
formative nature as the partnership moves through developmental stages. Cost–benefit ratio of dissemination activities is carefully
weighed.

Although the above summary provides a framework with which to view educational partnerships, we need to remember that partnerships are dynamic and complex
interagency relationships. The thirteen characteristics discussed in this chapter (goals;
context; outcomes; member characteristics; member commitment; roles and responsibilities; funding and other material resources; connections, sharing, exchanges; communications; decision making and action planning; group dynamics; inquiry, research
and evaluation; and stages) are interconnected. For example, problems to be solved or
goals to be achieved determine which relevant stakeholders to include as members of
the partnership. On the other hand, it is the partnership members who subsequently determine project goals, objectives, and priorities. In other words, goals suggest members, and members suggest goals. This is only one example of the interconnectedness
of many items.

Furthermore, as expressed by Clark (1998), although we have an idea of where
we are going and, as described above, sights we expect to see along the way, we are
working with a "roadless map" (p. 99). Fullan (1999) suggested that "even when you
know what research and published advice has to say you will not know exactly how to
apply it to your particular situation with its unique problems, and opportunities" (p.
28). This is confirmed in an empirical study (Borthwick et al., 2000) in which members
from ten partnerships were asked to identify essential elements of successful partnerships. Analysis found multiple perspectives on how partnerships should operate:

Some would be (a) goal-oriented with a short-term focus, some
would (b) emphasize the persistence/existence of the partnership, some would (c) expect to participate in a dynamic and
adaptable interagency collaboration, and others would (d) emphasize interactions involving attention to communications and
group dynamics. (p. 16)

To return to the metaphor of dancing used at the beginning of this chapter, having
a partner and knowing a few dance steps is not enough. You also have to know where
the slippery spots are on the dance floor and be flexible enough to move beyond the two-
step, dancing to the music or getting the orchestra to change its tune. Although the dance
may be tricky, collaboration is worth the effort. As expressed by Fullan (1999), "The true
value of collaborative cultures is that they simultaneously encourage passion and provide
emotional support as people work through the rollercoaster of change" (p. 38).

References

Bolman, L. G., & Deal, T. E. (1991). *Reframing organization*. San Francisco: Jossey-Bass.

Borthwick, A. G. (1994). School-university-community collaboration: Establishing and maintaining partnerships for school improvement (Doctoral dissertation, Kent State University, 1994). *Dissertation Abstracts International, 56*, 2052A.

Borthwick, A. G. (1995). *Establishing and maintaining partnerships for school improvement*. Paper presented at the annual meeting of the American Educational Research Association, San Francisco. (ERIC Document Reproduction Service No. ED 385 922)

Borthwick, A. C., Stirling, T., Nauman, A. D., & Cook, D. (2000, April). *Achieving successful school-university collaboration*. Paper presented at the annual meeting of the American Educational Research Association, New Orleans.

Boyd, B., Duning, B., Gomez, R., Hetzel, R., King, R., Patrick, S., & Whitaker, K. (1992, April). *Impacts of interagency collaboration on participating organizations*. Paper presented at the annual meeting of the American Educational Research Association, San Francisco.

Caplan, J. H. (1988). Public school and private university collaboration: A process for effecting change (Doctoral dissertation, University of Pennsylvania, 1987). *Dissertation Abstracts International, 49*, 667A.

Clark, R. W. (1988). School/university relationships: An interpretive review. In K. A. Sirotnik & J. I. Goodlad (Eds.), *School university partnerships in action: Concepts, cases, and concerns* (pp. 32–65). New York: Teachers College Press.

Clark, R. W. (1998). *Community-school-university partnership: Literature review*. Washington, DC: Hamilton Fish National Institute on School and Community Violence, George Washington University.

Clark, R. W. (1999a). *Effective professional development schools*. San Francisco: Jossey-Bass.

Clark, R. W. (1999b). School-university partnerships and professional development schools. *Peabody Journal of Education, 74*, 164–177 [Retrieved July 17, 2000 from WilsonSelect on-line database (Number BED100003111; ISSN: 0161-956X)].

Daft, R. L. (1989). *Organization theory and design*. St. Paul, MN: West.

DelPizzo, M. (1991). A naturalistic study of the salient themes of a school/business partnership (Doctoral dissertation, West Virginia University, 1990). *Dissertation Abstracts International, 51*, 3035A.

Etzioni, A. (1964). *Modern organizations*. Englewood Cliffs, NJ: Prentice-Hall.

Flowe, R. M. (1990). A model to predict institutionalization of school-business partnerships (Doctoral dissertation, The College of William and Mary, 1989). *Dissertation Abstracts International, 51*, 33A.

French, W. L., & Bell, C. H. (1984). *Organization development: Behavioral science interventions for organization improvement.* Englewood Cliffs, NJ: Prentice-Hall.

Fullan, M. (1993). *Change forces: Probing the depths of educational reform.* London: Falmer.

Fullan, M. (1999). *Change forces: The sequel.* London: Falmer.

Fullan, M. G., & Miles, M. B. (1992). Getting reform right: What works and what doesn't. *Phi Delta Kappan, 73,* 745–752.

Goldman, H., & Intriligator, B. (1990, April). *Factors that enhance collaboration among education, health and social service agencies.* Paper presented at the annual meeting of the American Educational Research Association, Boston. (ERIC Document Reproduction Service No. ED 021 744)

Goodlad, J. I. (1988). School-university partnerships for educational renewal: Rationale and concepts. In K. A. Sirotnik & J. I. Goodlad (Eds.), *School university partnerships in action: Concepts, cases, and concerns* (pp. 3–31). New York: Teachers College Press.

Goodlad, J. I. (1996). Sustaining and extending educational renewal. *Phi Delta Kappan, 78,* 228–234 [Retrieved July 18, 2000 from WilsonSelect on-line database (Number: BRDG97006691; ISSN: 0031-7217)].

Goodlad, J. I. (1999). Simultaneously renewing schools and teacher education: Perils and promises. In R. W. Clark (Ed.), *Effective professional development schools* (pp. 70–89). San Francisco: Jossey-Bass.

Goodlad, J. I., & Soder, R. (1992). *School-university partnerships: An appraisal of an idea* (Occasional Paper No. 15). Seattle, WA: University of Washington, Center for Educational Renewal.

Gray, B. (1985). Conditions facilitating interorganizational collaboration. *Human Relations 38,* 911–936.

Gray, B. (1989). *Collaborating: Finding common ground for multiparty problems.* San Francisco: Jossey Bass.

Gray, D. (1990). School-business partnership for school improvement (Doctoral dissertation, Portland State University and University of Oregon, 1989). *Dissertation Abstracts International, 51,* 1062A.

Greene, G. (1985). The nature and process of organization in a collaborative school-business partnership (Doctoral dissertation, University of Massachusetts, 1985). *Dissertation Abstracts International, 46,* 1489A.

Grobe, T. (1990). *Synthesis of existing knowledge and practice in the field of educational partnerships.* Brandeis University, Waltham, MA: The Center for Human Resources.

Grobe, T. (1993). *Synthesis of existing knowledge and practice in the field of educational partnerships.* Washington, DC: Office of Educational Research and Improvement. (ERIC Document Reproduction Service No. ED 362 994)

Harrington, J. G. (1990). School/university/business partnership: Collaboration in a tripartite partnership (Doctoral dissertation, Fordham University, 1989). *Dissertation Abstracts International, 50,* 3119A.

Havelock, R. G., Cox, P. L., Huberman, A. M., & Levinson, N. (1982). *School-university collaboration supporting school improvement. Volume IV: Comparison and synthesis of three cases.* Washington, DC: American University, Center for Technology and Administration. (ERIC Document Reproduction Service No. ED 225 971)

Hill, S. (n.d.). *New forms of collaboration.* Unpublished manuscript, University of South Australia at Magill.

The Holmes Partnership. (2000, June). *Members of the Holmes Partnership.* Retrieved July 24, 2000 from the World Wide Web: http://www.holmespartnership.org/members.html

Hord, S. M. (1986). A synthesis of research on organizational collaboration. *Educational Leadership, 43*(5), 22–26.

Huse, E. F., & Cummings, T. G. (1985). *Organization development and change.* St. Paul, MN: West.

Intriligator, B. (1986, April). *Collaborating with the schools: A strategy for school improvement.* Paper presented at the annual meeting of the American Educational Research Association, San Francisco. (ERIC Document Reproduction Service No. ED 277 089)

Intriligator, B. (1992). *Establishing interorganizational structures that facilitate successful school partnerships.* Paper presented at the annual meeting of the American Educational Research Association, San Francisco.

Kanter, R. M. (1989). *When giants learn to dance: Mastering the challenges of strategy, management, and careers in the 1990's.* New York: Simon and Schuster.

Kersh, M. E., & Masztal, N. B. (1998). An analysis of studies of collaboration between universities and K-12 schools. *The Educational Forum, 62,* 218–225 [Retrieved from WilsonSelect on-line database (Number BED198013863)].

Klohmann, E. L. (1988). Intergroup dynamics in a collaborative relationship: A study of an alternative high school and a sponsoring college (Doctoral dissertation, New York University, 1987). *Dissertation Abstracts International, 49,* 19A.

Levine, M. (1997). Introduction. In M. Levine & R. Trachtman (Eds.), *Making professional development schools work: Politics, practice, and policy* (pp. 1–11). New York: Teachers College Press.

Levine, M., & Churins, E. J. (1999). Designing standards that empower professional development schools. *Peabody Journal of Education, 74,* 178–208.

Lieberman, A. (1992). School/university collaboration: A view from the inside. *Phi Delta Kappan, 74,* 147–152, 154, 156.

Maeroff, G. I. (1983). *School and college: Partnerships in education.* Princeton, NJ: Carnegie Foundation for the Advancement of Teaching.

National Association of Partners in Education. (2000). Retrieved July 24, 2000 from the World Wide Web: http://www.partnersineducation.org/1.html

National Council for Accreditation of Teacher Education. (2001). *Standards for professional development schools.* Washington, DC: Author. Retrieved April 26, 2001 from the World Wide Web: http://www.ncate.org/2000/PDS_Stands_10-00.pdf

National Network for Educational Renewal. (2000). Retrieved July 24, 2000 from the World Wide Web: http://www.depts.washington.edu/cedren/NationalNetworkForEducationalRenewal.html

Padak, N. D., Shaklee, B. D., Peck, J., Barton, L., & Johnson, H. (1994, April). *A three-year examination of participants' perspectives of educational partnerships.* Paper presented at the annual meeting of the American Educational Research Association, New Orleans.

Payzant, T. W. (1992). New beginnings in San Diego: Developing a strategy for interagency collaboration. *Phi Delta Kappan, 74,* 139–146.

Ring, P. S., & Van de Ven, A. H. (1994). Developmental processes of cooperative interorganizational relationships. *The Academy of Management Review, 19,* 90 [Retrieved July 20, 2000 from ProQuest on-line database (ISSN: 03637425)].

Simmons, J. M., Konecki, L. R., Crowell, R. A., & Gates-Duffield, P. (1999). Dream keepers, weavers, and shape-shifters: Emerging roles of PDS university coordinators in educational reform. In D. M. Byrd & D. J. McIntyre (Eds.), *Research on professional development schools: Teacher education yearbook VII* (pp. 29–45). Thousand Oaks, CA: Corwin.

Sirotnik, K. A. (1988). The meaning and conduct of inquiry in school-university partnerships. In K. A. Sirotnik & J. I. Goodlad (Eds.), *School university partnerships in action: Concepts, cases, and concerns* (pp. 169–190). New York: Teachers College Press.

Smith, R. B. (1989). School-college collaboration: A case study of Lilly Endowment linkage grants in Indiana (Doctoral dissertation, Harvard University, 1988). *Dissertation Abstracts International, 49,* 2556A.

Su, Z. (1990). *School-university partnerships: Ideas and experiments (1986-1990)* (Occasional Paper No. 12). Seattle, WA: University of Washington, Center for Educational Renewal.

Teitel, L. (1997). The Organization and governance of professional development schools. In M. Levine & R. Trachtman (Eds.), *Making professional development schools work: Politics, practice, and policy* (pp. 115–133). New York: Teachers College Press.

Teitel, L. (1998). Separations, divorces, and open marriages in professional development school partnerships. *Journal of Teacher Education, 49,* 85–96.

Teitel, L. (1999). Looking toward the future by understanding the past: The historical context of professional development schools. *Peabody Journal of Education, 74,* 6–20

Thorkildsen, R., & Stein, M. R. S. (1996). Fundamental characteristics of successful university-school partnership. *The School Community Journal, 6,* 79–92.

Trubowitz, S., & Longo, P. (1997). *How it works—Inside a school-college collaboration.* New York: Teachers College Press.

Tushnet, N. C. (1993). *A guide to developing educational partnerships.* Washington, DC: Office of Educational research and Improvement. (ERIC Document Reproduction Service No. ED 362 992)

U.S. Department of Education. (1994, May). What GOALS 2000 means for you. *Community Update, 13,* pp. 2–4.

Van de Ven, A. H. (1976). On the nature, formation, and maintenance of relations among organizations. *Academy of Management Review, 1,* 24–36.

Van de Ven, A. H., Emmett, D. C., & Koenig, R. (1980). Frameworks for interorganizational analysis. In A. R. Neghandi (Ed.), *Interorganization theory* (pp. 19–38). Kent, OH: Kent State University Press.

Wangemann, P. (1989). Successful university-public school partnerships: The union of theory and practice (Doctoral dissertation, Brigham Young University, 1988). *Dissertation Abstracts International, 49,* 2066A.

Whetten, D. A. (1981). Interorganizational relations: A review of the field. *Journal of Higher Education, 52,* 1–28.

Williams, R. O. (1996). Professional development schools: Facing the challenge of institutionalization. *Contemporary Education 67,* 171–179.

Wilson, C., Clark, R., & Heckman, P. (1989). *Breaking new ground: Reflections on the school-university partnerships in the national network for educational renewal* (Occasional Paper No. 8). Seattle, WA: University of Washington, Center for Educational Renewal.

Zywine, J. (1991, April). *Views from the field: A perspective on school university partnerships.* Paper presented at the annual meeting of the American Educational Research Association, Chicago.

Section II

Collaboration Through the Eyes of the Partners

Model I

Collaboration Between a University and Professional Development School

The main purpose of this collaboration is preservice teacher training, although the schools also can serve other purposes, such as providing a location for students' fieldwork and fellowship training. The relationship between the school and the university may be formal or informal.

Chapter

4

Recipes for Professional Development Schools: A Metaphor for Collaboration

Pamela Gates-Duffield and Carol Stark

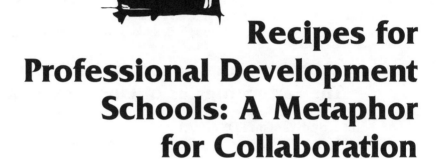

Muffins

1 egg	*Heat oven to 400*
3/4 cup milk	*Grease bottoms of 12 muffin cups*
2 cups flour	*Beat egg, milk, and oil*
1/3 cup sugar	*Stir in remaining ingredients*
3 tsp. baking powder	*Fill muffin cups 1/2 to 3/4 full*
1 tsp salt	*Bake 20 minutes until brown*
2 tbsp oil	

Variations: *Stir in apples, nuts, blueberries, bananas, cranberries, dates, berries, or any cup of chopped fruit (except melon)*
Substitute honey or brown sugar for sugar
Stir in 1/2 cup pumpkin & 1/2 cup of raisin with pie spices

Most of us have favorite recipes—recipes like the one above that have been handed down from family members or close friends—that we honor by preparing for those special feasts in our lives. Sometimes we keep the recipe true to its original owner, but many times, we change things—more spice, less sugar—to make it our

45

own. Out of these changes and new blends, we create a new and oftentimes healthier version worth celebrating. For us, the collaborative work of professional development schools (PDS) has been like this new recipe metaphor—honoring the old, changing some ingredients, and blending the mixture into a new creation worth celebrating. We have chosen to use the recipe metaphor to help us describe a multiyear PDS project between a middle school and its university partner and the collaborative partnership that developed as a result.

The recipe of our work and collaborative writing is delineated by the headings. Our voices, like the metaphor itself, alternately retain their distinctive flavors and blend together in an attempt to complement and honor our collaborative partnership. As with any process of collaboration, ours was not created in a vacuum. The PDS project was the vehicle for our collaborative efforts and directly influenced our work together. Although we use the recipe metaphor to describe our own experiences, it does not presume that all partnerships could or should be like ours. Instead, this is one of many stories of collaboration; it reflects the setting and purposes of our work together. As the metaphor suggests, the recipe is flexible as long as the basic ingredients remain.

Acquiring and Honoring the Recipe: The Early Struggles of Our Partnership

The early days of the PDS project at West Intermediate School were curious times because this was the second such project in the school district. Support from the school district and university was evidenced by the frequent visits from administrators during the scheduled professional development days and school improvement meetings and a willingness to provide needed resources in terms of space and clerical support. From the outset, there were concerns about issues of university control and central office mandates for change. By the time we began preliminary discussions with school improvement members from West Intermediate, however, the initiative for a change from a junior high school to a middle school had begun. In fact, West Intermediate had been awarded a two-year grant intended for the restructuring change—a process to begin work on becoming a middle school.

Pam's Voice

From my perspective at Central Michigan University (CMU), all of this presented a good and strong foundation for entering into a PDS partnership. It seemed evident to me that the climate of the school was one ripe for change—hadn't they indicated that through their work with the grant for restructuring? Little did I know about the politics of schools. Although there had been some resistance from parents in the early days of the PDS efforts at McGuire, that had been two years earlier, and I, in my naivete, thought we as educators were far past such resistance.

As conversations began with West faculty and staff, I quickly became aware of the tensions and suspicions they held. They seemed to fear that CMU would come in and take over in some way. As an outsider, someone fairly new to CMU and the educational arena itself, I was stymied by the levels of distrust exhibited toward CMU faculty. Perhaps because I had no history with either institution, or perhaps because I sought only to form collaborative relationships, not hierarchies, I asked a lot of questions, and listened closely to the answers. I was able to discover that the teachers with whom I wanted to work at West Intermediate held some deep concerns about letting the university into their classrooms. Would they be judged? Would they be told to do things differently by professor-types who had not taught middle school students in years—if ever? Were we just tying to gain entrance to use them as some sort of research experiment? The fears were real, and they ran deep. I only could surmise that these concerns were based on problems that had occurred with the university in the past. Curious, I asked about their affiliation (or lack of) with the National Middle School Project that was based at CMU because it was receiving great reviews and support across the state. Again, their initial interaction with the project's representative had left them suspicious of the university's motives. Throughout the early discussions about becoming a PDS, I continued to ask the questions of what kind of support was needed to continue the change process they had begun under their grant for restructuring. In response, I often received questions about what the university expected from them. I began to realize that even though one PDS partnership had been established in the district, there were no guarantees that other schools were necessarily eager to join forces with the university. I needed to learn from them how to negotiate within a new environment—one that suspected my motives and those of the university for whom I worked. It wasn't enough for me to simply want to be a partner; I had to become invested in that partnership through a common set of goals. We found a connection through our shared desire to become better teachers and learners for the sake of the students we taught—at the middle school and at the university.

Carol's Voice

I assumed the position of principal of West Intermediate School, with a seventh- and eighth-grade student population, in August 1993, moving from assistant principal of Mt. Pleasant High School, a position I had held for three years. The superintendent gave me the specific charge of making the transition from a junior high to a middle school more than a discussion item at faculty meetings. The conversation at West Intermediate about becoming a middle school had been, depending on with whom one spoke, a topic for a period of time that ranged from a few years to twenty years. A two-year, $50,000 grant awarded to West Intermediate for restructuring had resulted in no actual changes. It was apparent from parent concerns, media coverage, and general staff attitudes that action was needed.

During the previous school year, there had been discussion regarding the possibility of becoming a PDS. The subsequent vote indicated that the majority of teachers did not want to make a commitment to this PDS initiative, and the conversations about change ended. The discussions preceding the vote focused on previous contacts with CMU staff with whom the school staff had experienced uncomfortable situations. One such effort to include West Intermediate as a part of the National Middle School Project at CMU for restructuring middle schools ended with a decision by West Intermediate staff never to be involved in that initiative or with that individual. The CMU representative for the project who had met with the West Intermediate faculty indicated how they should be doing things without ever listening to what they were currently doing, what they had tried, or how they perceived they might need assistance in their efforts to become a middle school. The message the staff heard from the university "expert" was that she knew how to do their jobs better than they did. As a result of this difficult past, when I broached the subject of becoming a PDS partner with CMU that first fall, the negative reactions were speedy and emotion laden.

Another frequently expressed perception of PDS partnerships was that a partnership with CMU would only result in the loss of control of their school. Teachers believed the partnership gave the state and CMU the license to interfere; they were unable to envision any benefits to West Intermediate staff and students. They spoke of their reluctance to have university professors, who were not in schools dealing with the realities of public school education, telling them how they should be doing things and acting like they knew how to do it better.

Although no staff member ever completely voiced it, I felt that there was a dichotomy of perceptions. Many expressed their fear that these CMU partners would act as if they knew more than we did about teaching and learning in the middle school. I also think that some of these individuals considered the possibility that the CMU professors actually might know more and would discover their insecurities regarding their knowledge base and delivery of instruction in a middle school environment.

Pam's Voice

As both reflections show, we each entered the arena of collaboration with a particular set of expectations. The early work of the partnership mandated that Carol and I listen carefully to all the partners and then work to develop a PDS plan that would incorporate the ideas of all participants. What we learned early in the process, however, was that to move forward, we first needed to step back and listen to the voices of the teachers with whom we worked. We needed to understand the basis for their suspicions and work to allay their fears. These early challenges to create a cohesive team challenged us to form an alliance that grew into a full partnership over time.

The Basic Ingredients: How Do We Describe Our Partnership?

Pam's Voice

As with any recipe, there are certain ingredients that must exist for it to become a particular dish. With our muffin recipe, it is clear that whatever type of muffin we choose to make, whether it be blueberry, banana, or pumpkin, certain things remain essential—flour, milk, eggs, baking powder, salt, and a sweetener. The same can be argued for school–university partnerships, although the ingredients may seem a bit more elusive.

What we discovered was that the three primary ingredients were essential: trust, invested and informed participants at all levels (administrators, CMU faculty, and master teachers), and shared vision. When any portion of those three key ingredients is in short supply, the partnership suffers. From the university perspective, the ingredients most at risk are the shared vision and the invested and informed participants from the university. In our partnership, trust on the part of the university was never a problem; however, keeping a shared vision and invested participants from the university was an issue. In addition, the rapid turnover of higher level administrators can be a real problem for sustaining long-term investments in programs and initiatives. With each new administrator comes a new set of issues and agendas for change. With luck and continued briefing, some initiatives can survive, but many are phased out. To some extent, such was the case with our PDS projects. When West Intermediate and CMU began discussions of a partnership, the university climate was one of full support. The major funding agency at the time was the Michigan Partnership for New Education, and it invested substantial amounts of money into PDS projects across the state of Michigan. The key to the investment, however, was the university commitment to match funds. What that led to was a financial and human resource commitment from the university—one that offered a visible sign to university faculty and to the school district that this partnership was important. For us, as a university faculty, it meant that our teaching loads were reduced to allow time for us to work in schools with teachers and students to become partners in educational change. Faculty from both sectors—public schools and university—learned from each other, taking back new information and ways of doing things to their respective classrooms of students. For my own teaching, I felt grounded, knowing that I had current public school classrooms of teachers and students to validate the theoretical ideals I expounded.

For our partnership, the vision developed out of the six principles published by the Holmes Group (1990) in the publication of Tomorrow's Schools; they guided the way we began to think about our work together. The principles are the following:

1. Teaching and learning for understanding

2. Creating a learning community

3. Teaching and learning for understanding for everybody's children

4. Continuing learning by teachers, teacher educators, and administrators

5. Thoughtful long-term inquiry into teaching and learning

6. Inventing a new institution

Early in our work together, Carol and I began to see ourselves as vision keepers in that we understood the impact of those principles on the collaborative efforts in which we were engaged. As we did that, we began to realize that the vision we shared was in fact the basis for the partnership.

Carol's Voice

From my perspective, there were a number of basic ingredients that influenced the decision to begin a partnership with CMU when the proposal was again placed before the staff. The first was the directive from the Board of Education, which had been in place for several years, to transition from a junior high school to a middle school. The philosophical base existed at the Board of Education and central office level for this change; however, no specific directions or time line had been given.

Most of the teachers at West Intermediate were familiar with the Michigan Curriculum Framework, and several content area teachers were actively involved in realigning the curriculum at West Intermediate with the Standards and Benchmarks. In addition, the culture in the district supported the growth of teacher leaders and provided frequent opportunities for professional development and leadership training.

Pam and I were two additional ingredients, and neither of us had been a part of the original attempts for transition to the middle school and adoption of the PDS initiative. We were new faces who were not tied to previously failed efforts. Pam presented the components of the PDS initiative to the faculty again. We gave them a month to consider the benefits and responsibilities of entering the partnership with Central Michigan University, met again for additional questions, and asked for an agreement from all staff members to support the partnership. I indicated to them that my expectation was that all members would participate in the initiative, but that each individual could determine his or her level of participation. In addition, it was my expectation that no member would sabotage the work of his or her colleagues in our restructuring journey. A vote of support was each individual's promise that he or she would participate at some level and would not be a saboteur. The vote was 100 percent in favor of entering the partnership.

During that month of consideration, Pam and I had frequent conversations about our educational visions and our vision for West Intermediate. We discovered that we had similar views. We also discovered that we were both driven by what is right and good for kids and that we were both willing to fight the fight to make right and good things happen for kids. Pam also had enough conversations with the West Intermediate staff that they began to develop a comfort level with her. She listened and responded to their concerns with suggestions for possible solutions and changes that fit into their comfort zones and realms of possibilities. These conversations were the catalyst that allowed the staff to shift their trust significantly enough to make the commitment to the PDS partnership.

Another important ingredient was the funding that came with the PDS partnership. The staff had never had fiscal control over or responsibility for such a large amount of money. They were wary about whether the central office would really allow internal control of that amount of money and were curious if CMU would really turn over their contribution to a group of middle school educators. The process of making sound expenditure decisions became a significant part of the sense of responsibility of the study groups. They were proud of the fiscal sense they developed.

Master teachers and those teachers involved with realignment of curriculum were also critical participants in the change process. They understood the history of pain, the personalities of their colleagues, the need for change, and the politics of making any changes. Their leadership was instrumental to the speed with which we were able to begin the dialogue about how we wanted to structure ourselves to accomplish our tasks. Our district had established a culture that fostered professional development as a part of the teaching professional's role, and our teacher leaders at West Intermediate supported the focus and importance of professional development to learn the best practices of school restructuring. With these individuals, Pam and I became the "keepers of the vision" and rallied the staff when deadlines and difficult decisions needed to be made.

Trust and respect were vital basic ingredients, not prevalent at the inception of the partnership, that actually grew as we worked together on daily planning, gathering research data, and carrying forth the shared vision.

Blending the Old and the New:
Our Voices Merge to Solve the Problems

As with any recipe change, one can never be certain of the results while the product is under construction. Such was the case with our partnership. Even as the climate of trust grew, there was at times still a sense of skepticism about the process.

The perception of some of the staff as we began planning specific changes was that we needed permission from "central office" to implement them. I indicated that my experience with initiatives with which I had worked at the high school had not required permission from the superintendent or assistant superintendent for implementation as long as they were research based and fiscally responsible. As we implemented change at West Intermediate and did not suffer from intervention from central office, the concern disappeared and the question was no longer posed.

One of the most significant contributions of the PDS initiative was goal setting and the study group process. As a whole faculty, we determined each school year the areas on which we would focus our efforts. Study groups were formed for each focus area, and every staff member selected a study group with which to work. The study group process became the foundation of all of our efforts for change.

Pam and I each joined a study group, and Pam solicited other university professors to join the remaining study groups. Whether CMU professor or West Intermediate staff member, the roles and responsibilities of membership were the same. We served as equals, each with a responsibility to contribute our expertise to achieve the goals. Study groups grew into teams, developed trust, and expanded their horizons together in the search for what was best for our students.

The Transition Study Group examined the emotional needs of students transitioning from sixth to seventh grades and from eighth to ninth grades. Another study group that also sought to meet the needs of students was the Affective Needs Study Group. Other study groups included Restructuring, Inquiry, Cross Curriculum Language Arts, and Resources/Teacher Education. Throughout the process, faculty from West Intermediate and CMU worked together to find professional development opportunities to support the initiatives and goals set by the particular study groups. This blending of ideas, information, and ingenuity created a new community of learners that crossed institutional boundaries.

We learned from our CMU partners how to make decisions based on research, both from educational research studies and their accompanying recommendations and our own research. We learned how to implement action research, to evaluate programs, and make changes according to our research findings. We developed a decision-making consensus model that we used to support recommendations from study groups. I learned from previous experience that given the choice to change or not, most people will opt for not. Therefore, decisions presented to the staff were how to implement a recommended change, not whether to implement the change. Staff, who previously had not wanted any change, began to see the many possibilities to better meet the needs of students and to enhance their achievement. We were able to make several difficult changes in building configuration and curriculum delivery through the study group process.

My role as the building principal and instructional leader changed as well. I met with each study group throughout the restructuring process and was able to react to their proposals, offer suggestions or a different view, and discuss allocation of funds with them. I no longer had to be the driving force for change in our journey to becoming a middle school. It was exciting to watch as teachers became leaders of their study groups, grew personally and professionally, and began to ask hard questions of their colleagues about what was right for our students and school.

Other ways in which the school and university became intertwined were through the School Improvement team. Once the partnership began, the university faculty members were invited to participate in the school improvement team process as non-voting members. As part of that advisory team, university members were kept apprised of district and community agendas that sometimes influenced the decision-making process—all new experiences for most university faculty.

We experienced one particular difficulty that we never were able to completely solve. As we realigned curriculum to match the Standards and Benchmarks of the Michigan Curriculum Framework, parents began to question the differences between content and instruction at the middle school and the high school. In particular, the writing process became a kindergarten through eighth-grade initiative but was not adopted at the high school. In addition, high school teachers convinced parents that we were solely responsible for the teaching of grammar. With help from Pam, other university partners, and the assistant superintendent, we presented the aligned curriculum and our improved test scores to parents. We were able to convince most of them that our curriculum delivery was appropriate, but we did not convince the language arts teachers at the high school.

What we came to understand more fully as we worked together was that although we participated in study groups and worked to align our curriculum at West Intermediate, people outside of the partnership were not able to understand and therefore respect the collaborative efforts of the team. Their agenda did not match our agenda. It became important to remember that our partnership was limited primarily to West Intermediate and the programs we fostered. Collaborative partnerships are built on the ingredients of trust and invested and informed participants. Sometimes, as in our case, those ingredients of trust and invested and informed participants are restricted to the site. We learned that it was unrealistic to expect outsiders to understand the dynamics of our partnership and our site-based decision-making process because they had not made the commitment or the journey with us.

Changing the Flavor, Adding the Spices: The Vignettes of Successful Changes

Carol's Voice

We celebrated the thirtieth anniversary of the opening of the building during my tenure at West Intermediate, and despite many years of discussion about the transition to a middle school, the schedule still modeled a junior high school for most of those thirty years. As study groups began research and study of best practices, they made recommendations for change. It was as those changes, and others that I deemed important in our transition, were implemented that the behind-the-scenes conversations flourished.

One of the first changes I implemented was creating team areas by clustering classrooms by teams so that the social studies, math, and language arts teachers for each team had classrooms in the same area. Math teachers had been housed in classrooms on the second floor since the opening of the building. The move was scheduled to occur over the summer so that classrooms would be ready for use the following fall. Teachers boxed up their thirty-year accumulations of materials and they moved. It was that following fall that I learned there had been a huge debate among their colleagues whether the math teachers would in fact leave their departmental configuration on the second floor.

We implemented interdisciplinary instruction, preparing units that included combinations of two, three, and four core classes. Teachers on each team had a common prep hour to prepare these units, to discuss student achievement, and to meet with students, parents, and counselors. The fact that core team teachers had both a personal prep hour and a team prep hour meant that they taught one less section each day than noncore teachers. That issue surfaced sporadically and was always coupled with discussion regarding the overall benefits for the student and noncore teachers when teams met with parents.

We tried assorted combinations of block scheduling, none of which worked completely as planned. Classes such as band and choir, which were offered only one period a day and shared classrooms placed serious restrictions on creating a pure block for all students on each team. As a result, there was always a group of students on each team who could not be scheduled to benefit from the interdisciplinary instruction provided through blocks. This also limited using the blocks for team field trips and guest speakers because not all students could participate in these activities.

As we implemented the many components of a middle school, West Intermediate teachers were invited to present at both National and Michigan Middle School Conferences. When they returned, they shared the progress of other schools that were also involved in the process of transitioning to a middle school, information that validated our hard work and indicated that we were far ahead of other schools. This information served us well because at times it seemed we had accomplished so little and had so much yet to do.

Pam's Voice

Adding new spices to any recipe will change the flavor of the finished product. Such was the case of our collaborative work with the faculty at West Intermediate and CMU. As is often the case in university towns, many of the teachers in the district take their graduate classes at CMU. During our PDS work with West Intermediate, I had the opportunity to work with one of the English language arts teachers as my graduate student. She was pursuing a master's degree in English. She had taught at the Mt. Pleasant High School, and I had first had the opportunity to meet her as the teacher of French for my son and later as my youngest daughter's English teacher at West Intermediate. Throughout the years, we had often talked about the desire to work together outside of the PDS efforts, and through her graduate work at CMU, we finally had the chance. What was interesting for me, as a university professor, was the opportunity to interact with this teacher on multiple levels—parent to teacher, colleague to colleague, teacher to student. I can now imagine all types of horror stories that could have manifested themselves with this multiplicity of interactions, but fortunately, our work together was an engaging learning experience for us both.

Two professional interests that I had been actively researching and had been interested in for some time were in the areas of book groups and multiple intelligences. Although I had introduced the concepts and had given talks about both, I had not had the opportunity to apply these concepts to younger students for any extended period. Through Deb, I was able to observe both in action.

The first action research application that Deb instituted at West Intermediate was the idea of book groups. The program was designed to get middle school students and their parents to read and discuss young adult literature together under the guidance of Deb as facilitator. Each month the students and their parents would choose a book to read. They would read the book and return a month later for a structured discussion. Because it was an evening meeting time, the numbers remained low, but the discussions were insightful for both students and parents.

The other shared area of interest was the study of multiple intelligences. Through her research and the formal paper she subsequently used to complete her master's degree, I was able to discover how the theoretical side of the study met the realities of middle school classroom work. Through her work with middle school students, Deb seemed to make a conscious effort to engage all of her students in the study of English language arts. Her methodology was varied, and she concerned herself with finding new ways, supported by her research in the theory of multiple intelligences, to connect students to literature, poetry, and writing. Based on the exceptionally high MEAP testing scores and on student feedback, I believe her students left her classroom well prepared for the rigor of high school English classes.

The other "spice" that added an interesting and sometimes frustrating ingredient to the PDS recipe was my work with the 7–12 Language Arts Task Force. As Carol has alluded, there was significant tension and disagreement between Language Arts teachers in the middle and high school grades. High School teachers complained loudly that the students arriving from West Intermediate were not prepared for their high school English courses. This disagreement is not found only in our school district. As the teaching of writing has moved toward a workshop or process-driven approach, the chasm between middle school teachers and high school teachers of English has grown. Disagreements about what is taught, how it is taught, what is developmentally appropriate, and what is expected at the next grade level are found in many districts; ours is no exception. In an effort to bridge the gap, I agreed to participate in a task force that would attempt to address the misunderstandings and foster a climate in which teachers at both levels could work together productively. As I sat in meeting after meeting, I came to realize that although I had worked successfully in the PDS projects in both schools with a number of teachers, I was not able to act as an effective conduit for discussion in my own discipline. As a university professor who taught people to become English teachers in grades K–12, I knew the theory and practice of teaching English, and that should have provided some type of link between the two systems; however, I was wrong. Two things that had helped me to gain trust as a collaborative partner—my commitment to education and my commitment to the district as a parent—were now the very things that blocked my effectiveness. My three children had been students of many of the teachers sitting around the table, both at the middle school and at the high school. As a parent, I knew the assignments, the expectations, and the end results. As an English educator, I knew the strengths and weakness of those assignments and how things might have been done better. I could say little of substance without offending someone and thus putting my youngest daughter in a difficult learning situation. I was not an effective representative and knew it. Based on that set of experiences, I introduced a colleague who was not connected to the district and was a linguist by profession. Her input and work with teachers on aspects of grammar instruction has helped to move the task force in a more productive direction—or at least one that is certainly less potentially dramatic.

Creating a New Recipe: The Results

When a new recipe is complete, the taste test is done; if it has been a success, the celebration of sharing the new recipe with friends begins. Such is also the case with successful school–university partnerships. Although the work of change is difficult, the rewards are certainly worth the labor. Each time a successful event occurs, it is shared and celebrated to honor the hard work and accomplishments. Through that celebration comes a sense of recognition, and with that recognition comes a willingness to try again.

It was exciting as we made our own professional transitions to educational researchers. Our decisions were driven by the primary goal of improved student achievement. We made decisions within our consensus model of site-based decision making, supporting the research-based recommendations of each study group. The influences, which typically determine the structure and schedule of a middle school such as teacher prep hours and contractual limitations, became secondary.

The faculty at West Intermediate created a new school—through teaming and through study groups, they began to address the needs of their students in new and innovative ways. As new program initiatives became a part of the new school expectations, faculty began to see themselves differently—as researchers, as change agents, as professional educators. Attending and presenting their research at the National Middle School Conference became part of how they, as educators, began to promote the work of their restructured school. Their work became recognized by the district and through their national presentations.

The commitment of all of the teachers to support the principles of a PDS remained intact. Teacher leaders blossomed, adding renewed energy and revived idealism to many of the veteran teachers. We began to understand better that professional development was central to implementation of new initiatives.

The community watched and listened as we moved through our transition. We kept them up-to-date on our progress at parent meetings, through newsletter articles, and by responses to specific questions. Initial parental concerns were alleviated as we presented plans for changes accompanied by supporting research. We gathered student and parent opinions with surveys as a part of our evaluation process and made decisions about our programs.

Parents began to trust and respect our efforts to become a middle school. We became particularly aware of their belief in the middle school philosophy when layoffs eliminated five teachers. They immediately reacted, questioning the probable impact on their student's comfort and success at West Intermediate with the limitations on teaming with the decreased number of teachers. They obviously had listened to our research presentations and used the information as they expressed their displeasure with the layoff decisions. Unfortunately, these least-senior teachers were those most flexible and comfortable with change.

Pam's influence and support of our work became intertwined with all of our efforts at restructuring. Staff members did not question her sincerity or motives and trusted her recommendations for change. She was a driving force in maintaining the enthusiasm for our journey.

But, as with all good things, factors and personnel change. To continue the pace and productivity experienced during the first few years of the PDS initiative would have required a sustained level of funding and support from the administrative level at the university and district levels. That did not happen. Changes in key administrators—deans and superintendents—can and does affect the final product; they're part of the basic ingredients.

As we reflected throughout our work together, Pam and I discovered several ingredients that had had significant impact on the continued success of our recipe. Key central office administrators did not understand or respect the needs of West Intermediate teachers in their commitment to change, and as a result they often failed to validate our efforts and participate in our celebrations. Funding and the human resource support from CMU began to diminish. The most significant blow to our restructuring work came from the change at the superintendent level. Unfortunately, the new superintendent did not share the vision of the teachers in the district. He had no experience with a collaborative partnership with a university, nor did he believe that teaching and learning should be the driving forces in decisions regarding the use of resources in the district. We maintained our vision and continued our work and affiliation with Pam and the university, but the zest for change became more difficult to sustain.

Why Use Metaphor to Describe Our Work? Our Suggestions

The use of the recipe metaphor has been an interesting way for Carol and me to tell the story of our collaborative work together. For us, it functioned as a way to frame the different components that were needed to create a successful PDS experience. Obviously, in this recipe, we placed ourselves in the role of chef, but it would be incorrect to assume that we were the only ones whipping up this recipe of change. Without the support of faculty and administrators from the university and the district, none of the change could have occurred. To create a collaborative relationship between any school and university requires the input, hard work, and commitment of many; we had that support. Change happened because all of us wanted the best practices of teaching and learning for understanding for students at West Intermediate. Through the process of collaboration, we were able to meet the needs of students in new and innovative ways; and as a parent of one of those students, I am appreciative of that commitment from the faculty and staff.

The joining of a principal and a school staff is much like blending the ingredients of a recipe. If personalities are not compatible, if the principal is not able to respond to the learning and processing styles of the staff, and especially if the visions are not similar, they will never blend into a workable team. I am a person who thrives on the challenges of change. The staff at West Intermediate was ready to make the significant moves that would bring to fruition their years of discussion. We were an excellent blend. The availability of the PDS resources gave us the support we needed to take the risks and to actualize our vision.

Final Reflections on Collaborative Partnerships

As we worked together to create this essay, we were once again struck by the collaborative process, this time in terms of writing. Because Carol and I now have worked together for several years, we were curious about how the telling of our separate pieces of this collaborative experience would fit. After several discussions—over the phone, via e-mail, at a breakfast meeting, and later over more coffee at my home office—we landed on the framework of the recipe metaphor to structure our early writing efforts. That settled, we went away to our separate lives, now in different cities, to reconstruct the story of the work that had brought us together from our roles as professionals, to become colleagues, to end as friends.

As we came back together two weeks later over breakfast, we were pleasantly surprised at the initial writing efforts. What we said fit together and made sense. Later in the process, we would comment on how the stories—once separate voices—were blending together, just as the recipe metaphor suggested. By the final reading of this essay, we began to question one another as to who wrote what paragraph. The voices of the collaborative experience had blended together so well that to identify ownership of key phrases, we now had to check our own drafts. As we finished, we realized that, like our work in the PDS initiative, it no longer mattered who did what. It only mattered that we had been given the opportunity to work together collaboratively, did it well, and that in retrospect, the initiative had been worth doing, both for the students and for teachers with whom we worked.

References

The Holmes Group. (1990). *Tomorrow's schools*. East Lansing, MI: The Holmes Group.

Chapter

Learning Connections: Working Toward a Shared Vision

Robin Hasslen, Nancy Bacharach, Judy Rotto, and Jonathan Fribley

As the minutes of the morning ticked slowly by, six-year-old Alissa sat by the door, looking anxiously down the hallway. Her teacher reminded her that Alissa's long-awaited "book buddy" would be properly introduced when she arrived. Undeterred, Alissa continued to post herself at the door to the classroom. Finally, "Grandma Jean" arrived to begin her first mentoring experience as part of the professional development school (PDS) Book Buddy program. Assuming that this elderly woman was her *buddy, Alissa grabbed her tightly around the legs and looking up, said, "Ohhh, I have waited for you my whole life!"*

As part of a fledgling PDS partnership, those of us involved feel just like Alissa: We seem to have been waiting for this experience our entire professional lives! Having experienced enough of the new relationship to be simultaneously excited about it and yet aware of its challenges, we would like to share our reflections on the first year of this partnership between a university and a public school district. These two types of institutions have been taking journeys together for years. A more traditional journey is often directed by a university that determines its needs and enlists a school to fulfill them. There is no collaboration in the traditional model, no joint planning or decision making. The two worlds of schools and universities differ from each other in many significant ways (Collins, 1995; Darling-Hammond, 1994). It is inevitable that this relationship, like any new alliance, creates dissonance. At the same time, it is this very uncertainty that can lead to new and innovative ideas and make partnerships a complex yet exciting venture.

Despite the reality and abundance of these traditional relationships, the development of collaborative partnerships between public schools and teacher education programs has experienced tremendous growth since the mid-1980s. According to Darling-Hammond (1994), professional partnerships between public schools and universities "seek to reshape fundamental values, beliefs, paradigms for schools and school change while . . . negotiating two worlds and inventing new programs" (p. 21).

In this chapter, we will trace the process of the development of collaborative relationships within a school–university partnership. The significance of this journey can be seen in the very different dynamics at two schools within the same partnership.

Description of the Partnership

Our project, the Learning Connections Lab (LCL), began in earnest in the fall of 1997. St. Cloud State University is located in central Minnesota and has a student body of 15,000. Its College of Education graduates about 600 students a year, making it one of the largest teacher preparation institutions in the country. St. Cloud School District #742 enrolls 11,000 students. Site A Elementary has 39% of its students qualifying for free or reduced lunches and a 12% student-of-color population. Site B Elementary has 52% of its students on free or reduced lunches with a 22% student-of-color population.

Although St. Cloud State University (SCSU) has a rich history of collaborative work with area schools, no formal PDS structure was in place. Representatives from SCSU and the local school district met to discuss what a partnership could look like and collaboratively designed a vision and submitted a grant to the state for support. Participants in the LCL were ten Pre-K–3 classroom teachers from two elementary schools, university faculty and students, families, business partners, and service learning volunteers. At the end of the first year of collaboration, one site (Site A) experienced enough success to carry on; the other (Site B) lacked adequate commitment to continue.

With grant money procured from the state in hand, the journey toward creating a "shared vision" for innovative teaching strategies in literacy and lifework skills and providing a new field-based preparation program for preservice teachers was on its way. Because of the demands of the grant, the major goals of literacy and lifework for elementary students took the forefront, immediately creating some amount of dissonance between classroom teachers and university faculty, whose priorities focused on teacher preparation. Interestingly, difficulties with collaboration at Site B almost resulted in the LCL team's self-destruction because of the way in which differences were handled and the ensuing loss of trust among participants. The resolution of those issues, which differed drastically between the two sites, and the evolution toward a shared vision and away from individual interests was a painful yet exciting journey. From all experiences, both positive and negative, there are important lessons to be shared.

Collaboration Efforts and Perspective

Collaboration, unlike cooperation or coordination, is a pervasive relationship in which members contribute their resources to a new structure and then reap the benefits together (Kagan, 1991). Although the concept appears simple, we know the process is not. Collaboration is complex, unpredictable, and tends to be uncomfortable for many of the participants. Forming a new school–university partnership involves ongoing efforts at understanding cultures, establishing relationships, defining roles, developing curriculum, and delineating the decision-making process. It demands commitment from individuals who are willing to be reflective, flexible, and unafraid of change or confrontation—individuals described as "boundary spanners" (Lampert, 1991).

As we went about our work of collaborating, it became evident to us that additional knowledge about how to assess our collaborative efforts would be helpful. A 1992 work by Mattessich and Monsey titled *Collaboration: What Makes It Work* describes factors that make a collaboration successful. Although not intended specifically for school–university partnerships, the piece identified six factors necessary for successful collaboration: environment, membership characteristics, process and structure, communication, purpose, and resources. In an effort to describe as objectively as possible the successes and challenges of establishing a partnership, we provide perceptions in each of the six areas by the Site A teacher/coordinator, the Site B teacher/coordinator, and the faculty liaison at Site A. A response to these perceptions is provided by the university co-director of the partnership.

Environment

The environmental factors related to a PDS address what type of history of collaboration might exist between the institutions involved. The broader community's acceptance of the educational institutions adds to the environmental climate. The environment also includes the support, or lack of support, for the partnership. Obviously, the greater the support from as many groups as possible (political, social, economic), the easier it is to successfully develop and maintain a partnership.

Site A Teacher: Our elementary school has a history of collaboration and cooperation with the community and with the particular faculty person who is our liaison in the LCL. The importance of a positive relationship with the university participants is paramount and was perhaps the most essential piece of our success. The liaison was a former elementary teacher, a parent, and an occasional supervisor of student teachers in our building. She was familiar with most of our staff, had previously conducted research with us concerning multiage classrooms, and was perceived as a supportive, positive, and trusted colleague.

The five teachers involved in the partnership had a history of success with university methods students and student teachers. They were positive and assertive leaders in the school and had served as team instructional leaders and district grade level chairs. Most important at this point in the development of a partnership, these teachers were trusted and respected by nonparticipating teachers in the school.

Our school's proximity to campus was an added plus to the collaboration. Space for a partnership office in the school was limited, however, and practically nonexistent (a room slightly larger than a closet had to accommodate us). There was no room to provide classroom space for the university students, who had to return to the university for their content instruction

Site B Teacher: The context within which the collaborative relationship began at Site B was quite different from that of Site A. Some teachers at this site had experiences with both the university and school district administration that led them to question whether the collaboration would be positive. Teachers had concerns regarding district administrations' handling of previous conflicts at the site and the direction of some district initiatives. Some teachers' previous work with university student teachers and their supervisors led them to mistrust university follow-through.

Nonetheless, some individual relationships lent strength to the partnership. One university faculty technology specialist had worked at this site previously and was immediately valued for his focus on meeting teachers' needs. One teacher's comment that "if everyone from the university was just like ___ " expresses both the positive history that he brought to the site and the perception of negative history with others.

Site A Faculty: St. Cloud State University is one of the top-ten producers of teachers in the nation. One of the drawbacks in having such a large teacher preparation program is the inability to personalize our relationships with the schools. As a way to overcome this problem, faculty often choose to focus their efforts on a few schools. Over the preceding ten years, my work in preparing teachers had involved extensive work with Site A. My knowledge of the school, the teachers, and the students was extremely valuable as we contemplated this new collaborative effort. Reflecting on my past involvement as a university faculty member, however, I realized that our work "together" was not truly a partnership. It seemed that most often, I went to the school with my ideas, my students, and my agenda. I saw the LCL as a way to truly create a new manner of working *with* each other. My respect for the teachers evolved, and the support from the dean and the superintendent were extremely important to me as we moved forward.

On a professional level, I was feeling burned out by the politics and continual positioning of some of my colleagues at the university. I saw the project as a way to remove myself from the constant "drain" of university life. This community of scholars in the LCL became a new, invigorating support system for me. I knew that collaboration would be time and energy intensive, but knowing the players and the support from the administration, I was eager to begin.

Faculty Co-Director Response: The time was ripe for the establishment of a professional development school. In the College of Education, we had a firebrand dean who had had numerous positive experiences in PDSs and had an excellent rapport with the school district administration. Simultaneously, there was much disarray in the process of placement of the hundreds of teacher-education students annually, and the district was becoming overwhelmed by the haphazard way in which arrangements were made. Faculty in the college had established a comfortable role on campus. Moving into the schools was not highly desirable, nor was it perceived with much esteem.

As is obvious from the perceptions above, there was a definite difference in school environments and in participants at the two sites. Had we had more insight into how problematic those issues would become, we might have made changes in personnel early on in the partnership.

Membership Characteristics

Partners in a PDS should possess many attributes, the most important a willingness to respect other members of the collaborative. They must be willing to listen to and observe and attempt to understand others and others' school cultures. The players in a new partnership should be carefully chosen individuals who are committed to self-evaluation, are flexible, and are not afraid of change or confrontation. These people are the "boundary spanners," individuals who are willing to step outside of their cultures and into the fray (Lampert, 1991). It is also essential that key players such as school and university administrators be committed to the partnership with more than a verbal acquiescence to its value.

Site A Teacher: Differing levels of involvement at our site were apparent as some staff chose to take yearlong interns but not be involved in the intensive professional development activities of the project. Teachers involved viewed collaboration as in their own self-interest. There is a deep sense of caring and devotion to the children. There is a pride in the school and a bond that says that everyone working together makes this place a learning family.

As the year wore on, the teachers who had been meeting together weekly during school hours were becoming concerned with time away from their students. Although some were able to concentrate on the fact that they were becoming better teachers, others were concerned about the loss of time with some of the district's neediest students. Despite the high level of energy and enthusiasm demonstrated in this group, the toll exacted by the numerous goals of the grant began to show itself by springtime.

Site B Teacher: Membership characteristics contributed to the struggles at Site B. Especially important was that teachers and faculty by and large did not build trusting, respectful relationships. This may have been due in part to this group's use of its time together on tasks, largely to the exclusion of activities designed to create understanding or build relationships. In addition, some events occurred, often small ones, that made it more difficult for some of the less-assertive members of the team to feel safe in the group. Later, when conflicts emerged, the relationships between site members were not healthy enough to work toward resolving the conflicts.

Faculty at Site A: The school and university faculty at our site were all extremely dedicated teachers who were committed to meeting the needs of all of their students. This dedication and enthusiasm was contagious. At our weekly meetings, we steadily grew in our knowledge of and comfort with each other. Each meeting involved discussion of the K–2 learners, as well as preservice teacher preparation. There was no judging or critiquing, and often participants were relieved to hear others shared the same problem. Although the workload was overwhelming at times, the support and spirit were the glue that held the group together.

Faculty Co-Director Response: Although many LCL participants were acquainted from previous interactions with student teachers and were aware of differing
school cultures, there had not been recognition of the many misperceptions held about
each others' cultures. The realization that trusting relationships did not just "happen"
by working together resulted in the group's early change in agenda to concentrate on
team building. We became more aware throughout the year that some tensions could
not be resolved, partially because of school cultural differences and partially because
of individual differences.

Individual personalities were interesting to watch as predictors of interaction outcomes. At Site A, the coordinator was a twenty-eight-year veteran of the district and
highly respected by teachers, although positively and negatively perceived as a
"driven" person who was unable to walk away from the job. At Site B, the coordinator
was new to the school, a pre-K–12 licensed teacher whose most recent teaching was at
the preschool level. At times teachers felt that he was unable to understand their situation and that his expectations were too high. Together the two coordinators beautifully
complemented each other; one more a doer; the other more of a thinker. "Business as
usual" was the modus operandi at Site A, whereas at Site B, there was an underlying
tension that kept participants on edge.

University participants also brought to the table diverse philosophies and personalities. The Site A faculty was either more relaxed and comfortable with the fit or was
playing off the positive energy of the teachers. Site B faculty brought their wonderful
individual styles to a table already crowded with voices demanding to be heard. The
blend was difficult to work with, and the coordinator often felt responsible yet powerless to amend the situation. As a director, I often felt powerless to alter situations when
they called for addressing issues with colleagues.

Process and Structure

In any endeavor, it takes a sense of ownership on the part of the players to maintain a long-term commitment. There must be adaptability, flexibility, and trust as partners allow others to make decisions and create new structures and game plans.
Individuals should understand their roles and responsibilities despite the changes that
might occur in those during the early stages of a partnership.

Site A Teacher: There seemed to be a well-established foundation of respect and
trust among the teachers. Hidden agendas or personal jealousy or putting oneself on a
higher pedestal were not apparent. This attitude assisted the process of our goals im-
mensely. Teachers trusted the steering committee to be the leaders for all the participants and know that each voice would be heard by the representatives. Because the
university faculty was interested in coming into classrooms and working with teachers, there was a more complete understanding of where each one was coming from.
The university was not some place "over there." It was really a part of the school and
would be right there to nurture and assist us in any way for the good of all. At the same
time, faculty were visible and gave the idea that they belonged right in the middle of
our school.

Site B Teacher: Despite early discussions on the matter, key project structures remained unclear. Roles, decision-making structures, time lines, and benchmarks were opaque, changing, and sometimes missing altogether. Perhaps most important, structures were not in place to ensure that participants attended to the process. In the absence of knowledge and skills in collaboration, these were crippling to effective daily work. Site B never established processes and structures that supported successful collaboration

Conflict is inevitable in collaboration, and how it is resolved affects everything else. At Site B, unfortunately, the most significant conflicts were seldom addressed directly or in a timely manner. Instead, participants tended to talk to almost everyone except the person with whom they were having the conflict. This probably had several causes. The level of trust established was insufficient. A norm of collegial relationships did not exist. Furthermore, the teachers at the site had their own history of adversarial relationships. Some individuals in the project did not exhibit skills in building trust or resolving conflict. Whatever the source, the consequence was that conflicts festered until they could be ignored no longer.

The playfulness characteristic of Site A was absent at Site B. We didn't have fun. Participants' level of ownership also wavered, at times wanting a voice in all aspects of the project and at other points wanting someone to fix this thing for them. This may have been related to the lack of a clearly defined structure.

Faculty at Site A: One of the biggest challenges we faced was in defining each person's role. Whereas the teachers in the school seemed to define their role more easily, the university faculty struggled throughout the first year. Initially, university faculty members met on a regular basis to discuss the varying roles and levels of involvement with the project. Faculty that were not directly responsible for the delivery of the coursework for the interns felt disconnected. They were not sure of their roles, and each sought a "home" in the project.

There was some divisiveness about the faculty role, with some wanting each faculty member to do the same thing for the same amount of time. Inevitably, the issue of what the faculty were doing at Site A compared with Site B became a source of tension between the faculty, rather than a way to examine alternative methods. The faculty meetings that had been initiated in the fall ceased taking place at all.

Faculty Co-Director Response: In addition to accepting the differences inherent in our cultures, we knew from the outset that we needed to define a clear-cut decision-making process. An intricate plan was developed defining the process and the issues that demanded everyone's input as opposed to those that could be determined by a steering committee. As the year progressed, however, there were numerous occasions in which participants complained of having no voice. With the midyear connection of all members to e-mail, we were able to survey players more rapidly when decisions needed to be made. As with other tensions, we attempted to go forward with the recognition that we needed to accept these as growth producing, following Zeichner's (1992) democratic model in which all voices are necessary and tensions are a normal and positive outgrowth.

From the outset, participants were anxious about their roles and responsibilities. I had never been an administrator and found it very difficult to "lead" the group because of my democratic background. Although it was not expected (nor would it have been accepted) that I do so by the faculty, the teachers often perceived me to be remiss in my responsibilities.

Communication

Without appropriate, open, and frequent communication, a partnership cannot succeed. Individuals need to interact often to maintain a sense of trust and ownership. Keeping everyone informed and providing opportunities for input from all players are essential to collaboration. There can be numerous and varied ways of communicating, all of which should be used to meet comfort levels of individuals involved.

Site A Teacher: Communication was the key to our success. Restating views, reflective listening, and waiting for all to share their voice were characteristics of all in the group. This is not to say that some didn't verbalize more than others, but there seemed a respectful air about the importance for all to share their ideas. The weekly professional development times brought camaraderie and the exchange of ideas. Issues and concerns could be brought up, possible solutions suggested, and support provided.

Site B Teacher: Unlike Site A's situation, communication at Site B was not open and frequent. Despite the fact that team members met formally at least once per week and informally more often still, major issues were not discussed until a crisis point was reached. Because of the lack of safe relationships and processes, some participants were not willing to communicate with others about important issues or to contribute their voices to the work of the project. Oftentimes I heard voices that needed to be talking to one another rather than to me as the coordinator.

Faculty at Site A: Once-a-week site meetings, biweekly steering committee meetings, weekly faculty liaison meetings, and the various subcommittee demanded a considerable amount of time. Although time-consuming, these meetings were essential in keeping the lines of communication open. The weekly site meetings were pivotal to building trust and respect. The monthly "whole group" meetings were also valuable.

Communication can be extremely complicated when it involves multiple personalities with various communication styles. This was frequently apparent in our large group meetings. It was evident that certain individuals would overwhelm others and that some would simply cease to participate when they felt criticized or threatened. Others would continue to drill the same agenda session after session, feeling they were not being heard.

Faculty Co-Director Response: To provide equity in leadership, the partnership was directed by a university person (myself) and a school district representative (an assistant superintendent). Our differing experiences and cultures were quickly obvious in our interaction styles. The district co-director was accustomed to making decisions in an authoritarian manner, whereas I was overly sensitive to the need to be "democratic" (even when it became burdensome to the process). We perceived our roles differently, and it took much of the year before we were able to both appreciate the uniqueness and skills that we brought to the partnership. There were several occasions at which I felt the need to bring "warring factions" at Site B together in face-to-face negotiations. This strategy was uncomfortable for the participants. The teachers thought I should have greater say with the other faculty involved. The latter understood, of course, that we were peers and that I had no authority over them, and they had no need to be accountable.

The long-standing relationships at Site A lent themselves to relatively open communication. As some issues evolved at Site B, there tended to be some amount of comparison and competition between the two schools. It was assumed by Site B educators that they were perceived as the difficult group and Site A, the model PDS. Meetings at Site B tended to be high-energy sessions with food, fun, and sharing, but members never knew when a time bomb might go off, which added to occasional tension. When two of the three faculty members withdrew from the weekly site meetings midyear, the remaining team drew all kinds of conclusions without benefit of open discussion with those faculty members. Trust levels were all but nonexistent.

Purpose

It might seem obvious that initiating a partnership calls for a shared vision, but this is not always the case. Even a stated vision can be perceived differently by different players. Therefore, it is important to have concrete goals that are followed by written objectives and necessary steps.

Site A Teacher: There were many goals inherent in this grant project—perhaps as many as there were participants. It seemed we had to conquer the world for learners as well as unite the school district, university, and community as a whole. Teachers saw themselves as learners. They were dedicated and committed to providing open and accepting places where preservice teachers could bloom and grow for an entire school year with university faculty as supportive partners. The way in which we accomplished all of the goals could have been more focused. We could have simply stated that we would concentrate on one thing, but we didn't. We forged ahead, tried the best we could, and accomplished what we did. At our site, we felt confident that we had traveled a great journey, made some marvelous connections for all learners, and hoped to continue.

Site B Teacher: Ideological differences over purposes of collaboration, as well as beliefs about education, contributed to collaboration challenges at Site B. The enormous scope of the project affected this site as it did the entire effort. The daily successes of university interns and Pre-K–3 students, the final purpose for all of us, was perhaps the site's greatest asset.

Although all participants were clear about the basic purposes of the project, each understood that purpose from a different frame of reference. Many teachers saw classrooms as overburdened and believed that their students would benefit from university resources. Furthermore, many shared a perception that teacher preparation was out of touch with the "real world" of the classroom. Although faculty saw benefits to "real-world" classroom learning for the interns, they also believed that schools, and in particular this site, could benefit from other ways of understanding and working with children. Many teachers and faculty expressed widely divergent beliefs and practices around the level of self-direction to be provided children, intrinsic versus extrinsic motivation, reward-based discipline, constructivist learning, and "democratic classroom" values and practices, although they seldom expressed these to each other and very seldom in a manner that promoted dialogue. It is not a dramatic overstatement to claim that many teachers and faculty saw the project primarily as a method of providing resources for their institution and reforming the other institution.

Nonetheless, both teachers and faculty saw children and interns having experiences and gaining learning that was beyond what they had been able to offer previously. It was these results that led one teacher who struggled in many of the relationships with faculty to still say "this is a good thing."

Faculty at Site A: Certainly our biggest challenge was the complexity of this project. Had we not been pushed to accomplish multiple, complex goals we would have had more time and energy to invest in the process rather than the product. This focus on the here and now did not allow us to really analyze our practices and ourselves. Our weekly meetings tended to become "to-do" agendas, rather than opportunities to learn and grow together. One of the main goals of our collaboration, professional development, had taken a backseat to the daily functioning of the schools.

Faculty Co-Director Response: Because of the breadth of this work, we began developing committees around goals. When we gathered as a team to report on committee work, we were often met with disagreements, and people left feeling their good-faith work was for naught. Additionally, the divisions into small working committees at times resulted in individuals pursuing their own agenda with great enthusiasm and exhibiting less passion for other goals. The urgency of the classroom teachers to determine literacy and lifework curricula often left university faculty feeling that the issues of teacher preparation were not being addressed in a timely manner. During the year, we were able to relieve our own stress by deemphasizing some of the goals. Unfortunately, this situation of multiple goals resulted at times in an overall state of maintenance just to survive.

Resources

It is difficult to develop a PDS without a solid source of funding. The financial base should be hard money to alleviate the constant uncertainty about the continuity of the collaboration. According to John Goodlad, "Much of leadership is symbolic. But symbols, ceremony, and celebration will not go far unless they are backed up by resources" (1994, p. 110).

Site A Teacher: The grant monies that made this opportunity possible also almost made it collapse. To get the grant, the scope had to be large. Much of the last half of the school year was spent on lobbying for new sources of money. We only had one year to create and assess and then prove that what we had accomplished was worthwhile. The funding did, however, prove that we could blend institutions together, make our focus larger, and share resources for the greater good of all learners in both institutions and the community. This collaboration will continue to grow (even without extra funds) because of the continued efforts, strong sense of commitment by participants, and the realized benefits to all of the learners involved.

Site B Teacher: Every collaborative effort lacks certain conditions that would improve the odds of success. The above description suggests that history, skills, and attitudes all presented challenges for this site. Resources, especially finances to sustain the effort and leadership to move the project beyond the conditions of its birth, could have been key catalysts leading to a successful collaboration. Although the project received strong funding, I did not provide the leadership that might have taken advantage of the opportunity that money provided.

I did not provide the interpersonal skills and was not granted the legitimacy to lead others to act on the analysis of a variety of issues. I described several key elements of the site's difficulties as they were happening but was unable to get key players to agree to address them. Undoubtedly, inexperience contributed to the site leadership's ineffectiveness. The responsibility that leaders hold to ensure that key issues such as communication and trust were not sidestepped was not understood. The site leader did not fully understand the possible leverage points for achieving change. Inexperience also contributed to lack of recognition of the difficulties with roles described above in process and structure.

Faculty at Site A: The resources provided by the initial grant were wonderful. The money allowed us to have the time and materials needed to attain the multiple goals. The grant was limited to the first year, however, and even as the year began, we started to wonder about the future. Could we do this without funds? Additional resources were key to continuing our work together. As the district and university leadership met and decided on allocating internal resources to support the project, members were affirmed as the value of the project was recognized.

Faculty Co-Director Response: Although we were delighted with the grant funding that allowed us the luxuries of time for reflection, faculty and teacher release time, technology equipment and assistance, an outside evaluator, and curricular materials, we also felt constant stress for accountability. The university was solidly behind us, and the school district seemed pleased with our collaboration, but we knew that the funding agency would not extend monies without proof of student progress.

We were indebted to the outside evaluator who was able to very objectively assess the successes as well as the failures in the yearlong effort. She could perceive the progress apart from quantitative scores, and she was able to interview enough players of differing mindsets to provide us with a more distanced picture of whom we had become. A change in governor and political agendas found us without renewed funding at the end of the year. We have continued with adequate support from the university and school district and also without the added stress of inappropriate demands for accountability from a funding agency. Nonetheless, we are well aware of the fact that outside funding would be much more agreeable to progress in establishing future and additional PDS sites.

What We Have Learned

The first year of our partnership was an extraordinary learning experience for all of us. It was expected by some, including the funding source and the district administration and school board, that by the end of the first year our journey would have been complete. We certainly had learned enough during that time to fill an atlas, but the maps would not be etched in stone. In reflecting on the first year of our school–university partnership, it has become evident that the arrival at a shared vision was the "crowning glory" of the year

We realized too late that although funding was essential to get the partnership started, the grant we received forced us to undertake too many goals. Future partnerships would do well to attain funding that is solely focused on building the partnership without adding multiple new curricula. Our multiple foci, however, made it all the more exciting to see an "awakening" at the end of the school year when all players began to articulate the overall goals of professional development and teacher preparation. As we continued our journey with one-sixth of the funding of the first year, we were able to maintain the important criteria inherent in a professional development school model. The funding was important for the first year, but to realistically institutionalize the concept of PDSs, the work needs to be—and *can* be—accomplished in the absence of large amounts of money.

Although it was recognized early on that open communication and the ability to make accommodations were essential characteristics to collaboration, they turned out to provide the greatest challenges. We also needed to recognize the normalcy of "productive tensions" (Johnston, 1997) as part of a healthy collaborative relationship. We needed to "toughen up" and openly and honestly address issues and resolve conflicts. We needed to understand that a partnership has to be more than a school within a school or a clique of faculty within a college of education. We were never able at one site to accept the cultural differences and respect them, rather than attempt to change them.

The development of this new partnership also presented some challenges for our colleagues, both at the local school site and at the university. Individuals who were not directly involved in the project had a tendency to either ignore or make erroneous assumptions about the efforts. An important lesson we learned was to keep all constituents informed about the project. At the university, we also had to deal with issues of faculty load and reward systems. Grant monies allowed us to "buy" some of our teaching load to spend more time at the partner schools. Because of the time commitment needed to establish trusting relationships, this was essential. Yet as we entered the next phase of our work, we recognized the need for these partnerships to become relatively self-sustaining. University faculty also grew to realize the changing role involved in partnerships. The enormous amount of time and effort precluded extensive research efforts that did not pertain directly to the partnership. It was evident that the partnership needed to become the object of research, and the teachers had to become partners of the world of presenting and publishing. It was also essential that administration from the university value the work involved when making tenure and promotion decisions. Table 5.1 summarizes some of the major factors that facilitated and presented barriers to our collaborative efforts.

As we discussed the year and analyzed our own and the external evaluator's data about our collaborative efforts, we felt good about our work. We learned about working together and all of its concomitant benefits and challenges. We made significant changes in the way we prepare teachers, how we view our own professional development, and what we know about literacy development and lifework learning for Pre-K–3 learners. Most of all, we learned the value of collaborative efforts. We know we are moving in the right direction. We know honest, ongoing relationships are the key to a successful partnership. Through the hills and valleys of our work, we all continue to remind ourselves that the real benefactors are the children that come to us to learn and trust us to create for them a future of endless possibilities.

Table 5.1. Facilitators and Barriers to Collaboration

Facilitators to Collaboration	Barriers to Collaboration
• Resources to provide the time and incentive for people to participate	• Multiple expectations tied to receiving grant monies
• People who were willing to compromise and be flexible—"boundary spanners" (Lampert, 1991)	• Differences in the culture of the two institutions
• Open and frequent communication among all participants	• Lack of clarity of roles in the partnership
• Agreement of participants on a philosophical stance to teaching and learning	• Basic philosophical differences in teaching and learning
• Trusting, respectful relationships	• Prior negative history between individuals
• Support of administration from both institutions	• Inability to directly address conflict
• Prior successful relationships between the two institutions	• Uncertainty of future of project
• Proximity of schools to university	• Lack of physical space in the partner schools
• Desire to improve teacher preparation and teaching and learning	• Individuals with only self-servicing goals
• Clear process for decision making	• Lack of communication with colleagues

Alissa and Grandma Jean made it through the year also. Their relationship flourished and deepened. However, there were days when one or the other could not make the scheduled meeting. There were moments of frustration when one or the other might have been out of sorts. There were occasional disagreements about what to read or how time should be spent. But the two buddies stuck it out because they learned how to relate, they began to understand each other, and they knew that what they had established was satisfying and would endure.

References

Collins, J. (1995). Listening but not hearing: Patterns of communication in an urban school-university partnership. In H. G. Petrie (Ed.), *Professionalization, partnership and power: Building professional development schools* (pp. 77–92). Albany, NY: State University of New York Press.

Darling-Hammond, L. (1994). *Professional development schools: Schools for developing a profession.* New York: Teachers College Press.

Goodlad, J. L. (1994). *Educational renewal: Better teachers, better schools*. San Francisco: Jossey-Bass.

Johnston, M. (1997). *Contradictions in collaboration: New thinking on school/university partnerships*. New York: Teachers College Press.

Kagan, S. L. (1991). *United we stand: Collaboration for child care and early education services*. New York: Teachers College Press.

Lampert, M. (1991). Looking at restructuring from within a restructured role. *Phi Delta Kappan, 72*, 670–675.

Mattessich, P., & Monsey, B. (1992). *Collaboration: What makes it work*. St. Paul, MN: Wilder Foundation.

Zeichner, K. (1992). Rethinking the practicum in the professional development school partnership. *Journal of Teacher Education, 43*, 296–307.

Chapter

A Collaborative Journey: Study and Inquiry in a Professional Development Middle School

Cathleen Rafferty and Marylin Leinenbach

Marylin and Cathleen began working together in the early 1990s when numerous transformations were occurring at the school and the university. These changes were (a) the junior high converted to a middle school, (b) the middle school got a new principal, (c) the middle school became a professional development school (PDS) site, and (d) Cathleen joined the faculty at the university and was asked to be the PDS liaison for the middle school.

Marylin was teaching eighth-grade mathematics and had recently learned that the state had mandated the use of portfolios. Cathleen had been experimenting with portfolios in her teacher education classes and had mentioned that fact to several teachers in the building. Consequently, she was dubbed an "expert" and asked to lead a study group that would meet every other week during the school day. This chapter will detail Cathleen and Marylin's collaborative journey, which began in a portfolio study group at the middle school and continues to evolve today after Marylin joined the university as a half-time "teacher-in-residence."

Marylin and Cathleen's partnership was an outgrowth of a larger collaborative endeavor. In 1992, when Cathleen joined the School of Education (SOE) at Indiana State University (ISU), the SOE had just begun a PDS partnership with ten schools. Seven of these were located in Terre Haute, one of which was Chauncey Rose Middle School (CRMS), Marylin's school. School–university partnerships have created rich opportunities for informing teaching and learning at all levels. At ISU, beginning in 1992, this meant simultaneous nurturing of ten PDSs, including five elementary, one middle, and four high schools. Often PDS sites operate under various tenets or principles (e.g., Holmes Group, 1990; Rafferty, 1993, 1996), and schools affiliated with ISU are no exception. The following description and principles guide collaboration between ISU and ten affiliated PDS sites initially supported by monies from the Lilly Endowment and ISU:

A professional development school is a regular elementary, middle, or high school where public school and university personnel work together to facilitate higher levels of learning by all children in the school, to promote a better school environment for preparing teachers and other educational professionals, and to create a more supportive site for renewal of and inquiry by experienced teachers, administrators, school service personnel, and university faculty. Through the collaborative efforts of pupils in the school, community members, pre-service educators, practitioners in the school, and university faculty, a PDS becomes an exemplary learning environment in four respects:

1.   A PDS uses effective curricular, instructional, and administrative practices to help ensure that all students reach their full potential as students and as persons.

2.   A PDS provides for renewal, professional growth, and continuing education of all participants.

3.   A PDS serves as a site for pre-service educators to work in a stimulating learning environment with outstanding practitioners. In general, it allows prospective teachers and other educators-in-training to experience the full range of responsibilities of practitioners in their professional fields.

4.   A PDS supports inquiry, research, and exchange of professional knowledge. (*Planning for a Plan Committee*, 1991)

All of these principles are intertwined and mutually supporting, but the fourth component in particular has great potential to help ensure that other elements occur. That is, engaging in inquiry and research provides opportunities for renewal, professional growth, and continued learning about the most effective curricular, instructional, and administrative practices to help ensure student learning while creating a stimulating learning environment for prospective educators. In essence, then, school–university collaborative research or inquiry can be viewed as a form of professional development that also informs our practice, especially if the following tenets, described by Oja and Pine (1987), are followed:

1) research problems are mutually defined, 2) school and university collaborate to seek solutions to school-based issues, 3) findings are jointly reported and are used to solve mutually defined problems, 4) school faculty develop research skills and university faculty (re)discover field-based methodologies, and 5) faculty from both cultures are professionally renewed. (p. 97)

Furthermore, this type of inquiry can be subsumed under Freire's (1970) concept of praxis, which he defined as a combination of reflection and action on the world in order to change it, primarily because a major focus of this type of inquiry and research is to inform participants about classroom and school practices so that appropriate decisions can be made and action taken to improve teaching and learning.

Because of her previous ten years' experience as a middle grades teacher and her work with Judith Lanier and the Michigan Partnership for New Education, Cathleen was asked to be liaison for CRMS. As such, she became a multipurpose consultant and colleague for the school. It was out of this school-wide collaborative PDS role that Cathleen and Marylin began a multiyear journey (still in progress), which moved from study groups, to on-site graduate classes, to various collaborative inquiry and action research projects, to conference presentations, to publications, to the quest for National Board Certification, and to working together as teacher education colleagues. This chapter will tell Marylin's and Cathleen's stories as they have worked through a variety of projects and challenges as colleagues and friends since the early 1990s.

The Journey Began Through Portfolio Study Groups

Cathleen

Although I officially began my PDS liaison responsibilities during fall 1992, it took a while for me to "find my place" at CRMS. I spent a great deal of time at the school developing relationships with both teachers and administrators through a variety of activities that included attending faculty meetings, school improvement meetings, and team meetings, as well as working with groups of faculty and staff to write various grants.

It was important to me that I do a lot of listening and observing—particularly early in this new relationship—because I did not want to be perceived as "the university expert" who would come into the school and tell people what to do. I believe that school–university collaboration should be a true partnership in which the faculty from both "cultures" work side-by-side rather than operating in a hierarchical structure.

Eventually my participant–observer style paid off as a common focus emerged after the Indiana legislature mandated use of portfolios through PL19-1992. Several teachers knew that I was experimenting with portfolios in my teacher education courses and asked whether I would conduct a study group to explore portfolio use with middle school students. Because I was also chairing ISU's Collaborative Inquiry (CI) initiative, which is one of our four critical PDS principles, I suggested that we could write a proposal to seek financial support for our study group endeavor. Subsequently, we were awarded $400 to support site visitations to other schools using portfolios, substitutes for study group members meeting during the school day, refreshments for the meetings, and other related expenses during spring 1994.

Eight teachers comprised the first study group, which met every other Tuesday during the school day. We read, discussed, and analyzed numerous articles related to portfolios and portfolio assessment. Furthermore, we generated questions for a site-visitation group, synthesized our observations from the visit, and found ways to share our learning with other colleagues at CRMS. At the end of the semester, I asked whether anyone would be interested in piloting and studying the use of portfolios during the following school year. Marylin was the sole volunteer, and so we continued this part of the journey alone—at least initially.

Marilyn

By 1994, I had been teaching traditionally for twenty years, and my school was in the height of the "middle school change." Chauncey Rose, already a PDS site, had also become part of the Coalition of Essential Schools, and I was spending part of my summer in Nashville, Indiana, reading and discussing books and articles on the Nine Common Principles (Sizer, 1992a, 1992b). I had also been attending math conferences to learn about fractals, tessellations, the inquiry method of problem solving, and math manipulatives. I was feeling very frustrated because I was trying the new ideas with my students, but it was all so disjointed. Then my journey really began; I joined the portfolio study group at CRMS with Cathleen Rafferty, and my life changed.

During the study group time, we would read articles and discuss what we were thinking. This in itself was change. I wrote in my journal, "Teachers need a time to learn, plan, share ideas, and develop strategies and material." I remember being so excited the day we read the article, "What Makes a Portfolio a Portfolio?" (Paulson, Paulson, & Meyer, 1991). It was becoming clear to me that I knew I was on the right track. The students' work that was once disjointed would all come together under the theme of progress. I had the vehicle, the portfolio, which would play a significant role in my journey of change.

During these sessions with Cathleen, I would listen to the other teachers' ideas about what they perceived a portfolio would look like. At the next meeting, there was much discussion and sharing of ideas from teachers of all areas of the curriculum. We came to the conclusion that portfolios can take on many different looks and can have different purposes. You could feel the relief in the room.

The following week, we read an article that I still keep because it became the foundation on which I continue to build. It was "Planning for Classroom Portfolio Assessment" (Lambdin & Walker, 1994). This was exactly what the Nine Common Principles were stating: The school should help students use their minds well. Teaching methods should stimulate students to be active learners while teachers coach them. I was on my way and so very excited.

Cathleen continued that spring to push us in our thinking and to take us out of our comfort zones as we read articles about portfolios and why they would be important assessment tools. We talked about change and how change affected each one of us as individuals. We also discussed how this change in assessment would affect our students. With the advent of the twenty-first century, portfolios also make sense with interdisciplinary units and cooperative learning. Because of the reading of articles and conversations with my peers in the study group, I knew I wanted to continue with the concept of portfolios. I was hooked! Then Cathleen asked for volunteers to continue to study and pilot the use of portfolios during the following school year. There was a gleam in my eye and a smile on my face as my hand went up. I was on my way to a life-changing journey!

Continuing the Journey by Piloting and Studying Portfolios

Cathleen

Although I was the official leader of the project—at least from Marylin's perspective—I can honestly say that I learned as much as, if not more than, Marylin did. We met nearly every week, sometimes several times a week during the 1994–1995 experience. In retrospect, I guess I did not realize at the time how much Marylin relied on me to take the lead. It was very important to me that we proceed as equal inquiry partners because I was personally uncomfortable with the "university expert" model. As a former classroom teacher with ten years of experience with the middle grades and as a teacher educator prepared to do truly collaborative PDS work, I made a conscious and deliberate attempt to foster democratic and collegial relationships with my public school counterparts. What I probably underestimated, however, was the power of traditional roles and expectations at this and other PDS sites. (A synopsis of our first collaborative project follows, but more detail is also available in Rafferty & Leinenbach, 1996.)

We introduced portfolios to the students in September 1994 by comparing and contrasting them to more traditional types of assessment. We learned subsequently that many students thought the portfolio's purpose was to "showcase their best work." After lengthy debriefing sessions, we realized we had not adequately helped students understand the purpose, rationale, and procedures for portfolios in eighth-grade mathematics primarily because we had not fully clarified these aspects for ourselves, let alone how to convey them to the students.

From this frustration emerged some powerful insights that ultimately convinced us we needed to involve students in decisions regarding *their* portfolios. For example, students determined that grammar and mechanics should be included as grading criteria for their math portfolio. Students did not mind being "guinea pigs" but felt it was unfair that an "experiment" should impact their grades.

During the debriefings after class sessions involving student decision making, Marylin and I always observed with both satisfaction and humility that eighth graders were more than capable of making decisions and defending their positions. Although we were chagrined not to have recognized this earlier, we were determined to capitalize on student insights during second semester. This turned out to be a critical turning point for us as collaborative research partners because we clearly understood the importance of involving students in their own learning and assessment. We also realized that in many respects, the students were also co-researchers. I was able to share our work with my teacher education students, which provided an important credibility-building opportunity for me as well. Stories about Marylin and her students serve to anchor various instructional and assessment methods that I share with my teachers-in-training. Because I do not have my own classroom, being able to work with Marylin and her students affords me valuable "reality sessions," which in turn benefit future educators.

By second semester, students demonstrated a keen ability to make and defend their choices regarding the portfolio process. Nonetheless, after evaluating spring portfolios, we learned that we were just beginning to understand how to help adolescents with a mathematics portfolio. Marylin's final journal entry says it best: "I've learned so much about my students and I'm a better teacher for it…. I know that portfolios will be used in all of my classes on a regular basis as a result of our learning this year."

Marylin

When school began, under Cathleen's guidance, I was feeling my way through portfolios. I was trying problem-solving techniques with my students, using a new book, and trying very hard to be "coach" instead of lecturer. Because I was going in so many different directions, I would become frustrated, and Cathleen would be my calming force, helping me to put things into perspective. Cathleen would review my journal, giving me critical insights and themes, asking me to recall when certain happenings occurred and what had precipitated my revelations.

Using the knowledge I had gained reading the articles in our study group, I had determined that the purpose of the portfolio was to show progress. Because I had written all over my journal, "*START SMALL*," I chose my third-hour math class to begin the use of portfolios. In the first few weeks of school, both Cathleen and I prepared the students for portfolios. At this time, we also began writing in mathematics. I can still remember the looks on their faces when they said, "Writing? In math class?"

By early November, I was pleased with the portfolios. Cathleen was spending time in the classroom on a regular basis, getting to know the kids. She was still pushing me in my thinking by giving me articles to read. One of them, "To Do or Not to Do Portfolios? That is the Question" (Wasserstein, 1994), became a revelation. The portfolios were *my* interpretation of what they should be; they were simply scrapbooks. I was making the decisions for the class. I was not having one-to-one discussions with the students on assessing their work. Cathleen and I spent many hours discussing where to go next.

By early January, frustration set in—both in myself and in my students. The students felt like guinea pigs. They told me, "Math and portfolios—too much!" For me, there was never enough time. My school was committed to teaching algebra to all eighth graders, and I was under pressure. It was time to make choices. By talking it over with Cathleen, I decided to back off of algebra for a while and gave each student a copy of "Planning for Classroom Portfolio Assessment" (Lambdin & Walker, 1994). By reading this article, the students began to see the whole picture, understanding what their portfolio could contain and demonstrate. They would choose five pieces, write an introductory letter to the reviewer, and provide written summaries regarding their choices.

A week before the semester ended, I began allowing math time for choosing the pieces of evidence and writing the summaries. I wrote in my journal: "The deadline for turning in the portfolios is Tuesday. Material must be typed. I can't wait!" And "I did not make it clear—was there a grade involved here? No! What would happen if you did not turn one in? NOTHING! I did not plan ahead."

This was truly a learning experience, and I needed Cathleen's expertise for the next steps. The idea that I was a researcher was still so new to me. I still considered myself "just the math teacher"; Cathleen was the researcher. Because of my deepening respect for her insight, I once again turned to her for advice, asking, "Now what?" After a lengthy discussion, we decided that we needed to involve the students, so we discussed the winter portfolios with them. All agreed they could have been better. The consensus was that we needed to be the best we could be, and that included attention to spelling and grammar. We asked ourselves, "Where do we go from here? What will the spring portfolios look like?"

I wrote in my journal, "Another great class—Cathleen and I are amazed what we get from the students. I am in awe—I never thought to tap into the wealth of information the students store. In twenty years of teaching, I have not given eighth-grade students enough credit. Revelation—I need to listen more.... My students and I would not be at the point we are now without the expertise of Cathleen Rafferty.... It's been a good relationship between Cathleen and myself. We needed what the other was good at doing. My students, my teaching, our classroom—all were hers for whatever. I did not have the experience or the studying to run the research project. My students respond well to Cathleen. She treats them like adults, and they always know she values their opinion. Collaborative inquiry works!"

Expanding the Journey

Cathleen

In addition to working with Marylin to pilot and study portfolios in her eighth-grade mathematics class, I was also continuing to meet occasionally with the original portfolio study group during fall 1994. I began meeting with a new portfolio group late that fall and into spring of 1995. In many respects, at least in the early stages, portfolios were the "glue" that kept me working with a variety of teachers, including Marylin.

Both the continuing group and the new group operated in a similar fashion to the original. By the end of the 1994–1995 school year, it was apparent that although we had read and discussed much, only Marylin had actually implemented and studied the use of portfolios with her students.

None of us in the class knew exactly what to expect when the class convened in late August 1995, not even Marylin and I who had now worked together for well over a year. Marylin was now teaching sixth grade and needed to reconceptualize portfolios with a new population of students. Fortunately, the teachers and I pooled our collective wisdom and experience to brainstorm activities that would assist us as we piloted portfolios and to determine the most meaningful ways to assess, document, and evaluate our learning. By now I had worked with many of these teachers long enough that they expected this democratic approach. Sometimes I still sensed that some just wanted me to "tell them what to do" but others, particularly Marylin, really valued co-constructing their own learning experiences. From my perspective, it was gratifying to know that traditional school–university roles and expectations could be blurred. Nonetheless, it was becoming apparent that it was a long-term process.

From the revised course title, "Piloting and Studying Portfolios," we concluded that we should keep a log or journal in which to record reactions and ideas from readings, discussions, class activities, and the pilot project itself. In addition, because CRMS was affiliated with the Coalition of Essential Schools, it made sense to do a final exhibition in which we would present evidence of student work and our own insights about how portfolios influence our teaching.

Various activities comprised our weekly sessions, including reading and discussion of articles and chapters related to portfolios, journal writing and sharing of insights, identification of the purpose for using portfolios in our classrooms, delineation of indicators or types of evidence to support the portfolio's purpose, "Critical Friends" visits to classmates piloting portfolios, presentations about portfolios to colleagues in other schools, creation of a Portfolio Framework to assist others in starting the process (see Rafferty et al., 1996), and development of rubrics to assess our journals and final exhibitions.

As the semester progressed, we became our own support group and safety net, even though we represented different grade levels and subject areas. In fact, on many occasions we noted how much we had learned as a result of the diverse perspectives in our group. Because I had an ongoing interest in Marylin's portfolio work, I also spent extra time in her classroom

Marylin

I had made the decision to move to sixth grade the previous spring because I wanted to leave the traditional method of teaching algebra and concentrate more on portfolios and the creative side of mathematics. When I made the move, Cathleen and I were uncertain about necessary modifications, particularly for using portfolios with the special-needs students in the collaborative mathematics class. Together we read articles with LeeAnn, the special-needs teacher, and were convinced that performance-based assessments, to be included in the portfolios, would give us deeper insights into student thinking and understanding.

I wrote a note to Cathleen in October. "Come to the classroom soon. The students have written their own stories and made drawings using tangrams based on *Grandfather Tang's Story,* (Tompert, 1990). They are so proud." When Cathleen visited the classroom, she was in awe of the students' abilities in manipulating the tangrams, something she found difficult to do! Several students, both special-needs and regular-education students, were so proud to show her how to do it. This experience would not have been possible had it not been for this team-teaching opportunity in a collaborative mathematics classroom.

As the first semester ended, the following thoughts from my journal captured this first portfolio experience with sixth graders, both regular-education and special-needs students:

The portfolio is so powerful. I saw children today reflect and write on their progress.... All portfolios are finished. I have really enjoyed reading them. I gain insight by reading their reflective essays and the parent comments.... I am maturing also in my thinking. Cathleen continues to help me form the reflective questions for the students about themselves as learners.

It also helped that I was part of the class that Cathleen taught at Chauncey Rose. I learned so much as a result of the diverse perspectives of our group. LeeAnn and I were able to share with the group our thoughts on the use of portfolios in a collaborative math class. We both felt that one of the major benefits was that portfolios help level the playing field. When students work in groups of three or four, there aren't any distinctions between the special-needs and regular-education students. In addition, students who had low self-esteem felt better about themselves. They were actively participating in class and seemed connected to their peers. Finally, portfolios gave the special-needs students a choice—probably for the first time in their school careers. We included them in the process of what, how, and why a skill is being learned.

LeeAnn and I expected our students to do exhibitions, and an extra bonus of our graduate class was that LeeAnn and I were expected to do an exhibition at the end of the semester in front of our teacher peers! We were not only leveling the playing field between regular-education and special-needs students, but as teachers we were also modeling the behaviors we expected from our students.

Redirecting the Journey Through Action Research and Teacher Portfolios

As is too often the case in school reform efforts, emphases change. Not long after the graduate-level course in which teachers piloted and studied the use of portfolios in their classrooms, the state legislature rescinded mandated portfolio use. After that time, Cathleen and Marylin continued their collaborative work, writing and presenting about portfolios in mathematics classrooms, but not many others persisted in their efforts. Cathleen also remained as the PDS liaison to CRMS, continuing as a multipurpose consultant and grant writer for the school.

Cathleen

During discussions with the principal and assistant principal in 1996–1997, it was evident that "standards" had replaced "portfolios" as a reform focal point, and I was asked to offer another on-site, graduate-level course that would address a variety of standards. Concurrent with this increased focus on standards at the public school was a similar focus for teacher preparation. As such, I was able to merge multiple layers of standards into a course that underscored the need for simultaneous renewal across a school–university partnership. The course, CIMT 595—Exploring Standards to Improve Instruction and Assessment, involved seven teachers (including Marylin) in the study of both teacher-education-related standards such as the Interstate New Teacher Assessment and Support Consortium (INTASC) Principles and National Board for Professional Teaching Standards (NBPTS), and various content-area standards from groups such as the National Council for Teachers of Mathematics (NCTM), the National Council of Teachers of English, the International Reading Association (NCTE/IRA), and so forth. After negotiating with class members, we determined that in addition to readings and whole-group discussions related to the standards, each class member or collaborative team would conduct an action research project, make connections to at least one set of standards, keep a reflective journal, and present results and insights to colleagues at semester's end.

Both Marylin and her special education team-teaching partner, LeeAnn, were enrolled in the class. Because they had previously made observations such as, "When students work in groups of three or four, there aren't any distinctions between special-needs and regular-education students," they decided to pursue several questions regarding portfolio use in a collaborative mathematics class. Among the many insights gained from this project was that there are a variety of instructional and assessment approaches that have great potential to "level the playing field" for students labeled as "special needs" or "learning disabled." By actively engaging these students in a collaborative mathematics class via use of portfolios, manipulatives, and other strategies that actively engaged them in their own learning, it was often difficult to distinguish these students from their regular-education counterparts. (See Rafferty, Leinenbach, & Helms [1999] for additional information about this particular inquiry focus.)

In addition to ongoing portfolio assessment insights, it was rewarding and instructive to work with teachers who, despite incredibly heavy workloads and busy lives, took the time to be reflective and analytical about their teaching. In other words, as a result of this particular on-site course, I began to understand how some of these teachers might respond to the rigors of the National Board Certification process.

Marylin

It was at about this time that I teasingly asked Cathleen, "Please, how about if I stay in my comfort zone just for one year, OK?" Of course, I knew in my heart that the answer was, "No," so I enrolled in the on-site class. It was during this particular graduate class that I first heard the words *National Board Certification* and *Standards* from various subject-area organizations such as NCTM. Once again, LeeAnn and I joined together to do an in-depth study and comparison of the NBPTS standards, the INTASC principles, and the NCTM standards.

For our project, LeeAnn and I decided to do a math project that would incorporate the concepts of proportions and geometry. We believed that the project explicitly and appropriately connected the standards from the NBPTS, the INTASC Standards, and the Curriculum and Evaluation Standards for School Mathematics released by the NCTM (1989).

During the following school year, I learned how important this redirection, this studying of the standards, would be to my professional development. What I did not realize at the time was that I was building the foundation needed to begin the journey for National Board Certification.

Committing to Self-Reflection Through the National Board Certification Process

Cathleen

Once again I found myself offering a graduate "class" to support teacher learning at Chauncey Rose Middle School. This time, however, the focus and process were quite different. Because of our work at the school, which is a PDS site affiliated with ISU, eight teachers made the commitment to pursue National Board Certification (NBC). At the time, and even currently, the local school corporation had no mechanism to recognize or reward teachers who achieved or even pursued this rigorous national voluntary and advanced certification. Fortunately, grant monies in the form of a stipend to defray the $2,000 NBC process and a tuition credit for three hours of graduate work supported these teachers.

From my perspective, providing support to eight teachers pursuing a variety of NBPTS certificates was among the most difficult professional development activities I have attempted. Even though I had previously worked with all but one of the eight teachers in at least one graduate-level course taught at the school, I did not have enough understanding of their reflective abilities and dispositions, especially as they pertained to the type of in-depth analysis required for the NBC entries. The one exception, of course, was Marylin.

Through our work together across many years, several graduate classes, and numerous collaborative inquiry projects focused on portfolios, I had witnessed the development of Marylin's confidence in her research and writing skills. By the time she tackled National Board Certification in 1998–1999, we had presented at several national conferences, such as American Educational Research Association and National Middle School Association, and coauthored articles. She knew how to think deeply about herself as a teacher and her students as learners, as well as how to capture that thinking on paper. She had been doing it for several years already. In fact, within the last year or so, Marylin has finally begun to provide suggestions to *my* writing. The first time this happened, I noted it with a smile, and we both understood how far we had journeyed as colleagues and friends. Furthermore, what I think Marylin came to understand most as a result of her pursuit of NBC is that although the process is anything but "easy," it is certainly achievable if one is willing to dig deep into a reflective and analytical process designed to have teachers explore their underlying rationales and philosophies of the teaching and learning processes.

Another critical attribute that Marylin possesses is the desire and disposition to do whatever is necessary to help students understand. She is passionate about finding multiple approaches to teaching and learning so that *all* students can be successful. For her, it is not just another platitude, it is a way of life because she embodies the words of Robert Fried, author of *The Passionate Teacher:*

To be a passionate teacher is to be someone in love with a field of knowledge, deeply stirred by issues and ideas that challenge our world, drawn to the dilemmas and potentials of the young people who come into class each day or captivated by all of these. A passionate teacher is a teacher who breaks out of the isolation of a classroom, who refuses to submit to apathy or cynicism. (Fried, 1995, p.1)

Marylin

Why National Board Certification? Why not stay in my comfort zone for awhile? Previously I had received many honors for my teaching, such as being one of thirty-six 1998 honorees nominated for the prestigious American Teacher Award from the Disney Company. I remember the thrill of being notified that a producer and two cameramen from Disney would be spending two days in my classroom, recording my teaching and interviewing my students. Of course, I asked Cathleen if they could interview her too, because I realized that I would not have been in the position for this award had I not known her! Our working relationship had evolved into one of deep friendship, and we always supported each other.

Stay in the comfort zone? It was not to be. It was time to do deep self-reflection on the last five to six years and the effect my journey had on my teaching. This self-reflection was to be done through the process of the NBC portfolio. I knew this journey was not going to be easy, but what I was not totally prepared for was the amount of time I would put into this project.

With the critical insights I gained from analysis done on NBC entries, I had the true epiphany. In working so closely with my students, through using everything I had learned in working with Cathleen, and by doing the deep self-reflection, I knew that I needed to continue to do the following:

- teach in a concrete, hands-on manner, believing that *all* children can learn mathematics and that it is my job to find the right strategies to accomplish this;

- level the playing field of special-needs and regular-education students by raising expectations and providing adequate support so that children know they can succeed;

- engage my students with strategies that make them active participants in their own learning, rather than passive receivers of knowledge; and

- encourage teamwork, demonstrate connections, and stimulate creativity.

As mentioned previously, in the spring of 1994 after the study group was finished, I understood that I was on the right track. More than four years later, the reflection that I did for the NBC section "Developing Mathematical Understanding" once again proved that I was on the right track. As Cathleen had encouraged study group members to become lifelong learners, so, too, do I encourage my students so that they are active participants in their own learning.

When Cathleen and I were working with the third-hour eighth-graders in the fall of 1994, we asked them to be trailblazers. Now, after the deep reflection for the NBC section, I know that I must continue to encourage my students to persevere as they work through challenging problems. My students as learners will begin to realize the relationship between their decisions, their actions, and their successes.

As I look back on the years of working with Cathleen, I see her influence on me as a learner *and* as a teacher of my students as learners. Both Cathleen and I create an environment in which students are empowered and motivated. We both create an environment in which students feel comfortable taking risks in the form of attempting new approaches, asking questions freely, and being critical of their work through self-reflection.

As a teacher, I learned many things about myself throughout this year. I learned self-discipline. I learned that I am capable of multitasking. (Sadly, I never did learn how to cook supper and write on the computer at the same time, and there were many burned suppers!) I gained confidence in my writing ability. Most important, however, I began my study of multiple intelligences and how it affects my students, their learning, and what I as a teacher can do to support them (Gardner, 1993a, 1993b).

Current and Future Journeys

Both Marylin and Cathleen have recently experienced new professional growth opportunities. During summer 1999, Cathleen was named chairperson of the Department of Curriculum, Instruction and Media Technology at ISU. Marylin has increased her teaching responsibilities to include work with preservice teachers at ISU.

Recently John Lounsbury, noted middle-grades expert, asked Marylin to respond to an assignment for the *Middle School Journal*. Before she e-mailed her response, she asked Cathleen to edit it. Cathleen smiled, sighed, and then asked Marylin when she would finally be confident enough in her writing not to need someone else's approval. "Yes," Marylin thought. "Cathleen is still pushing me, and she is right." Because of all the work they have shared since the early 1990s, but especially because of the NBC process, Marylin finally knows that she can write.

Certainly, the fact that nationally recognized researchers seek a public school teacher's input confirms that the "university expert" model finally acknowledges the importance of practioners' experience, wisdom, and insights. Nonetheless, our example is but one of the many faces of school–university collaboration. Given this, we pose the following questions.

Is the type of collaborative relationship that we, Cathleen and Marylin, have typical of school–university partnerships? Are we representative of faculty members at either the school or university level? Is the nature and type of work that we chose to pursue what the Holmes Group envisioned in *Tomorrow's Schools* (1990)? Is there some sort of formula that others might apply if they, too, wanted to emulate what we have described herein?

Honestly, we do not know the answers to our questions. Readers of this chapter and the others contained in this edited volume will have to determine for themselves whether what we have done, how we have proceeded, and the impact that we have had represents time well spent. At the time of this writing, even we are uncertain what future opportunities will be available for us. Nonetheless, we are confident that wherever the journey continues to lead us, we will collaborate as a learning team as we maintain our focus on improving teaching and learning opportunities for all of our students—both those in the middle school and those who will teach them.

References

Freire, P. (1970). *Pedagogy of the oppressed*. New York: Seabury Press.

Fried, R. L. (1995). *The passionate teacher*. Boston: Beacon Press.

Gardner, H. (1993a). *Frames of mind: The theory of multiple intelligences*. New York: Basic Books.

Gardner, H. (1993b). *Multiple intelligences: The theory into practice*. New York: Basic Books.

Holmes Group. (1990). *Tomorrow's schools: Principles for the design of professional development schools*. East Lansing, MI: Author.

Lambdin, D. V., & Walker, V. L. (1994). Planning for classroom portfolio assessment. *Arithmetic Teacher, 42,* 318–323.

National Council of Teachers of Mathematics. (1989). *Curriculum and evaluation standards for school mathematics*. Reston, VA: Author.

Oja, S. N., & Pine, G. J. (1987). Collaborative action research: Teachers' stages of development in school contexts. *Peabody Journal of Education, 64*, 96–115.

Paulson, F. L., Paulson, P. R., & Meyer, C. A. (1991). What makes a portfolio a portfolio? *Educational Leadership, 48*(5), 60–63.

Planning for a Plan Committee. (1991, Fall). Unpublished manuscript, Indiana State University, School of Education, Terre Haute, IN.

Rafferty, C. D. (1993). Animal, vegetable, or mineral: What is a professional development school? *Contemporary Education, 64*, 223–225.

Rafferty, C. D. (1996). Making rhetoric a reality. *Contemporary Education, 67*(4), 187–190.

Rafferty, C. D., Emmert, B., Helms, L., Herner, S., Jacobs, K., Leinenbach, M., Mallory, C., Pell, B., Smith, A., & Turner, S. (1996). Using study groups to promote a culture of inquiry: Two cases. In A. M. Raymond, C. D. Rafferty, & K. M. Dutt (Eds.), *Collaborative action research: Case studies of school-university initiatives* (pp. 32–39). Terre Haute, IN: Curriculum, Research and Development Center, School of Education, Indiana State University.

Rafferty, C. D., & Leinenbach, M. (1996). Blazing a portfolio trail—without a crystal ball. *Middle School Journal, 28*, 27–32.

Rafferty, C. D., Leinenbach, M., & Helms, L. (1999). Leveling the playing field through active engagement. *Middle School Journal, 30*(4), 51–56.

Sizer, T. R. (1992a). *Horace's compromise: The dilemma of the American high school*. Boston: Houghton Mifflin.

Sizer, T. R. (1992b). *Horace's school: Redesigning the American high school*. Boston: Houghton Mifflin.

Tompert, A. (1990). *Grandfather Tang's story: A tale told with tangrams*. New York: Crown.

Wasserstein, P. (1994). To do or not to do portfolios: That is the question. *Kappa Delta Pi Record, 31*(1), 12–15.

Chapter

7

Blending Voices, Blending Lives: The Story of a New-Age Collaboration with Literature and E-mail

Susan Steffel and Chuck Steltenkamp[*]

Once upon a time, collaborative relationships consisted of people working together on a single project, at a single location, during a single time. The project we discuss in this chapter is none of the above. Rather, it represents three classroom teachers, in three different locations, over the course of three years, and it involves university and high school teachers and students corresponding with each other about literature via e-mail. Our partnership is really a virtual collaboration. Most of us have never met each other, yet our story demonstrates that strong relationships with literature and with each other can indeed develop.

Our project grew out of a need to find meaningful ways for Susan's university students to experience firsthand the benefits of using response theory with real-life secondary students. The university is located in a small town with only one large high school. To avoid the headaches of organizing transportation and on-site visitations, Susan toyed with the idea of using e-mail to allow for "virtual" travel.

*The authors wish to acknowledge the contributions of Dodie Zolman to this chapter.

These e-mail exchanges have been going on for three years now, and although changes have been made to smooth out the process, the initial project remains pretty much the same. The findings are what surprised us. Not only did students become more engaged with each other, they became more engaged with literature and with us. Taking away the physical distinction between student and teacher allowed all of us to blur our roles and develop new insight and empathy for literature and for understanding each other.

Susan Steffel, a faculty member in the Department of English Language and Literature at Central Michigan University, started the project with Chuck Steltenkamp, a teacher at Troy High School, whom she has known for years. Dodie Zolman, a teacher at Grandville High School, joined the project after the program's first year. Both Chuck and Dodie are veteran teachers who have maintained their passion for teaching. Both exhibit the energy and positive attitude that teaching requires. Let us share with you our story through narrative and excerpts from our own e-mail correspondence. The three of us tell our collective story: Susan is the narrator, Dodie the transcriber, and Chuck the reflector. We believe that our voices speak to the varied levels and layers of collaboration. Dodie's e-mails focus on "the project" and comment on the day-to-day activities as they occurred in real time. Chuck offers reflection on "the process," looking back after three years. Susan describes the collaboration, offers her own insights, and serves to tie everything together (similar to her actual role in the project). We believe that our three perspectives convey the realities of our work. The reader will be able to form a more complete sense of the project by weaving together the stories and perspectives of each of the three participants. Come along with us and experience our "once upon a time."

Characters and Settings

Susan's Story

I began my career as a secondary English teacher, and after eighteen years at that level, I left to try the challenge of training secondary teacher-education students for the realities of the classroom. For the last nine years, I have been teaching a literature methods course for English majors and minors pursuing their secondary teaching certificate at Central Michigan University-Mt. Pleasant, located in the center of the state. My goal has been to provide for my students a realistic experience that is based in theory, pedagogy, and practice. Although the course has been successful in having the university students experience for themselves the power of response to literature in a student-centered classroom, they have remained skeptical about the use of literature circles, response journals, and other conventions of response theory in actual secondary classrooms. Immersed in the traditional paradigm in which the teacher "presents" the literature, they were having difficulty sustaining the response approach when they began student teaching.

I started this project with enormous expectations. Even after teaching for almost thirty years, I still tend to go full throttle into new projects. The positive potential always overshadows the negative. I knew that there would be glitches in the process, especially because I didn't really know the teacher at the other end of the original project. I was trusting the colleague who put us in touch with each other and the positive impression I had from our initial telephone conversation.

I fully expected the project to be a success. I was excited, my students were excited, and my partner teacher was excited. It had to work. Of course, I knew that there would be some minor trouble. I anticipated some student resistance, but I couldn't wait to get started.

Dodie's Story

I am a veteran classroom teacher, and I was looking for more authentic ways to engage my students in our class discussion about literature. Actually, it was serendipitous that we began our project. Susan and I didn't know each other; in fact, we still haven't met face-to-face. We were brought together by a university colleague and mutual acquaintance who encouraged us to contact each other. Susan called me one Sunday evening, and I knew immediately that we were going to have a good time working together.

It was through these first informal conversations that we developed this project. We discussed the possibility of some type of correspondence between our university and high school students, possibly letters or journal exchanges. Susan raised the possibility of using electronic mail, and we continued our discussion of the project using e-mail ourselves, further developing the time line and getting to know each other.

During that initial phone call, I was excited, energetic, and positive. Susan's overwhelming desire to try things that might somehow benefit her students was evident. In my e-mail message to Susan, I wrote, "Hi Sue! You made my night! I am so glad we are going to be able to do this project. I'm glad you're willing to do it. I think it will be so beneficial to my students." I was eager to begin, and my hopes focused on the desire to turn my kids back on to reading. I wrote to Susan, "I have thirty students in my Contemporary Issues class—most do not plan to go on to college and many are convinced they do not like to read though I am hellbent on changing that idea!. . . My students are good kids but many have been turned off by school because it is either too difficult for them or they see no benefit (yet) from attending. They are excited about some of the topics we will be reading about so I know they can get interested. I just know this is going to be a lot of fun!"

The project began very slowly with both of us gently persuading our students to participate. Secondary students were both intimidated and intrigued by the possibility of corresponding with "those college students," and the university students were anxious to interact with the high schoolers and try out their "teacher stuff." The dynamics of the project were more complicated for the university students. They were not only fighting the fear of learning a new computer skill, they were also afraid that they wouldn't measure up to the high school students' expectations. What if they were discovered to be frauds?

Sue was looking for more input and a variety of audiences for her university class, and she expanded the project to include another high school connection.

Chuck's Story

I have known Susan for many years, although I was living now on the other side of the state. The two of us had a graduate school connection and would regularly see one another at professional conferences. Eventually, we ended up in grad school again, working toward our doctorates. As two full-time high school teachers, we supported each other and commiserated as we struggled to balance our teaching with the perpetual night classes, weekend classes, and summer classes required of us. By the time we completed our dissertations, we were fast friends.

It didn't take long before we discovered that we missed the intellectual stimulation we had shared during our own schooling. We decided to begin meeting once a month to discuss a common professional reading and swap our classroom stories. We continue to meet, more or less regularly, as schedules permit.

My goals for this project focused on reconnecting my college-bound students with literature. My e-mail to Sue points to my concern that my students' responses to literature had become passive in a traditional classroom: "I am aware that even with my best efforts, sometimes literature study can become a dull and one-sided academic exercise that focuses primarily on narrow responses which I control and which offer students' responses little range. Consequently, I was hoping to reach students who have become conditioned to offer only sage answers if any at all—to questions which are shaped by someone who will eventually give them a grade."

The Plot Thickens

An engaging plot incorporates twists and turns to maintain the reader's interest. Through these twists the characters are forced to take risks, and our plot was no exception.

Risks

None of us ever seriously considered that there would be any major problems. Susan and Dodie brainstormed for potential books to use for this project. They were looking for books that would be easily accessible to both groups. It needed to be a well-written, quality piece of literature, but not necessarily a "classic." It had to be engaging and focus on issues important to young adults. The book Dodie and Susan selected was one Susan had read it but never used it in a class. She wrote to Dodie, "I have never taught this book before so if you or any of your students come up with some great ideas, I am all ears!"

Dodie assured Susan that it was a powerful story of an adolescent girl. The novel, *Ellen Foster* by Kaye Gibbons, was certain to generate strong responses. Using an unfamiliar book would be a risk for both Susan and Dodie.

Despite the unknown risks, Susan's university students had readily agreed to do this project. They were eager to begin. One volunteered to collect money for the books; another volunteered to wheel and deal with a local wholesaler to negotiate the best price. Another volunteered to drive and pick up the books.

In contrast, the book Chuck and Susan agreed on was one that he was already using in his eleventh-grade literature class. *Ordinary People* by Judith Guest was the topic of their first e-mail exchanges. In this case, Susan was less anxious because not only had she done this project before, this time she was familiar with the novel.

Complications, Conflicts, and Reality Checks

We faced another twist of plot when we failed to consider that the high school students might not be as motivated as the university students were. We soon found out there were a number of other complicating factors.

Naively, Susan had anticipated that her role in this project would be one of the respected professor. She would encourage her students, revel in their success, and continue her own exciting conversation with her partners across the miles. She planned to be a peripheral observer, leading the discussion among her students who would be sharing their strategies and findings. Susan set the project up to be self-driven, and her students were to approach this as one-on-one action research. They knew that they were to save all of their correspondence, experiment with leading the discussion, observe the responses of their partners, analyze the nature of their discussion, and reflect on the entire project.

As in any story, the characters face a number of plot-altering conflicts. For us, those never seemed to end. From technology to human insecurity, we all needed encouragement. With all this flux, Susan had to give up the need to control, and she ended up being a much more active participant.

The Technology Factor

Susan did not anticipate that her preservice students would not be computer savvy. As a high school teacher, she was perpetually learning computer skills from her students and believed that most high schools had computer labs and proficiency requirements. After all, we have heard for some time now how computer literate today's students are. It turned out that Susan was far too optimistic for her first foray into the universe of technology.

Wrongly assuming her students to be computer literate, Susan began outlining with them the use of multimedia, the Internet, and interactive software in the literature classroom. It took less than a minute for her students' eyes to open wide and their mouths to drop. Beyond confused, they looked panicked. Further discussion informed Susan that although able to compose a paper using a word processor, the majority of them (at the time of the 1998 collaboration) were not familiar with the Internet or even with e-mail.

Susan discovered a surprising truth. Rather than all being proficient users of technology, not only were many of them nonregular users of e-mail, some hadn't even bothered to activate their university-supplied e-mail accounts. Her first challenge was to assist these students in mastering the use of the university server, remembering their brand new passwords, and negotiating the ins and outs of sending and receiving mail. The incentive was there. These college kids were motivated to learn and to begin their conversations with their assigned partners. How difficult could it be?

It seemed, however, as if there were no end to the trivial problems: the labs, the availability of computers, commuting and living off campus, using stations that didn't have printer capabilities, storing messages, and so on. Likewise, Dodie's replies to Susan included similar encounters: "I do not know what 'Authentification Warning' was about either. I am not very technologically literate either. This will be like the blind leading the blind!" And, when Dodie's new school server continued to have problems, she was forced to use a fax to communicate with Susan. Her fax message read, "Our

Internet lab is not working properly yet, so please urge your student to send their messages to me so I can print them at home and take them to school. I would hate for the kids not to be able to read their messages."

Chuck ran into technical difficulty as well. He was also an e-mail novice but either had more assistance available or was more comfortable asking for it. He wrote to Susan, "We were typical educators who understood the importance and potential of using the computer for literature discussions, but faced certain obstacles: primarily, we lacked the technical knowledge and comfort zone necessary to oversee a project like this. What were we thinking?"

Issues of Insecurity

The dynamics of the project were more complicated for the university students. Not only were they fighting the fear of learning a new skill, they were also afraid that they wouldn't measure up to the high school students' expectations. The book selected for tandem reading was one that was unfamiliar to the university class. That old paradigm of the all-knowing teacher still haunted them, but they were calmed to hear that their high school counterparts were also intimidated by them. Chuck wrote to Susan, "I know there was some worry and fear about communicating with college students, especially seniors, but your students seem so human. They all give English teachers a good name." And in a following message:

 Another fear involved the students themselves. Our idea was to pair high school students with college students, including older adult students. How would they respond to each other, not having met and only communicating on-line? Clearly, there would be gaps in the experiences, and we were uneasy as to how—or if—these gaps could be overcome with dialogue. One of my worries was that the students would depart from the text and use their contact with each other as largely bull sessions.... My concern not only proved to be groundless but was probably the most successful aspect of the project connectedness.

When problems were solved on one end of the project, they began on the other. Finally mastering their own difficulties and eagerly anticipating the first responses to their initial messages, Susan's university students were met with silence. "You have no new mail," became a taunt. Day after day, they became increasingly more frustrated. They second-guessed themselves and doubted their own ability to connect with secondary students. "Why haven't they written?" they would ask. Susan and her students learned from Dodie that the technology connection had broken down on the other end. For weeks, Susan's students had to send messages to Dodie at her home account, and she would print out the messages and pass them along to her students. The high school's brand new system server didn't quite have the bugs out. Eventually, most of those issues were resolved, and students were able to e-mail directly for the limited time remaining in the semester.

Changing Roles and Time Demands

Instead of being an advisor to the project, Susan ended up being a much more active participant in it. Her roles included those of troubleshooter, trying to discover just what the problem was and then solving it; tech specialist, assisting students using her own limited proficiency; and cheerleader, keeping attitudes positive and momentum going.

These combined roles required an enormous amount of time, much more than Susan anticipated. Both university and secondary students would forward messages to her to pass on to their respective partners. Each student required an immediate response. They were trying, after all. Susan found herself working at the computer most evenings, often until late at night. Instead of having one partner, she was carrying on multiple conversations, serving as the mediator for these student partnerships. There was never enough time. She felt chained to her computer, as did Dodie and Chuck, who commiserated with her. Dodie wrote, "I know how time-consuming reading all that mail can be…. Chuck also noticed that his role changed as the project evolved. "At first I saw myself in a traditional central role, initiating and controlling my students' responses through our class discussion first, and believing that this would be passed on through their e-mails. Fortunately, I was mistaken."

In reflecting on the process, not only did Chuck acknowledge that his role had changed, he acknowledged that the project changed the overall design of his classroom. He wrote to Susan:

> As I mentioned previously, students became more comfortable with their partners, and their dialogues frequently departed from being text-driven to being more reflective about their own lives. The book became a jumping-off point from which they could discuss their relevant daily details. Instead of central facilitator, I faded into the background to the role of the engaged cheerleader. Our class discussions became enriched by sharing the responses of university partners seemingly far away but now made very close and active through my students…. I was especially gratified that a few of my teenage students were thrilled with the rapport and response of their partners—some old enough to be their parents! They were finding an empathy with them that I did not expect when the project began. For years, I have listened to teenagers complain that adults are condescending to them and have listened to adults complain that teenagers do not listen to them. Expecting exactly that, I was pleasantly surprised.

Freed from the responsibility of a teacher-centered classroom, Chuck focused on developing his own e-mail expertise: "Slowly, I became more valuable as a technical advisor…. I had been learning from my students for years. Yet, by using e-mail more myself … I was more comfortable in helping those who needed it."

Dodie and Susan seemed to address problem solving in similar fashion. Just like Susan, Dodie also served as moderator, troubleshooter, and cheerleader. The almost-daily messages from Dodie to Susan had been sent late at night and helped to diffuse our frustration. Dodie's upbeat sense of humor motivated and reassured Susan.

Chuck and Susan, on the other hand, did not do as much sharing of their frustrations. Chuck solved whatever he could on his end, assuming that Susan was doing the same. Whatever the reason, his trust in Susan was motivating. Chuck wrote to Susan, "I knew that the students' various successes and shortcomings of the project were a two-way street. Fortunately, I knew you well enough to know that whatever happened, you were anxious enough for the project to succeed that you would draw upon any resources you could to motivate your students."

We All Needed Encouragement

We tried new things like exchanging pictures on-line. Few of these efforts ever worked, and we again relied on humor to cope. Our constant encouragement of each other and our students kept us from giving up. Dodie wrote to Susan, "Sending a picture of your kids was a great idea. I ran right down to our tech teacher and asked him if it would be possible to send a picture via e-mail. He rattled off a set of instructions and said he would come to my class tomorrow and take a picture and try to send it to your students. I have no idea if this will work, but I am very excited about it. I am one of these people who loves all this new-fangled stuff, but I don't know how to do any of it." Although Susan was never able to receive her digital picture, some of her students did and graciously brought copies to class to share. Dodie then received Kodak glossies of Susan's class, courtesy of the U.S. Postal Service and Susan. Both Dodie and Susan have realized at that point that they should have asked for their students' help earlier.

In a story, plot is forwarded by the interaction of characters. Chuck noted the importance of their mutual support in sustaining each other: "Susan's encouragement was crucial for me. We shared our frustrations as well as our successes, and I was heartened by the fact she ran into many of the same glitches that I did and was not too proud to say it when they occurred. We were fortunate that our collegiality was such that it allowed us to admit our mistakes and insecurities to each other without embarrassment."

The Control Issue

Susan has had issues of control. For her, it was always a challenge when collaborating to take the leap of faith and trust that her partners were as involved as she was. Given the physical distance between us in this project, it was even more of a personal challenge. Each of us qualified as a major character in this story, but in Susan's role as university coordinator, she was responsible for managing both projects. To maintain true collaboration, however, she had to avoid second guessing the intentions of her partners and let some things go. It was also a constant struggle for Susan to avoid micromanaging the student discussions. She had purposely left them to direct their own conversations, wanting to observe the directions of the conversations and the content. Beyond the issues of technology were a fair number of situations over which we had little or no control. Not only did we have to deal with our own frustrations, we needed to reassure our partners and mollify our students.

External Conflicts

Lack of Correspondence

Dodie was concerned about her students' lack of participation. We were all at the mercy of "senioritis." Dodie wrote to Susan, "Please tell your students not to get too upset with the lack of response from my kids. At this time of year, they feel overwhelmed when asked to do anything. Their minds are elsewhere and it will only get worse. Tell all of your future English teachers that second-semester seniors are just wonderful human beings!"

Chuck, on the other hand, experienced the reverse with my university seniors, as is indicated from his e-mail message:

A few times during the project, my students would complain about their partners not having much to say, or worse yet, not even being caught up with their reading. My high school students were incredulous that college students would actually blow off assignments. Though I was quick to blame my own students for shortcomings, Susan reminded me that she had some of the same frustration with her students. My secondary students were guilty of the same lethargy at times, yet would hold their university partners to a higher standard and complain louder.

Scheduling Conflicts

Scheduling was difficult, and neither class met in a computer lab. Nonetheless, although the high school classes did have the option of scheduling lab time, the university class did not have that option. Labs were unavailable during class meeting time, and students had to fit their e-mail in with their other coursework. Moreover, a number of Susan's students did not live on campus. These nontraditional students faced the challenge of arranging extra time on campus to complete this assignment if they did not have Internet service at home. For Susan, this probably was the biggest problem to overcome. She made her office available and formed computer buddy groups. Eventually, students developed a system, and the positive rewards of the correspondence took over.

Issues of Calendar

Students who, for whatever reason, were unable to correspond regularly caused another frustration for both sides of the project. School calendars aggravated this problem. The first semester we attempted this project was in the spring. None of us remembered that university and secondary school calendars place spring break a month apart. The high school kids were annoyed when, for an entire week, most received no mail.

Issues of Attendance

From the other side, university students were frustrated and confused when their partners seemed to disappear for unknown reasons. It was a good dose of reality for these preservice teachers about how the changing dynamics of attendance can impact classroom planning. Dodie would e-mail regularly with attendance updates. Both Dodie and Chuck would correspond with Susan's students who asked for help with delinquent partners.

Internal Conflicts

Interference or Support

Initially, at the university level there was little input from Susan's superiors. After the project was off the ground, Susan was able to secure a substantial university technology grant that provided further technology training and enabled her to purchase new equipment to continue this project. The grant provided a welcome validation of her efforts in this project.

Dodie often received help from her computer technology colleague, but there were also occasional situations where decisions had been made without informing her. In her message to Susan, Dodie wrote, "What a day! We went down to the lab to send messages and all the computers had been turned around ... and were not in the same order, so students were terribly confused as to which computer to use (most have their messages stored on the hard drive). So, needless to say, many students did not get a message off today. It never ends, does it?"

Chuck was grateful for the lack of interference, but with a touch of sarcasm, he argued the importance of support. He wrote to Susan, "Considering that our project was not, as the saying goes, illegal, immoral, or fattening, it wasn't surprising that we didn't have any interference. I am cautiously optimistic that we would continue to have the same administrative support if we were to need significant funding or time to accomplish this project.... I believe that collaborative projects such as ours are worth the time and effort, even if they were to run less smoothly than ours did."

Professional Insecurity

It wasn't just our students who experienced insecurity. To some extent, each one of us was concerned with how our partners would view us. In his e-mail to Susan, Chuck shared his concerns:

In teaching, like any other field, there is rampant insecurity among its practitioners. This insecurity, regardless of the teaching level, can dampen the enthusiasm with which one or both partners participate in a collaborative project. The fact that we are long-time friends helped to alleviate insecurities that might have hampered our progress. There are precious few productive partnerships between secondary schools and universities, even ones within the same geographical areas. Improved institutional cooperation would facilitate projects such as ours, established between university and secondary departments and, ultimately, between teachers and their students.

Analysis of the Text:
How Did We Determine Success?

Regardless of the difficulties, we declare the project a success. Measured by the university students' project papers and evaluations and the endorsements of the high school partners, we are convinced that we should continue. Other measures of success include e-mail conversations that continued beyond the class project. A number of students each semester choose to continue their dialogues with their high school partners. Some just continued the exchange, but some actually selected new books and read them together.

Many students commented that they were disappointed that the project ended just as they were becoming comfortable in the medium. The use of e-mail opened up a whole new world for them.

The university students began responding as teachers. Andrea shared, "If I learned one thing throughout the course of this project it is to have patience, understanding, and not to prejudge or expect too much." And Melanie reflected, "A week went by with not getting a response to my last e-mail message, and I immediately wondered and doubted myself.... Instead of getting down and letting my fears get in the way, I wrote back and tried to be friendly with him. I tried to give him the impression that I was truly excited (which I was) to talk to him about the book."

An outstanding proof of our success is that a number of university students have incorporated various versions of the e-mail exchange into their classrooms while student teaching. Others have incorporated it into their own classrooms as beginning teachers, and still others have formed cohort groups among themselves after graduation.

Dodie also measured success by her students' responses and wrote the following to Susan: "This e-mailing is a powerful motivator! I am just thrilled to see my kids typing their little hearts out and getting excited about this project. It is such a positive experience for them."

Reflection

Resolutions and Conclusions

As teachers, the three of us each gained insight into the kinds of responses that our students have to literature outside the classroom. This insight, in turn, changed our classrooms. The project also provided an opportunity for us to team teach. Perhaps most important, it allowed Susan, as a methods instructor, to stay in touch with the secondary classroom, and it allowed a couple of secondary teachers the opportunity to positively affect how future secondary teachers are trained.

As with any project, some experiments work better than others. Certain teachers are more adept at implementing and promoting projects, whereas others wish to maintain control over the discussion and direct the conversations. Many teachers need to learn technology skills right alongside of their students. Unfortunately, many secondary schools remain woefully undersupplied. If they have computer labs, many do not have Internet access. The situation is improving, but slowly.

What It Takes to Work

We are convinced that these one-on-one collaborations work because they're initiated at the classroom level. It is the personal relationship between classroom teachers that drives the project. It doesn't matter whether that connection is based on a fifteen-year friendship or on a stranger's telephone call. Collegiality results when teachers work together for a common purpose. Trust, sharing, and dedication form the basis. It's the same for discussion of literature. These teachers believe in the potential of their students—they love kids, love teaching, and love literature.

As with our students, the better we grew to know and trust each other, the more we could risk. In so many ways, our relationships paralleled those of our students. They interwove with the students. It was no longer "them and us," but a collective "we." This project was a success for all of us.

A project's success also depends on students who, although perhaps inspired by their instructors, develop and demonstrate the same key attributes that are necessary for teachers: commitment, flexibility, energy, and stamina. As a result of this project, the teacher–student roles blurred, sometimes disappearing completely. Teachers took on the role of student, and students took on the role of teacher. It became a blended classroom, incorporating "yours, mine, and ours." We became equal participants in this extended learning community as the project took on a life of its own.

Perhaps most gratifying for Susan was sharing her students' reflections about the project. They no longer wrote from the point of view of a student; they spoke from the perspective of a teacher. Our story no longer had minor characters. We had all become major characters.

Comments from students testify to the success of the project. Kim wrote, "I guess that's what being a teacher is all about—sticking with it and keeping on trying." And Jessica shared, "Even though we have never met, I have a great respect for Mrs. [Dodie] Zolman as a teacher. I hope she knows how successful this project has been, regardless of the glitches…. I have learned how persistent, patient, flexible, and ingenious a teacher must be in order to have success in this way."

No one can argue the power of a story. As teachers, this project has changed us, our classrooms, and our students. Those who would argue for cultural literacy insist that we all bring the same experiences to our reading of literature. We argue that through sharing our responses to literature in the context of our individual stories we end up not only with a fuller understanding of the original story but one enriched by the stories of our lives. The project began in an effort to study student responses to a story. We all began with our own fears, expectations, and experiences, but together we created a new story—our story, still honoring the individual voices and contributions, but merging as a whole our voices and roles.

The three of us see ourselves as colleagues, collaborators, and friends. Regardless of the future of these projects, we have formed strong relationships through literature. What we wished for our students, we have experienced ourselves. We truly do learn from each other. We form a community of learners. We share with you our collective story, and our individual stories, and hope you will allow us into your own, enlarging the community so that we together with literature may live "happily ever after."

Chapter

Our "Stealth PDS": An Undetected Professional Development School Relationship

Adrienne "Andi" Sosin and Ann Parham

The school–university partnership described in this chapter is a long-standing collaboration of more than thirty years' duration, between a public school, called Center-City School, and Metropolitan University,* which contains a professional school of education. During the thirty-plus years the relationship between Metropolitan and Center-City has been in existence, varying personalities, pressures, and opportunities have influenced the quality and intensity of the partnership, yet the collaboration has persisted, and each institution has found that keeping this continual relationship active is mutually beneficial. We have humorously termed it a "stealth PDS," because of its invisibility to all but those who know about its existence.

The authors of this chapter are a university teacher educator and a public school teacher, now retired. We have each been involved to varying degrees in the collaboration for more than ten years and relate the events from our vantage point as active participants. We add our own personal stories of collaboration and friendship and share anecdotes and lessons we have learned. We hope that our story will help others improve their own school–university collaborations.

*We have used descriptive pseudonyms to shield the identities of the institutions.

Context

Center-City is an urban public school, built in the 1960s. Today it remains in relatively good repair, with wide, attractive hallways and large, sunny classrooms. A brick school, it is situated on the rim of a public low-income housing project of brick high-rise apartment buildings. Center-City has many of the problems urban schools generally face. More than three-quarters of the students qualify for free lunch at the school, an indication of low socioeconomic status. The school's students are multiracial; about half of the students are Hispanic, and a quarter each are African American and Asian. English is not the native language of most of the children's families. Many of the Center-City students live in the surrounding public housing project or in a set of middle-income apartment houses around the corner. A number of children living in homeless shelters attend the school, with their attendant problems of transience, and many students travel to school from across the city, creating lateness problems. Although it is a zoned school, few white or middle-class children who live in the area attend Center-City because their families either obtain variances for them to attend other schools within the district, or they are sent to parochial schools. Test scores and other indicators of performance are low in relation to the rest of the school district. Center-City receives Title I and other funds and is part of a funded state initiative, called the Community Schools Program, a program designed to raise achievement by involving parents and community organizations.

The other entity in this case study is Metropolitan University, a comprehensive undergraduate and graduate multicampus university. Metropolitan's School of Education sponsors preservice programs for teacher certification in elementary and secondary subjects, undergraduate, graduate, and advanced degrees in educational administration. Students study early childhood development to qualify for elementary teaching certification or can gain secondary certification in English, mathematics, social studies, the sciences, or modern languages. Although these programs are now being revamped in response to new state regulations and national accreditation standards, during the period discussed in this chapter the teacher education programs were traditionally organized and university based. The Metropolitan campus, situated in the downtown center, is essentially an urban high-rise building. Some undergraduate students live on campus in a high-rise dormitory, but most commute to the university by train or bus. Many of the Metropolitan students are the first in their families to attend college. Many work part or full time to pay their tuition. These students are particularly concerned with the amount of out-of-class time needed to commute to field experiences or student teaching and often request school placements in the area.

The Past

The historical data for this case study was collected primarily through interviews with participants, both at the school and the university. Where written documents were available, these were used to supplement interview accounts. The recent events of the case study are primarily taken from the authors' and others' recollections of events, from interviews, and from any written documentation available.

According to interviews with former faculty of Metropolitan's education department, when the school–university relationship with Center-City began during the early

1960s, it was between a newly built elementary school and a newly established teacher-education program. The university's primary connection with the local schools was for traditional student teaching. Elementary schools located within walking distance from Metropolitan became favored sites for student teaching placement because their easy accessibility allowed faculty supervisors to conveniently schedule visits to evaluate the student teachers, and students were able to easily get to and from classes at the university. This ease of access fostered a sense of familiarity with the schools in the area. The faculty became acquainted with schools' staff and teachers, and the teachers became familiar with the faculty and the features of the teacher-education program.

Interviews and letters regarding the early years of the relationship provide information about the tone of the first relationships developed with all the local schools. A respectful distance was maintained between the college and the schools. Placement of student teachers with cooperating teachers was entirely left to the principals, as a gesture of respect for their professional judgment. According to the former chair, the university's faculty regularly visited the cooperating schools, but the faculty did not attempt to offer professional development services to the school. Professionalism and a hands-off attitude marked the early days of the relationship between schools and the university.

Over time, many strands of connection grew from the university's student teaching program. Teachers and principals at the local schools developed strong relationships with supervising faculty from the university. The principals often hired successful student teachers upon their graduation, who as alumni became cooperating teachers for new student teachers. Cooperating teachers received a voucher that waived tuition for a course at Metropolitan each time they had a student teacher in their classroom. Many cooperating teachers took courses at the university and formed relationships with their professors. Some teachers earned advanced degrees in educational administration, including one teacher who later became the principal at Center-City. Thus, Metropolitan's teacher education program developed a cadre of loyal administrators and cooperating teachers at Center-City and in the other local schools.

The era of the 1960s and 1970s was marked by multiple substantive connections between Center-City and Metropolitan. In addition to student teaching, there was an interactive relationship in which faculty from the university conducted curriculum development and other projects at Center-City. Teachers who were interviewed about that period remember participating with the faculty in different projects. Each semester, Metropolitan's education faculty taught demonstration lessons to Center-City's children while preservice education students observed the lesson through one-way glass. The teachers recollect that incidental, but not unintentional, professional development at the school served as a quasi-laboratory for the university's curriculum development projects and demonstration lessons. Even during this period of maintaining respectful distance, and despite the uneven balance of benefits, the relationship contained many seeds of currently desirable teacher-education practices.

During the late 1970s and early 1980s, there was a general trend of school closings in response to dips in the birth rate and a lower population of school-age children and a commensurate decline in teacher preparation. Consequently, the relationship with Center-City and the other local schools dwindled. Nonetheless, as the late 1980s and early 1990s brought resurgence in interest in education by the public and a rise in the birth rate, Metropolitan's teacher education program revived and reached out to the city schools. By 1990, Center-City again was a regular student teaching placement site. It had an energetic new principal, who was interested in reaching out to the university and to other community agencies.

From the inception of the new administration, Center-City underwent a significant change, influenced by the new principal's dynamic leadership and by the district's implementation of an intensive staff development effort. Many parents enthusiastically and publicly got involved in the school's operations. Funds were solicited from various contributors. Center-City used school district, city, state, and private support to develop a themed middle school, implement an inclusion program for special-education students, develop cross-age classes, provide Reading Recovery services for early intervention, participate in the district's implementation of the New Standards, and engage in other educational innovations and creative ventures. Test scores rose, and Center-City became an example of a successful turnaround in an urban school.

Our "Stealth" PDS

Concurrent to the Center-City's improvement during the early 1990s, the literature about professional development schools (PDSs) began to appear. For teacher learning that benefits all stakeholders, PDSs can be exciting places. Scholars and accrediting institutions strongly recommended PDS arrangements for teacher education (Goodlad, 1988; Holmes Group, 1986, 1990, 1995; National Council for Accreditation of Teacher Education [NCATE], 1997). As the articles appeared, Metropolitan's faculty discussed the efforts of other teacher preparation institutions and schools to establish PDS relationships (Lemlech, 1997; Levine, 1997; Teitel, 1997).

Ideas from PDSs became part of the Metropolitan faculty's conversations with teachers and administrators at local schools, including Center-City. Although there were many impediments to formalizing a PDS during the time described in this chapter, the PDS concept greatly influenced some aspects of the partnership between Center-City and Metropolitan. Even though there was little official interest in creating a PDS with Center-City, the PDS literature increased our desire to move our institutions closer to the PDS model. The two of us humorously called our school–university relationship a "stealth PDS" because it was not outwardly visible, but also because in our collaboration we saw many, if not all, of the characteristic conditions discussed in the PDS literature (NCATE, 2001).

Our Major Strands of Connection

Student Teaching

Student teaching, an apprenticeship to a mentor teacher, is required by state certification regulations. The certification requirement made Metropolitan's student teaching program the most important of its strands of connection with the local schools. It was vital for Metropolitan's director of student teaching to successfully negotiate for enough student teaching placements each semester so that every student teacher could be placed in a lower-grade and in an upper-grade classroom. To accomplish this, the student teaching director made frequent visits to each school and met with principals and teachers to discuss the student teaching program and any problems that came up.

Generally, each local school principal accepted two to six student teachers each semester, depending on the availability of cooperating teachers. Through regular visits to the schools, the director became familiar with the teachers and administration of each school in which the university placed student teachers and developed strong relationships with principals and particularly effective cooperating teachers.

During the 1990s, the interchange with Center-City became more extensive than it had been in the past, partially based on strong student teaching relationships. When Metropolitan developed special projects, it was considered natural to bring them to Center-City. The relationship between Center-City and Metropolitan University gained strength fostered by both university faculty initiatives and the school's willing participation. Thus, the strands of connection that were originally based solely in student teaching multiplied as other initiatives were developed.

The Teacher Opportunity Corps

One of the first initiatives to enhance the relationship between Center-City and Metropolitan was the Teacher Opportunity Corps (TOC). A state-funded grant program, TOC was designed to increase the number of minority teachers. Both TOC and a later federal grant award for Urban Community Service became major outreach programs for Metropolitan's school of education. More than sixty education students were selected from traditionally underrepresented groups. These students were placed in the local schools for weekly field experiences with mentor teachers, who received a small stipend for their participation. A significant number of TOC students went to Center-City, and many Center-City teachers were recruited to be TOC mentors. Appearances at Center-City by the TOC students and their supervising Metropolitan faculty were regular and visible. The TOC program substantially increased the extent of Metropolitan's faculty involvement and knowledge about the school and the school staff's knowledge about and connection to Metropolitan.

An On-Site Reading Methods Course

Beginning in 1990, an on-site reading methods course augmented Metropolitan's role at Center-City. Center-City was a desirable site for the reading methods class based on its location, its diverse population demographics, its characteristically urban classrooms, and its long-standing relationship with Metropolitan. The goals of the university professor in taking the reading methods courses to Center-City were to provide preservice education students supervised and structured experiences in working with children in basic literacy activities and to give the students opportunities to interact with teachers in a true-to-life urban school situation. For five years, the reading methods classes met at the school weekly. The course professor coordinated with participating teachers, who allowed time for the students to work with small groups of children. Some cooperating teachers gave the students greater autonomy to take control of small groups, whereas other teachers often demonstrated lessons and distributed specific texts to be read with the children. Immediately following their classroom experience, the class met for reflection on theory and practice.

One special feature of the on-site course was that Center-City's parents were invited to participate in the class on a noncredit, informal basis. The parent's participation was the result of negotiations; it was the school's quid pro quo to meet its

Community School program objectives. Some parents attended regularly, some spo-radically, but with few exceptions the parents made a positive contribution to the class. Their participation was especially valuable at the end of the year when they engaged in role plays of parent–teacher conferences with the education students, providing them with a real-life parental viewpoint.

The positive outcomes of this experiential approach to the reading methods course were both immediate and long term for all the participants. The students appre-ciated their real-life experiences in the school, and there were substantial gains in the students' instructional abilities. Parent participation enriched the class sessions, and parent feedback was positive. Weekly visits to teach the on-site course afforded the professor with regular opportunities to meet teachers and other school staff, both for-mally and informally. These contacts provided entrée for education students and other Metropolitan students to learn about the school's multifaceted operations. The number of student requests for student teaching placements at Center-City increased. Opportu-nities increased for education students and the parents to take part in the events and culture of the school and to develop connections with each other and with the teachers, staff, and administration.

The Community School Advisory Board

Another strand of connection for Metropolitan developed through membership on Center-City's Community School Advisory Board. The goal of the Community School program was to develop an active set of stakeholder organizations and local supports to raise a school's achievement levels. The state legislation mandated that each school form an advisory board constituted of neighboring community agencies. As a university representative, Metropolitan's reading methods professor was invited to serve on the advisory board. Quarterly meetings of the advisory board kept Metro-politan's faculty aware of the school's status in the district and of the school's activi-ties. The advisory board also provided opportunities for members from all the community organizations to interact on current and proposed projects. In this way, the communication encouraged by membership on the Community School Advisory Board developed into an additional strand of connection in the relationship between Center-City and Metropolitan.

The Literary Bridge

The connections developed by membership on the Community School Advisory Board became an important factor when funding for a family literacy project became available to Metropolitan's School of Education. The funding enabled Metropolitan's educational outreach office to offer a series of computer workshops in the university's academic computing laboratory. When this program began in the mid-1990s, com-puter hardware and software in homes and schools were not nearly as ubiquitous as they are now. Computers were unfamiliar, to the point that many people were afraid to touch them for fear of breaking them. Because Center-City was a close partner for Metropolitan's faculty, it was the school on which the outreach office focused for the proposed project. Drafting the proposal brought together the school personnel and uni-versity coordinator, who met often for planning and preparation. Metropolitan's fac-ulty coordinator arranged for the use of the academic computing laboratory and recruited and trained multilingual tutors from the education student body. Center-City's parent liaison recruited the first class of twelve parents, the computer classroom's capacity. To provide the parents a level of comfort, a tour of the university was arranged for them, becase the university was considered a distant and formidable institution. The parents' curiosity about computers and the availability of free instruction provided a strong incentive for them to attend the workshops.

The workshops were taught by a mathematics and computer science professor at first but later were led by graduate education students who intended to teach English, business education, or technology. At the weekly workshops, the parents learned computing concepts and used word-processing software. Most of the parents were native Spanish speakers, and some had low levels of English literacy. A few parents had not graduated from high school. The parents' varying literacy levels were supported by individualized attention from the faculty, Center-City's staff, and the education student tutors. Some parents prepared their resumes during the computer workshops and used them to find employment. One parent prepared to take the General Education Diploma examination. As the Internet developed, it also became a regular topic in the workshops, along with the introduction of other types of software. The familiarity with computers that developed in the workshops prompted the leaders of the Center-City Parents Association to authorize purchase of a computer to have at the school. All the parents who participated developed awareness about computers and self-confidence in their ability to use technology; they also improved their English skills.

Once the project began, Center-City's Community School liaison, a strong advocate of parent empowerment, suggested that a way for parents to contribute to the school's literacy goals would be to use the available technology to publish the school's literary magazine, *The Literary Bridge*. The idea that parents could provide this service to the school empowered and stimulated everyone's imagination. The computer workshops were transformed into *Literary Bridge* workshops, where the compositions children wrote were typed, children's art was scanned, and the document was laid out. Workshops also met at Center-City on weekday evenings, where parents read the children's compositions, selected themes and artwork, and learned about writing process. From 1995 through 1999, *The Literary Bridge* was desktop-published, copied, and then distributed to each year's graduating class as a memento of their graduation.

The Literary Bridge represents a tangible contribution by the university to Center-City's literacy effort. The computer instruction enabled the parents to meaningfully participate in its publication, and many parents expressed personal growth and success resulting from participation. Each year, parents assumed a greater share of the responsibility for the shape of the finished publication. Qualitative indicators—including parent attendance and attitudes; the support of the teachers, the principal, and the community school liaison; and the student teacher-tutor's and faculty's reflections—were largely positive. Children are proud that their compositions are published in *The Literary Bridge*. Word-of-mouth requests for spaces and parents' continuing attendance from year to year have been sufficient to keep maximum attendance at the workshops each year. A number of Center-City parents and children have attended the university's annual outreach recognition ceremonies, attesting to their positive experiences.

The *Literary Bridge* project benefits the university as well as Center-City. Student teachers gain from the opportunity to tutor and conduct instruction in keyboarding, computer concepts, and literacy development. Graduate students have developed action research projects about parent involvement and about adult literacy development. The program's success motivated the university's dean to continue to fund stipends for student teachers as tutors and to support scheduling the academic computing facility. Engaging in this collaborative project also strengthened the other relationships between the school and the university. In many ways, this project represents how a school and university can cooperatively engage each other to support each institution's goals in substantive ways.

Stresses and Influences on the Relationship

There have been many stresses and influences on the relationship between Center-City and Metropolitan. The long-term association and strong personal friendships and professional relationships between the people from Center-City and from Metropolitan are positive influences. Geographic proximity, which enables Metropolitan's students and faculty to get to and from Center-City easily, is a major positive influence. Nonetheless, close geographic proximity also has placed stress on the relationship. The many teacher preparation institutions that share the city rely on local public schools as resources for practice teaching and research. Requests for field experiences and student teaching placements from higher education institutions give school and district leadership the opportunity to foster the relationships they perceive to be in their best interests.

At one point, competition caused a stress in the relationship. In this instance, a breach of connection was saved by the actions of cooperating teachers who were part of the cadre of Metropolitan's alumni at Center-City. When these teachers became aware that Metropolitan's student teachers had been turned away to take another college's students, they found alternative classroom placements for the other student teachers and preserved their roles in Metropolitan's student teaching program. Their long-established connection and loyalty caused them to protect their strands of connection between Center-City and Metropolitan.

Over the recent past, there have been other difficult situations that have stressed the collaboration. These problems are not uncommon to any school–university collaboration. For example, the problem of facility overcrowding is common to urban schools. Meeting space is a scarce commodity in most schools and is an especially difficult problem for courses meeting on-site in urban schools during the school day. The class often had to meet in hastily arranged spaces, some of which were difficult to adapt to planned activities. Sometimes, meeting rooms were so busy that the students and professor waited in the hall. Some education students, especially those who preferred the more hospitable university setting, complained to the professor. In dealing with space issues, flexibility was a key requirement. A focus on the positive benefits of the students' experiences was vital to keep a lack of quality meeting space from causing a rift.

The most difficult stresses came from issues raised about teaching philosophy, methods, and the value of teacher education. Challenges based on "town-versus-gown" issues are difficult to resolve, but their resolution was vital to maintaining the school–university connection. Some alternatively certified Center-City teachers were vocal in their opinions that the study of education was "a waste of time." Their criticism that, "the university doesn't teach the way it really is" contributed to an unsympathetic environment for the education students. Because these comments could have undermined the relationship, it became important to deal with them proactively, in a positive manner. Upon becoming aware of the issue, Metropolitan's faculty liaison approached the teachers and engaged them in substantive discussions. The teachers were able to voice their concerns, suggestions, and opinions, and as a result they came away with a greater understanding of their role in preparing student teachers. Some of these teachers later became cooperating teachers. Attention to concerns and keeping a focus on the positives of the relationship were essential in meeting the challenge of criticism.

Another stress to the relationship between Metropolitan and Center-City resulted from the many pressures leveled on school administrators and teachers. Test scores that did not meet the district's standards resulted in intense pressure on school personnel from the district administration and state regulators. An intensive and structured literacy program was implemented to improve reading test scores. It became increasingly difficult for Metropolitan's student teachers to bring in materials they constructed and to create lesson plans that did not conform to the strictly defined literacy methods. Restrictions on the conduct of the literacy period eventually led to an incident with a reading methods student in 1995. The incident demonstrated the level of stress that surrounded Center-City's reading scores. The principal explained that he could not risk giving the children's time to student teachers. He was fearful that test scores would suffer if the regular teacher or the approved program were not the sources of instruction. The principal's lack of confidence in the university's methods instruction was sufficient reason for the professor to relocate the reading methods course to another school.

Despite the stresses and negative influences, the relationship between Center-City and Metropolitan was maintained, protected by insulation from multiple connections. Because these events took place in the mid-1990s, there have been major staff changes at the school, including two subsequent principals, changes in assistant principals, and a large turnover of teachers at Center-City, including some key cooperating teachers. The most recently appointed principal has been receptive and eager for a continuing relationship between Center-City School and Metropolitan University. The warm reception she has given to student teachers and faculty provides indication that the thirty-year relationship will continue. The mutuality of benefits in partnering with a university persists, including continuation of the student teaching and TOC placements, the *Literary Bridge*, and now *America Reads,* among other projects.

Our Story of Collaboration

Andi's Reflection on Collaboration with Ann

Ann became my friend and collaborator in 1990 shortly after becoming my professional contact at Center-City, when I made the first overtures toward bringing my reading methods class on site. The principal introduced Ann to me as the parent liaison to coordinate involving parents in the on-site reading methods course. I watched Ann lead a parent workshop, and her ability gave me confidence that she would be a very good ally. For five years we collaborated in making my reading courses successful experiences for all the students, parents, teachers, and children involved in them. In this way, Ann and I established a working relationship that has continued to grow over the past ten years.

Ann was more than a liaison at Center-City for me because we connected in discussions of educational practice, philosophy, and the issues involved in what we were doing at Center-City and with the university students. As a member of the school staff, Ann was able to speak to teachers or clue me in as to how I could approach difficult situations. She interpreted and shared school happenings, so I was aware of the internal stresses and pressures the school faced. We shared literature about PDSs, read selections about teacher and collaborative action research (Noffke, 1997; Oja & Smulyan, 1989), and began to laugh about our "stealth PDS." Ideas about teacher learning in communities (Cochran-Smith & Lytle, 1999) led us to visualize our efforts not just as local and specific to our situation but as a part of a larger movement toward forging better relations to benefit education and society.

When I became aware of a foundation grant opportunity to involve a school and its parents in a family literacy effort, I contacted Ann. Together we crafted a proposal to develop workshops in computer literacy for parents that grew into the *Literary Bridge* project. In 1998, we traveled to San Diego to talk about our collaboration at the meeting of the special interest group for School–University Collaborative Research of the American Educational Research Association.

Ann and I became close friends through our work together. We were relatively comfortable talking to one another about the events that happened on a day-to-day basis. While discussing nitty-gritty organizational and personality issues, I learned about Ann's family, and she learned about mine. We didn't discuss personal issues to any great degree and are still tied to each other mainly through professional topics, yet we have developed a deep friendship. We both believe that our vision of a professional development school relationship between Center-City and Metropolitan will benefit all parties. We now realize that we are partners with similar objectives.

Ann's Reflections on Collaboration with Andi

When I began my career in education, I envisioned years of working to meet the challenges of students, staff, and of the educational bureaucracy. At Center-City, I was first a classroom teacher, then case manager for a board of education initiative for parents called Project Return, and finally a full-time parent coordinator, where I served as liaison with teachers, parents, and the community. Learning that a reading course for education majors would be held at Center-City was an exciting discovery because the university offered the possibility of enhancing my program for parents. I was introduced to Andi, the professor who taught the course, and was impressed by her enthusiasm. When I familiarized her with the parents' initiative, we began to explore the prospect of a partnership. Andi demonstrated a keen awareness of the needs of parents and was willing to work with me toward the development of a parent literacy program. In addition to inviting parents to participate in her classes, she planned "hands-on" activities to help parents and university students interact. During each semester, I was invited to conduct role-playing sessions with education majors enrolled in her class. Our involvement extended to both classes and to extracurricular activities. Andi encouraged me to meet the university staff and to become familiar with other university linkages with the surrounding community. As our relationship grew, we planned many special activities that served to underscore our school–university partnership.

Andi worked tirelessly to resolve issues that were university based, while I dealt with school-based issues. We agreed philosophically as to educational goals and were committed to strengthening the partnership. Together we used thoughtful negotiation to complete each task. Through the bond that we had formed, we were able to develop a program to serve parents and improve the viability of Center-City's connection with the university.

Upon retiring from the school system, I discovered that my collaboration with Andi served to strengthen my skills. Andi recommended that I consider becoming a clinical supervisor of student teachers, and I taught a course called "Parents, Schools and Communities" for education majors. As I reflect on the experiences I gained from working with Andi, I have a growing respect for the importance of our partnership and our opportunities to mutually open doors and seek solutions.

Our Lessons

This chapter uses a case perspective to analyze the benefits and problems in forging and maintaining a school–university partnership. Our experiences have taught us that several factors are crucial to school-university collaborations such as ours. The following factors are our lessons learned.

Information and Communication

In a school–university collaboration, the parties need information about the goals of the alliance and the means by which those goals are to be reached. Clarity around issues that arise needs to be addressed on an ongoing basis by school and the university liaisons' frequent communication and by being together in the school on a regular basis. Their presence and their familiarity with the individual needs of the participants support the continuation of collaboration. For example, visits by the student teaching director, weekly visits to teach an on-site course, and membership on the community school advisory board provided opportunities to communicate and exchange information about current problems and goals and provided an opportunity to share the successes of individual efforts. Through sharing information, teachers, administrators, and professors were able to discover similar goals for student achievement and similar desires to collaborate in reaching those goals.

Focus on the Positives

In generating school–university collaborations, it is important to focus on collaborative benefits to all the stakeholders, both at the school and at the university. Advocates need to be vocal about how the positive aspects of the relationship outweigh any negative aspects. All the programs we have described worked to increase familiarity and expand the number of participants in the relationship. Our long-term association of close ties among the personnel involved assisted both entities in gaining support from external sources. As friends, we were able to honestly discuss our differences while maintaining our basic allegiances to the school and university. We found it important to meet criticisms and give people opportunities to vent their frustrations when things did not go as planned. As advocates for the collaboration, we publicized the successful aspects of the relationship and focused on the positives.

Insulation Through Multiple Connections

Insulation provides the ability to transcend obstacles, regenerate interest in new collaborative efforts, and reengage following differences. During a period when there is a lack of trust between the university faculty and the school staff, important relationships may need to be hidden to protect them, which is why we coined the term "stealth PDS." An example of insulation through multiple connections took place when the on-site reading methods course was discontinued. Despite the ending of that strand of connection, student teaching and other programs continued without interruption. The insulation provided by the people involved in the collaboration protected the other strands of connection from disruption.

Commitment

Commitment to the relationship implies that university faculty and school personnel all acknowledge that they learn together, that they develop mutual respect, and that they are willing to take the actions needed to sustain the relationship. Commitment requires that people involved step forward to defend the relationship from negative pressures. In our school–university partnership, we recognized that we were partners with different objectives, but we and all the others involved were committed to maintaining what we felt were important benefits to our institutions. We showed our commitment in the many hours we put into the various projects we undertook. We were willing to expend energy and take risks on behalf of our school–university relationship.

Conclusion

In this case, many threads of connection and relationships overlap each other. The Center-City and Metropolitan relationship has already spanned thirty-plus years, during which administrators, teachers, and faculty have come and gone. The physical proximity and shared ideals of the school and university have combined to forge a relationship that has withstood both external and internal pressure.

The purpose of this chapter was to describe the experiences of one university and one school involved in collaborative work. Although as authors of this account, we believe that all concerned would benefit if the loosely knit relationships described here were more tightly bound. This is not an easy task, nor is it necessarily a straight trajectory. It doesn't take many people to keep a school–university relationship going. Our experience is that a few focused participants from different segments of a school's stakeholders allied with university proponents of collaboration can sustain multiple partnership strands, giving the relationship opportunities to intensify. For us, now part of Metropolitan's faculty, we hope to work with the new Center-City principal to embrace our partnership and energize collaborative projects at both the school and the university.

References

Cochran-Smith, M., & Lytle, S. (1999). Relationships of knowledge and practice: Teacher learning in communities. In A. Iran-Nejad & P. D. Pearson (Eds.), *Review of research in education* (Vol. 24, pp. 249–305). Washington, DC: American Educational Research Association.

Goodlad, J. I. (1988). School–university partnerships for educational renewal: Rationale and concepts. In K. A. Sirotnik & J. I. Goodlad (Eds.), *School-university partnerships in action*. New York: Teachers College Press.

Holmes Group. (1986). *Tomorrow's teachers*. East Lansing, MI: Author.

Holmes Group. (1990). *Tomorrow's schools*. East Lansing, MI: Author.

Holmes Group. (1995). *Tomorrow's schools of education*. East Lansing, MI: Author.

Lemlech, J. K. (1997). Guest editor's introduction: Professionalism and partnerships. *Teacher Education Quarterly, 24*(1), 5–7.

Levine, M. (1997). Can professional development schools help us achieve what matters most? *Action in Teacher Education, 19*(2), 63–73.

National Council for Accreditation of Teacher Education. (1997). Standards for Professional Development Schools. Washington, DC: Author. Available on-line: http://www.ncate.org/2000/PDS-Stands_10_00.pdf

National Council for Accreditation of Teacher Education. (2001). Standards for Professional Development Schools. Washington, DC: Author. Available on-line: http://www.ncate.org/2000/PDS_Stands_10-00.pdf

Noffke, S. (1997). Professional, personal, and political dimensions of action research. *Review of Educational Research, 22,* 305–343.

Oja, S. N., & Smulyan, L. (1989). *Collaborative action research: A developmental process*. New York: Falmer Press.

Teitel, L. (1997). Changing teacher education through professional development school partnerships: A five-year followup study. *Teachers College Record, 99,* 311–334.

Model II

Consultation

In the consultation model, one or several university faculty members work with one or several teachers. The faculty members, in the role of consultant, provide resources and expertise to the teachers. Other stakeholders may also join as collaborators. The main purpose of this partnership is improvement of instruction and teachers' professional development.

Chapter

Sailing the Ship:
A Collaborative Journey

Judith A. Robb and Donna Cronin

The marvelous richness of human experience would lose something of rewarding joy if there were no limitations to overcome. The hilltop hour would not be half so wonderful if there were no dark valleys to traverse.

—Helen Keller

In agreement with Keller's sentiment, we replace the Olympian metaphor with a broader pelagic one. The sea connotes a vast area to traverse with no definitive path, no visible shores, no concrete "hilltop" of aspiration. Our successful journey of collaboration required formation of a highly functioning crew to navigate unknown waters toward a hazy destination, experiencing crests and troughs of both gentle and threatening waves, seeking smoother waters for the journey, but unclear about how to recognize the far shore, the *right* shore, or the means to reshape it. This chapter is about capturing the richness of human experience during the voyage.

Introduction

Six teachers from a suburban junior high school and the university faculty member who worked with them had no idea of what they were entering into at the start of a school-year journey that held much promise. We were one of four school–university teams formed during the course of four years to become the Mathematics and Science Collaborative. The impetus for this collaborative began in a snowy seacoast school parking lot on a dreary winter afternoon. The junior high school principal and the university supervisor of teaching interns working at that school continued their long-standing conversation about connecting teachers and university faculty around issues of reform-based teacher education, particularly in mathematics and science. They envisioned a seamless, lifelong, recursive learning cycle that would begin at the entry-level "exploring teaching" stage for young college students and then never end. The goal would be to renew teaching and learning in the company of others who had the same goals. The same long-standing conversation was continued the next day at another junior high school between two other teachers and the same university supervisor. Teachers and principals from two more schools embraced this hazy vision, plus additional university faculty and an advisor from the state department of education. Together they wrote and secured a federal grant to reform the teaching of middle school science and mathematics through collaborative action research.

We were a group of excited individuals, poised to make big changes in the teaching of mathematics and science who began with an on-paper structure for collaboration and an enthusiasm for reform, but an unclear plan for implementation and an unfocused vision of results. In hindsight, none of us understood the complexities of change nor recognized fully that any real change or true collaboration is a very slow and sometimes paradoxical process. Fullan's (1993) observations on school change could have been grounded in our experience: "The way that teachers are trained, the way that schools are organized, the way that the educational hierarchy operates, and the way that education is treated by political decision-makers results in a system that is more likely to retain the status quo than to change" (Fullan, 1993, p. 3).

We focus our story on the collaborative process that evolved between the university faculty and teachers at one of the junior high school sites, as understood and purveyed through the experiences and dialogue of two participants: the university faculty liaison to that site and a teacher working at the site during the collaborative project period. The story has to do with the successes and failures of university faculty and teachers involved in building a team who not only changed the way in which mathematics and science were taught at their school but also contributed to systemic changes in the school's philosophy and structure while experiencing a series of epiphanies at both the individual and team levels. How did teachers come to "see themselves and be seen as experts in the dynamics of change," a perception that Fullan (1993, p. 4) viewed as requisite to true change? We try here to give equal attention to the crests and troughs inherent in the rich experience of the voyage toward perceptual and literal change. We interpret *now* what happened *then*.

Communication Problems

Unspoken Assumptions

Initial Expectations

At the start, the teachers at this very traditional junior high school believed that university faculty would direct, lead, and facilitate curriculum change while providing grant-funded financial support. The university faculty had a different view, one in which teachers and university faculty would co-develop the elements of curriculum change, with the university not necessarily taking the lead. The latter was a deliberate philosophical stance on collaborative action research emphasizing a "work with" rather than "work on" posture in which all participants would contribute a particular expertise and co-construct the "grand plan" and its implementation (Oja & Smulyan, 1989, p. 24). Initial curriculum reform expectations held by both groups seemed compatible at the start, but we had not openly articulated each of our positions. It took some time to understand that our real-life images of what would happen, and especially *how* it would happen, were very different. Each group had entered into a formal collaborative arrangement with a different set of unspoken assumptions and expectations, each unknown to the other.

Solicitation of Participants

Because the school science department chair and principal had been involved in a number of the grant-writing sessions, the university grant directors assumed that the teachers involved were well aware of the grant parameters and had a plan in mind for getting started. Directors hoped to involve at least six teachers plus principals from each of the four schools, but, maintaining their egalitarian, nondirective stance, deliberately left the particulars up to each site. Privately, the directors expected that some sort of volunteer solicitation process would be used. At this particular site, the chair of the mathematics department, who had not been involved in the initial grant writing, chose the participating teachers herself. As instructed, she limited the total number to six, meaning that less than half of the eligible teachers would be "allowed" to participate. Participants, preselected by the math department chair, were "invited" to join the project. In the following passage, Donna describes her invitation:

I was standing in the doorway of my classroom one day, and the department chair came in from the hallway to ask if I would like to be part of a math/science project with the university. She said it was something about integrating curriculum. In answer to my query, she said, "We don't know yet who else will be involved." I thought "we" meant the university who would explain to us what would happen. A science teacher was named as a potential "good partner" for me. The offer to join the project was described as contingent upon whether or not I would be able to work with this science teacher. "Oh sure." I said. (Personal recollection, July 2000)

The next day, Donna asked one of her well-respected colleagues and friend whether she had been asked to join the project. The answer was "no." The invitation was never issued, and Donna's colleague said she was "hurt" because she was not asked to be part of this new team. From the department chair's perspective, she was choosing the people who she thought would be most interested in the project but did not want to overburden busy teachers with details at this early stage. Finally, Donna took it upon herself to recommend her friend to the math department chair, who said: "She can join, but she has to find a science partner." Although the six participants, three pairs, were finally identified, it is apparent that, before the project even began, there were hurt feelings and an exclusionary principle in place regarding the selection process. A negative attitude toward the math department chair was also developing.

Commitment

Given their own experience, the chosen participants were concerned about a possible school-wide perception of peer exclusion and were poised to downplay any appearance of elitism or dispensation from usual duties. On the contrary, although they viewed participation in the project as a good opportunity for the school and for their students, participating teachers highlighted an assumption that they would be required to contribute time to the project, the parameters of which were still unclear, that went above and beyond the usual expectations of them as teachers, sometimes without tangible remuneration. Hence, some participants privately worried that they could not fully meet the grant expectations despite their enthusiasm. For example, one woman who was dealing with child-custody issues, worried about committing her time, at the start of the school year, for the following summer workshop. Oblivious to unrevealed individual worries of this sort, project directors required such a commitment of all thirty participants from all four schools, early in the school year, as established in the original grant language. Teachers did not voice these personal concerns to the directors at first for fear of being excluded or appearing to "whine." Later, when improved trust elicited voice, a number of personal accommodations were made for and by individuals and teams who developed creative arrangements for full participation outside the original parameters of the grant.

Thus, the project began with the directors unaware of important issues. For their part, the directors did not ask for feedback on the particulars and were, in fact, quite pleased that teams had been identified and were ready to begin. Although in hindsight this missing discourse on crucial issues seems like such an obvious communication breach, both the directors and the teachers thought at the time that they had a common understanding of the selection process and project expectations and could readily deal with the few minor obstacles that might surface. This early communication gap became an underlying factor and unrecognized model portending a failure to identify and solve problems in a timely manner as the project went on.

Teachers and School Administrators

The newly formed "team" viewed the school administrators as encouraging their efforts, but somewhat disinterested. The principal confided to one of the directors (Judy) that he hoped the teachers would truly become a mathematics–science team that would feel empowered to make decisions bordering on site-based management. He hoped they would change the curriculum and influence the school culture toward more of a middle school philosophy and practice. His strategy was to stay out of the way and let it happen. He never conveyed his hopes or deliberate noninterventionist approach to the teachers. Judy conveyed the principal's general sentiments to the team but did not describe his specific hopes. The principal did not publicly acknowledge the team, which was a "sore point" that they expressed to Judy and a concern that was at odds with their desire for low visibility within the school. The team acknowledged its paradoxical stance but hoped that "John would at least meet with us as a group." The concern was heightened by the fact that a team of social studies and English teachers had already formed at the school and was perceived to be meeting regularly with the administration.

Our interpretation of these early conditions is that the math–science team felt undervalued by their school administrators and that they might be viewed as "inferior" to the other team. The math–science team also felt they did not receive adequate instruction from Judy or the other director, and they were skeptical of Judy's ability to "read" their principal. The principal had a strong belief in the abilities of the math–science team members to effect change but did not want to interfere with their work, preferring to leave direction to the university grant directors who preferred to take a nondirective role! Once again, although all parties spoke to each other regularly, there was little accurate, substantive communication about perceptions or expectations.

To get started, the teachers found short time blocks to meet individually with the university liaison, Diane, to develop a plan, a course of action. Although it now seems ridiculous that teachers who constituted pairs within a team met *individually* with the university liaison, the class schedules were construed as an insurmountable obstacle to freeing more than one teacher at a time during his or her regular planning period.

Teachers and the University Liaison

Graduate Student as Liaison

From the directors' standpoint, Diane was a perfect choice to work with these teachers. She was a former middle school science teacher pursuing a doctorate under Judy's faculty advisement. Her academic interest was teacher belief systems and what it takes to change them. From the teachers' viewpoint, they felt Judy had abandoned them; she had been there at the start of the school year but spent less time in the school after Diane arrived. It was never actually explained by the two project directors that each of them (the directors) had undertaken initial logistical responsibilities at two of the four schools but never intended to serve over time as regular liaisons from the university.

Anxious to do something concrete with their students, the teachers became extremely frustrated when a "Grand Plan" did not materialize during the first few weeks. They described a sense of "going in circles; always discussing and never doing." Diane reported back to the university liaison meetings that the teachers were resisting her efforts to help them get started. The liaison group suggested that she help the math–science partners identify concepts common to both curricula and work on joint lesson planning. Heeding Diane's suggestion, and happy to have a direction for starting, Donna and her science partner reviewed their respective curricula and found no "natural connections." Diane suggested looking at "percent" and "formulas." Heeding that suggestion, the partners discovered that, although these concepts may be a natural basis for content articulation, they were addressed differently and at different times in the school year within each subject area curriculum. Donna began to feel that the science curriculum had a lockstep, unreasonably rigid sequence, whereas her science partner could not understand why Donna could not just teach the appropriate mathematics when the need was apparent in the chronologically ordered science curriculum. Donna bristled, citing her deeply held philosophy that "mathematics is a discipline unto itself, not the handmaiden of science." Furthermore, she believed strongly in a developmental approach to the teaching and learning of mathematical concepts and couldn't just "plug in" to the science curriculum. Neither partner confronted their philosophical biases but rather blamed Diane for giving bad advice. The pair finally suppressed their differences and agreed on an ill-fated plan to teach fractals during the study of crystals.

Other pairs of teachers began examining their existing curricula in an attempt to identify interdisciplinary themes within grade levels. The one common area of agreement was a focus on the integration of mathematics and science teaching that would reflect reform efforts as embodied in the *National Council for Teachers of Mathematics Standards* and the American Association for the Advancement of Science's *Benchmarks*. But how to start?

By winter, Donna and her colleagues deemed the effort a failure and declared their intention to "jump ship" (Kull, Andrew, Bauer, & Oja, 1995). There was a pervasive feeling of frustration and distrust among the teacher members of the "team." Furthermore, the teachers did not like the fact that their university liaison was a graduate student with less middle school experience than they had. They viewed her as having little or no more expertise than they had and found her difficult to work with. Upon reflection, Donna believes that she and the other teachers regularly subverted Diane's efforts, explaining to her politely why each of her suggestions "wouldn't work in *their* classrooms." In retrospect, Donna feels they were annoyed that a full-time faculty member was not working with them and unfairly judged Diane, not really giving her ideas much of a chance. Diane was frustrated also and reported at the university liaison meetings that this team had done nothing concrete. In an attempt to be truly helpful, she focused her attention on answering housekeeping-type budget questions posed by the principal and two department chairs: If substitute pay were not used up, could it be moved to a different budget category? If the principal secured a seat for the science department chair at the upcoming nascent State Science Standards meeting, would the grant pay for it? (meeting minutes, November 13, 1992). Diane had an abrupt, efficient manner. She was most comfortable in the liaison role when she could record questions, get the answers, and report back. She was perceived by the teachers as "unfriendly," but they did not voice their concerns to the project directors at that time. Instead they "talked behind their backs," overtly polite and hopeful until their frustration level reached a fever pitch. (journal entry, summer 1993.) It was then, during late winter, that they called: "Help! We are ready to jump ship!" (Kull et al., 1995)

On the university "side," Judy was loosely monitoring the situation at Donna's school, mainly by talking regularly with Diane and receiving her version of the story. On the school "side," one teacher later commented on their behavior during this period: "We were definitely not a team, and our interpersonal skills needed much work for any of us to be effective in the change process" (journal entry, summer 1993).

In our current analysis, Diane, who was newly enrolled in the doctoral program and whose experience had been teaching adolescents and undergraduates, was unused to the role of peer collaborator. It became clear later in other situations that although she was an outstanding researcher and writer, Diane was generally not well-suited to interactive fieldwork. The project directors were slow in recognizing this poor fit. There was clearly not yet enough trust on either "side" for candid dialogue regarding Diane and her role, which was fuzzy at best. Donna and Judy believe that the consistent, immediate, direct, supportive, expert involvement of an acceptable university liaison with the teachers is crucial to success. He or she must establish credibility as an ally and colleague while gently guiding the group when they are ready for it and responding to disparate requests simultaneously. The role often requires helping the group to articulate its needs and frustrations while moving toward achievement. Interestingly, the teachers at this site later decided that they could handle the work on their own and would be willing to replace Judy, the second university liaison, with a different, low-key, responsive graduate student who was carefully introduced and "eased into" the role.

Faculty as Liaison

Judy became Diane's replacement. This change in liaison came about at the request of the middle school teachers who had finally met as a full team, only to discover that all of them were experiencing a growing dissatisfaction with their lack of progress and, as they perceived it, lack of direction from Diane or the university faculty. Rather than immediately "jumping ship," they appointed a spokesperson to call Judy and explain their feelings.

The directors met quickly, removed Diane from the site and asked her to serve the project as an administrative assistant back at the university. In assuming the liaison role, Judy was concerned about the amount of time it would take, given the expectations of the middle school teachers at that site. A chemistry-professor–turned–science-educator had assumed a similar role at another site where teachers had high expectations for his involvement. He found it difficult and time-consuming to anticipate and meet teachers' needs but felt that the work was important. Another site, whose teachers were accustomed to collaboration, recognized the university liaison as an expert in curriculum development and sought specific input from him at their monthly meetings. A fourth site, because of a number of issues, including illness and a variety of time constraints, had spotty interactions with the university liaison. In retrospect, that site made the fewest gains over the course of the project. In all cases, the liaison role included continuing summer and school-year interactions, which were not rewarded within the university. On the contrary, because this work did not constitute mainstream research or sanctioned teaching responsibilities, it was viewed as an "add on," which would not "count" for promotion and tenure. Several faculty were hoping to develop a collaborative action research agenda that would result in publication.

As the "new" university liaison, Judy had to adjust her own thinking. Her natural approach would have been to involve teachers in a team-building, hands-on math and science workshop in which, together, they could experience and debrief some innovative teaching strategies with new materials. An earlier attempt on the part of science and education university faculty to provide just such an experience for teachers from all four schools (organized mainly by Judy) had failed miserably, however (Kull et al., 1995). The response to that experience was, "That was nice. So what? If this is all there is, I'm not sure I'm interested." Worse yet, on the occasion of that workshop, Donna's math department chair asked participants to complete an adult-development survey that would pinpoint their particular stage of development. Teachers from her own school were livid at the thought of their department chair having personal information about them. They became suspicious that Diane, too, had been doing "research on them." In truth, the department chair was carrying out an assignment given in a course taught by one of the directors, who did not anticipate such dire consequences. This seemingly innocent act of surveying the group, perceived as a major breach of trust by the teachers, is exactly the kind of action that must be thought through in light of the collaborative goals of the partnership. At the time, it also rang the death knell for any research expectations held by university faculty.

We learned that all planned activities, no matter how enriching (and certainly harmless) they seemed, should have the prior approval of those who would be involved. Our understanding of the "survey incident" was helpful in avoiding a future potential disaster regarding the summer schedule as discussed later in this chapter.

Having failed in their initial attempts at collaboration and change, the teachers at Donna's school, although still a bit skeptical, wanted the new arrangement to be successful and were willing to do their part to make it so. Moreover, the directors had established some credibility by responding to their concerns as soon as they were voiced. Teachers also appreciated the fact that they had some say in manipulating the budget to suit their needs. Judy appreciated their cautious enthusiasm and was careful to ask for recommendations from the team before suggesting a course of action. Judy was well aware of the strong personalities and abilities of these teachers but later wrote the following in her journal:

I was struck by a perception among the teachers that certain things could NOT be accomplished because of the school structure. For example, one pair could not meet during the school day because they did not have a free period in common. The teachers were unwilling to approach the administration about freeing one of the teachers from a study-hall duty in order to create a meeting time. They were worried about asking for "special favors," and they did not believe that the request would be granted! "Ridiculous," I thought. Aloud, I said: "Do you think I could help?" I was empowered by the team to approach the administration. The vice-principal was very receptive, and worked with me to grant the relief-from-duty request in a way that would connote a "change" of duty, rather than a "relief," thus obviating any appearance of favoritism. (Project documentation, 1993)

Donna and Judy both view this schedule reordering as a critical incident within the development of their collaboration for several reasons. First, the teachers were willing to try to make a change in the sacred structure of the school day, but it would not have occurred to them to try if it were not for the university collaborator. Second, the teachers directed the effort and were pleasantly surprised at the positive result. Third, Judy willingly accepted the job of ombudsperson, thus gaining credibility even if she were not successful. Fourth, Judy began to better understand the school culture: There was an egalitarian imperative associated with role of the teacher. The role of the teacher is to teach children in the regular classroom (door closed) and perform custodial duties related to children in venues such as study hall and lunchroom. Being excused by the administration from that role, in any context, but particularly in the context of individual professional development, would carry an elite status that the teachers had been wary of from the beginning and which the administration understood. True to Fullan's observation, school culture mitigated against professional collaboration.

At this early point in the project, the teachers still felt that the "university presence" held special power. The power differential was viewed as helpful because the teachers determined how that power would be used. Team actions that could be perceived as elite or exclusionary were often attributed to "university expectations," permitting the team to require the university liaison to be the prime communicator, thus institutionalizing a form of scapegoating. The teachers also began to see themselves in the expanded roles of curriculum specialist and peer collaborator. Judy recognized her expanded role as ombudsperson, one that she hoped to outgrow as the project went on. Judy studied anew the school culture, recognizing how important it was to carefully pick the issues that warranted a digging in of heels, lest her credibility with the administration be used up by nonessential tasks. She took her cues from the teachers and employed the approach of "gentle recommender" with all parties. Donna and her colleagues felt satisfied that the new arrangement would work. The school administrators were satisfied that a known "go-between" was nearby.

The teachers focused on scheduling, noting that our new arrangement allowed four of the team members to meet with Judy one class period each week. The other two team members were able to meet with Judy once a week during a different time block. At last we felt that our ship was moving, if not sailing, and, most important, everyone felt that they were part of the same crew. Judy felt that her new role was indeed *new* and would take a lot of time and effort. How could she reconcile this role with her usual university responsibilities? The answer to this came later when an action research agenda began to take shape.

Elements of Success

External Validation

A turning point for the project was a collaborative decision at the school to hold a mathematics and science fair, not just a *science* fair as usual, in the spring. Partners worked on integrated curriculum projects to prepare for the fair. The theme was "consumer products." Donna and one of her math colleagues had developed a favorite graphing exercise in which they presented a series of line graphs to students who then made up their own interpretations.

Donna shared these graphs and stories with her science partner, Linda, who showed the graphs to her students and asked if any of the graphs fit the data they were collecting for their consumer products experiments. Students began a more careful data analysis while looking for "best fit" to the existing graphs, eventually realizing the need to construct their own graphs, which they did. The state department science consultant, who had been judging this science fair for years, commented that he had never before seen such a rich integration of mathematics and science in students' work at this level. He was very impressed, praised the teachers, and talked throughout the state about this success within our grant-funded project—and in such a short period of time! This recognition from an important outside official had an astounding effect on the teachers. They felt successful in their interdisciplinary efforts and could point to a real artifact of reform-based change. At the same time, preparing for the science fair had been hard work, and everyone now realized that this kind of collaborative, reform-based work was difficult. We now understood that storms would likely have to be weathered throughout the voyage but should not require us to "jump ship!"

The example above had an additional effect on Donna. In her teaching of mathematics, line graphs had been treated as "already existing" and presented to students primarily for interpretation. Emphasis was on reading axes and units. Occasionally, students had to represent given data through graphs, but they were not required to construct graphs from original data. Within the course of the overall project, Donna began to think of graph construction as the more important concept. She and Linda eventually developed a consumer product testing unit in which, among other things, students graphed the results of experiments they designed to answer the question: Which product has the best thermal retention qualities? On one of Judy's visits, she witnessed a seamless movement of students from the science class to the mathematics class for continuation of the same experiment.

Cultural Assimilation

By the end of the spring, we all felt good. Math and science teachers continued to collaborate on joint lessons, implement them, and reflect on results. Taking time away from study-hall duty for professional planning was deemed not only justifiable but valuable. Soon students were asking "Is this class math or science?" Teachers liked that. Students noticed the collaboration and responded positively: Math and science teachers worked together to do something for *them.* Teachers had broken the cultural mold at their traditional school. They opened their doors to each other, asking for critique of their own teaching and querying colleagues about thematic intersections. They no longer reflected Barth and Sagor's notion that teachers were like a "group of preschoolers engaged in parallel play . . . who rarely turn to one another during the school day except during their thirty-minute lunch period, where informal norms often forbid any kind of professional talk" (Sagor, 1992, p. 2). Interestingly, lunch meetings which had previously been "bitch sessions," became efficient "listing sessions," in which several teachers would draw up a list of questions and suggestions to present to Judy during her visits. In retrospect, it is surprising to both Donna and Judy that, despite dramatic, visible changes in conduction of activities during the school day by the project team, the teachers on the team still believed that school administrators did not fully support the project.

Judy continued to meet with the groups of four and two, became a co-planner, and often was invited to participate in the lesson itself. The teachers appreciated her constructive feedback. She joined the lunch sessions and began to co-construct the lists of team needs, thus becoming a full-fledged team member as well as a project director. Donna describes Judy as a "regular team member" by this point in time. Judy describes herself as an "almost-regular" team member because she was not a full-time member of the school community. This is an odd situation for a university professor who begins to take on the exciting norms of teachers in flux, teachers who solicit her expertise, while simultaneously fulfilling university expectations that seemed old and stale by comparison, held no immediate reward, and were, in fact, in sharp conflict with the role of school collaborator. This new role required a lot of time on Judy's part which the teachers understood and appreciated. She was now spending at least one day a week at the junior high school while also serving as overall project director. The one-course grant-funded release of time was not enough. Spending any less time at the school would also "not be enough" to sustain the changes that had begun—one more paradox.

Despite some occasional "bad weather," we were now experiencing fair winds and following seas, unaware of gathering storm clouds.

Learned Lessons

As the school year drew to a close, the expanded "project planning group," which consisted of one teacher representing each team, principals (only one of whom came regularly), and the university liaisons and directors, decided to hold another meeting of all participants. Mindful of the failed session in the winter, the directors sent an organizational memo *after* participants were asked for input. An excerpt reads:

A quick poll of the "membership" tells us that . . . is the best day for most of us to meet . . . to share our progress so far and work in teams to plan activities for the summer and for the next school year. Below is a tentative agenda based on the feedback we have received from many of you regarding the last large-group session. We heard some frustration at not being able to learn what other teams are doing and not having enough time for your own team to get together to plan. So . . . [the meeting agenda] is not "written in stone," but is meant to respond to the needs we have heard expressed by many of you. You may wish to designate a spokesperson for the "sharing" session. If you have any materials (lessons, organizational plans, minutes of meetings, articles, etc.) you wish to distribute, we can duplicate them for you . . . Thanks for your continued interest and work. (Memo, May 1993)

The group also invited a faculty expert on team building, noted in the memo, to be on hand for consultation and for feedback to the planning group on his sense of how the project was going. Donna's copy of the memo has a handwritten notation: *Bring graphs*. Everyone felt that this meeting invitation held just the right amount of responsiveness and direction on the part of the planners.

It was at this meeting that Judy learned that "our" team had believed themselves to be "behind" the other teams in their progress toward project goals. The sharing session put them at ease, revealed that the process and realization of gains had been slow and arduous for all teams (notes from full group sharing session, May 20, 1993).

Transformation

Co-Planning

Teachers, University Liaison, and School Administrators

We then discussed the upcoming Summer Institute. The schedule for the institute, as written into the grant proposal two years before, had been offered previously to participants for comment and returned to the planning group with polite, abundant notes in the margin. For example, from Donna's school: "Could we discuss regression and line graphs instead of box and leaf plots?" "Three of our team members already know a lot about cooperative learning—could they do something else?" In truth, the summer schedule did not exactly fit any of the teams' needs, although they felt that bits and pieces might be useful. One team said that unless the schedule were changed, they would not be coming: "We can do it without you." Now there was a full-fledged storm upon us. Our chemistry-professor–turned–teacher-educator came to the rescue:

> After some thought that night, I arrived at an alternative plan that seemed to address the issues raised by the teachers. I presented it, with a bit of trepidation, that day at [a] . . . staff meeting. I was nervous because I was about to suggest that a carefully crafted plan—one okayed by [our funding agency]—be set aside. My written notes: "If we believe in constructivism as a base for decision-making, then summer should: a) start from where each team is; b) allow them to explore their understandings of their projects; c) seed this work with expert advice and with injection of higher order questions concerning teaching and learning and what integration of mathematics and science may mean; d) respond to content-knowledge requests on an "as needed" basis; e) the focal point remains the team and its ideas throughout the institute—this will develop commitment to each other and to the goals of the project. (Kull et al., 1995, p. 66)

He went on to add that we worried that the plan might be "delusional . . . how were we going to manage plugging teams and people [faculty experts] in and out 'as needed' over a three-week period and achieve some concrete learning goals?" (Kull et al., 1995, p. 66) At our next meeting, the planning group received expert assistance from one of the school principals who constructed a blank schedule form, each team filling in desired subject-matter instruction, consultation, and team planning sessions. The "final" schedule was a hodgepodge that brought various groupings together at various times, but it satisfied everyone, including the university faculty who felt that certain teams needed particular experiences (e.g., Donna's team needed sessions with our team-building expert, and another team needed help with their orienteering unit from our forestry expert). Miraculously, everything fell into place.

Donna and Judy share summer images of team planning that took place in an old, hot seminar room at the university, huge windows raised to catch the breeze and a view of the green, tree-framed quadrangle. We covered the walls with planning paper and filled it all. Partners went outside, seated on the grass or at picnic tables with mathematics and science books and materials such as balls and ramps to refine and record the activities they had developed or adapted during the school year. We ate picnic lunches and swam in the pond-like outdoor pool across the street at the end of the day.

By July 6, the team had developed an outline of joint math–science topics for the ensuing school year, including a "culminating (cumulative) activity" at the end of each quarter. The newly learned forestry and microscopic techniques were incorporated into their curriculum plan.

The Regional Junior High School teachers still felt that they were working more as partners than as a team, so, after checking to see if he had been helpful to other teams ("well worth it," the others said), the team requested assistance from Charlie, the faculty expert on team building. Judy was excused because the teachers felt that they had problems that they had to solve themselves with the help of a facilitator, and, besides, Judy would eventually go away, and they would still expect to work together. At one point, Donna recalls asking Charlie, "What can we do to become a team?" The answer was, "Donna, you could start by being quiet and listening to your colleagues!" Team rules were devised. They would emphasize turn taking, trust, tolerance of failure, requirement that decisions be made only by the team and not by individuals, public modeling of success designed to involve more teachers in the school. They would begin each meeting with an agenda, make summary statements during the meeting, rotate the roles of facilitator and recorder, spend five minutes at the end polling members as to "what went right and what went wrong with how we worked together as a team." They also agreed to call Charlie while "it was still fixable (team notes, July 22, 1993). At the end of the Summer Institute, teachers from Regional Junior High School assessed their progress and reported it to the full group: "This summer we arrived as pairs but we were really six strong personalities—very territorial—looking out for ourselves.... We evolved into a team.... Our Team Sheet gives a brief synopsis of activities by grade level, and if anyone is interested, contact us" (team notes, July 21, 1993).

The group recognized that they had come a long way, were proud of their accomplishments, and felt strongly enough about their work to share it with other junior high teachers. They credited Judy with helping them "move forward" but credited themselves with accomplishing new goals within a still-traditional junior high format. There remained one last rocky shoal for the team to navigate that summer.

Teachers, School Administrators, University Liaison

Now that the teachers had co-planned activities, they wanted something specific from the school administration: Each teacher pair wanted back-to-back math–science classes containing the same students. This was, in effect, a subversive approach to introducing block scheduling that might also require heterogeneous grouping of students rather than the current homogeneous grouping by ability. With Charlie's help, they devised a plan for inviting the principal and vice principal to the university ("neutral turf") to discuss their accomplishments and requests. Judy was invited to greet everyone—and then leave! Although Judy had expected her role of ombudsperson to the administration to eventually disappear, she felt a little left out, particularly because her own colleague, Charlie, was quite clear about the importance of excluding her. This is where professional trust comes in, and a talk with Charlie about softening her proprietary attitude helped Judy. It was the right time to begin a slow exit.

Donna and her colleagues issued the invitation to their administration to join them for a meeting in the summer. The teachers were highly skeptical of the whole idea, believing that the principal and vice principal would not come or, if they did, would not grant their requests. Again with Charlie's assistance, a previsit strategy session was devised that cited their appreciation for administrative support (a political statement), their team growth over time, their new knowledge, their curricular and teaching accomplishments, and their requests for the upcoming school year (team notes, July 19, 1993). Much to the team's surprise, both administrators not only came to the meeting but also agreed to a set of short- and long-term commitments to meet both the stated and implied goals that would likely move everyone toward a middle school model. Recall that this shift was one that the principal had silently hoped would happen. In the long-term, efforts would be made to include more of the school in project plans and move to an increased block scheduling of "teamed" students. The teachers were over-joyed to receive an immediate thank-you note from the principal that read, in part, "I appreciated the opportunity to hear what types of activities you folks are engaged in and the potential this type of approach has for becoming contagious with our staff.... It really appears as though what you folks are doing is exciting. I admire your drive, and your motivation to keep current in your fields" (letter from principal, July 20, 1993). There was also a caveat which, in an understated way, acknowledged the team's power to effect change: "Do remember to keep us informed about what you're doing and we'll do everything that we can (obviously not everything you'd like) to make it work" (letter from principal, July 20, 1993).

All of the short- and long-term goals were eventually accomplished but not with-out a few rough seas. Judy met each Friday with the team, but her role changed. Teach-ers now knew what they wanted, and it was Judy's job to find grant support. For example, it was felt that the vice principal might need a consultant who was familiar with block scheduling. Could the grant pay for it?

Action

Local Changes

As teachers became more empowered, they made a presentation to the school board, wrote regularly in the parent newsletter, and held a parents' night when students were the teachers who actively engaged their own parents in hands-on mathematics and science activities. Eventually, strong modeling and subtle invitations increased the numbers of involved teachers. Linda (with the good wishes of her colleagues), the project faculty, and three teachers from the other project schools coauthored a collabo-rative action research paper they presented at the American Educational Research As-sociation, which was later published in a special issue of the *Journal for the Kansas Association for Supervision and Curriculum Development* (Oja et al., 1996). Others presented workshops and papers at various conferences held by professional organiza-tions, including the National Middle Schools Association, the National Science Teach-ers Association, and the National Council for Teachers of Mathematics. Science and mathematics teachers even attended each other's conferences. These activities repre-sented a dramatic change in the teachers themselves. Donna and her colleagues origi-nally had little confidence in their ability to create change or to influence the administration, much less to share their now-valued work with others at national meet-ings. On the contrary, they had to be persuaded initially to leave their classrooms, even for short periods.

Long-Term Legacies

Eventually, the Regional Junior High School became a middle school in a newly constructed building. The principal retired. New teams were formed. The project ac-tivities and curriculum guides were "packaged up" and housed in a curriculum library accessible to all teachers. Donna is now department chair in a school that may elimi-nate departments because of the new, more democratic structure. She feels that this would be just fine. Donna is also a doctoral student in education and plans to conduct an ethnographic study on the concept of "teaming," having already enlisted the help of her project colleagues from the four schools and, of course, the help of Charlie, who will briefly exit retirement to help her. Judy is a bit wistful at the loss of the kinship and support she felt from "her team" as she slowly moved back into full-time campus work. She has written about the "lessons learned," and taken them to heart in organizing a full district collaboration between the university and the schools surrounding the University of New Hampshire's urban campus, where she now directs the Teacher Education Program. This new collaboration has moved quickly and successfully, largely because of the navigation lessons learned here.

Conclusion

Real Communication

Our first-year voyage of collaboration reflects a number of important themes that connote both barriers and enhancements to success. The first and most important is communication. In collaborative arrangements, communication problems are directly proportional to the number of participants and the diversity of cultures from which they come. The larger the number of participants and the more diverse the cultures, the more difficult it is to effectively communicate, even when there is a pervasive belief that not everyone has to contribute equally or in the same way.

In our case, participants were teachers, school administrators, and university faculty from teacher education, educational administration, the sciences and mathematics. We believe it is essential to establish a new culture that embodies the goals and folkways of the collaborative project while recognizing the norms of the original, long-standing cultures that still ground each participant. Collaboration is most successful when the elements of that culture are understood and discussed through direct communication. When the going got tough, we spent a great deal of time communicating about surface-level issues: Can we change that budget category? Will the grant pay for . . . ? Although this mode might be helpful in revealing the trappings of a culture, *real* communication occurred only when participants could identify and voice what they needed from each other and what support they needed in dealing with a variety of cultural imperatives: "We need more time to work together on . . . sit with us and plan . . ." Real change happened when we all literally worked side-by-side, "walking a mile in each others shoes," coming to understand and appreciate what each person had to offer, and recognizing the power in collective, collaborative work. We also learned that some people are not well suited for collaboration and should not be put in a situation that requires a full commitment to it.

New Lenses

We feel strongly that in doing this kind of work, one cannot necessarily rely on implementation of "tried and true" actions that have worked well in the past. The failure of our first large-group, hands-on activity is a good example. If we had polled the group before that session, we would have known that it was not what they needed or wanted at the time. Although it may not be easy to accomplish, it is important to establish an "anticipatory buy-in" of all participants to events and actions that are crucial to the project.

Donna and Judy concur with other researchers who have noted the power of moving out of the day-to-day setting to do creative work, as long as real-world application is kept in mind. Summers on and near a peaceful university campus provided an idyllic setting, and we took full advantage of it. We studied laboratory techniques on an oceanographic vessel, in the forest, on a mountain, and at a glaciation site rich in representative geologic formation. We also relaxed, shared, and wrote amidst inspirational surroundings on the university quadrangle.

Beyond the Expected

Collaborative work takes on a life of its own. The Mathematics and Science Collaborative project was originally about connecting university faculty with school faculty and administrators to bring about reform-based changes in the teaching of mathematics and science. What the project became was a reform-based development of integrated curriculum and a profound restructuring of the school and its philosophy. The reshaping took place along the way and is still going on. Teacher beliefs and actions changed dramatically.

Finally, as a result of this collaborative voyage, Donna and Judy, like most of the other participants, experienced profound personal and professional change. We each revealed and critiqued our basic philosophical assumptions about pedagogy, about peer relationships, and about the ways in which we carry out the day-to-day activities of our lives. It is somewhat ironic that we both feel this *individual* change, as the result of collaborative interaction, is the most important result of our work together.

References

Fullan, M. (1993). *Change forces: Probing the depths of educational reform.* New York: Falmer Press.

Kull, J. A., Andrew, M. D., Bauer, C. F., & Oja, S. N. (1995). The effects of a mathematics and science integration project. *Research in Middle Level Education Quarterly, 19*(1), 59–84.

Mathematics and Science Collaborative Portfolio (1992–1995). Unpublished meeting notes, minutes, memos, letters, journal entries.

Oja, S. N., Kull, J. A., Kelley, F., Gregg, B., LaChance, D., Moreau, D., & Turnquist, B. The voices of teacher-directed change (1996). *Journal for the Kansas Association for Supervision and Curriculum Development, 14*(1), 35–51.

Oja, S. N., & Smulyan, L. (1989). *Collaborative action research: A developmental approach.* New York: Falmer Press.

Sagor, R. (1992). *How to conduct collaborative action research.* Alexandria, VA: Association for Supervision and Curriculum Development.

Chapter

10

Developing School–University Intellectual Partnerships: The National Humanities Center's Teacher Leadership for Professional Development Program

Richard Schramm, William E. Bickel, Rosemary H. McNelis, and Cathy K. Pine

During the past decade, the National Humanities Center, an institute for advanced study, has sought to test, refine, and disseminate a complementary alternative to the traditional skills-based workshops that dominate teachers' professional development experiences today. The center has attempted to accomplish this through its Teacher Leadership for Professional Development Program and its predecessor, the Secondary School Faculty Development Project (see Bickel, Hattrup, & Pine, 1994; Pine, Bickel, & McNelis, 1998). This alternative program, an inquiry-based seminar model, requires the crafting of productive collaborations among teachers, university faculty,

131

and the center's own staff, as teachers fashion study groups around substantive ideas and texts in collaboration with university scholars. Based on an eight-year evaluation of the work, we describe here the origins of this initiative and the nature of the collaborative structure, as well as the benefits and challenges experienced in the collaborations and the elements essential to successful collaborations of this type.

Program Description

Origin

The Teacher Leadership for Professional Development Program grew out of work started at the center in 1990. It was designed to test a model of professional development that brought high school teachers together in close collaboration with university scholars as a community of active learners in a study group centered around serious ideas that the teachers had identified. Initially, the work focused on the accomplishment of a number of teacher participant-related outcomes (e.g., building academic community, enhanced teacher control over in-service training). By 1997, when it had become apparent that the professional development seminars were achieving these largely individualistic ends, the center decided to expand the focus of the project. It added two broader goals of a more "systemic" nature, with the intent of institutionalizing its model of professional development seminars. These expanded goals were aimed at developing a new role for teachers, that of professional development seminar coordinator, and providing the ongoing technical assistance necessary to make teacher-designed, teacher-led professional development seminars a regular part of a school's life (National Humanities Center, 1999).

An important aspect of the development of the coordinator role was the center's decision to emphasize the recruitment of National Board Certified Teachers to serve in these positions. Board certification, the center believes, functions as an apt screening device in the selection of potential coordinators, for it suggests that a teacher possesses the qualities of leadership, initiative, professionalism, and commitment required of a coordinator. The prominence of board-certified teachers in the program led to the inclusion of middle and elementary schools in recent program implementations because relatively few board certified teachers worked in high schools in 1997. The center is currently testing the redesigned initiative in fourteen sites around the country.

Why This Model?

This model offers an approach to professional development that accords well with recent efforts at educational reform and the concomitant calls for an enhanced professionalization of teaching (Hawley & Valli, 1999; Little, 1993; Shulman, 1999). Teachers who are expected to engage in substantial educational reform, in "the reinventing of teaching," must have professional development tools that go well beyond the traditionally available "skill development" programs. Teachers must become "knowledge workers" (Shulman, 1999, p. xiii), meaningfully engaged with substantive ideas in a collaborative environment with their peers (Hawley & Valli, 1999). Schools become places for teacher as well as student learning. The National Humanities Center's model of teacher-designed and teacher-led collaborative professional development meets the aforementioned criteria. It enables teachers to build programs of structured and sustained inquiry around questions they define as important to their professional growth. It brings them together as a community of active learners in a focused study group around serious ideas and substantive texts, and it includes college or university scholars within that group as equal partners in the inquiry. The approach also allows teachers to graft their personal interests onto larger school priorities and explore both through collective study. Indeed, it affords teachers the opportunity to take a "big picture" perspective. When given the chance to design their own seminars, teachers have asked large questions about the context and meaning of their work. Elementary school teachers, for example, have chosen to study the world of young children. High school teachers have opted to explore adolescence, and teachers at all levels have inquired into the implications, educational and otherwise, of the changing demography in the United States. In each instance, whether a formal part of the seminar or not, the evaluation process has provided solid evidence that teachers have related these topics to their classroom practice and to the broader life of their schools.

Although it is clear that this model of professional development advances a new, more professional idea of the K–12 teacher, we recognize that it is not suitable for every teacher or every professional development priority. Mentoring may do more for novice teachers than seminar participation would. Similarly, the implementation of a new math or reading program would be better served by more traditional forms of professional development.

Nonetheless, for topics in which the goal is increased understanding or new content knowledge, this model is highly effective. In past implementations, teachers have selected a wide range of seminar topics. Realizing that the model will have to address state and district concerns if it is to be institutionalized, teachers have, in recent implementations, focused more closely on such concerns. One school, for example, is using the model to meet a district mandate for diversity training. Another is using it to address a district interest in the relationship between brain research and learning. Still another is developing a seminar around state-mandated language arts standards. Within these areas of study, teachers selected the issues on which they wished to focus, and they decided precisely how to address them. In so doing, they maintained the principle of teacher design and leadership that is central to the model. As teachers become more familiar with the model, they no doubt will adapt it to other purposes. Regardless of how teachers use it, however, the model requires them to reflect upon their professional development needs; to frame an inquiry; to read, think, and exchange ideas. In short, it requires them to be intellectuals.

Program Cycle

The first year (the "Focus Year") consists of a series of steps that move fifteen to twenty-five participants through a process of framing a topic for collective inquiry. The process gives a school a structured way to do the homework necessary to make intelligent and efficient use of the scholarly resources of its partner college or university. The outcome of this process guides the coordinators' identification and selection of scholar consultants, who then assist the teachers in refining their proposal into a detailed seminar syllabus and identifying study materials. The second year is the "Study Year," during which the participants and their consulting scholars explore the syllabus, which they created together, in a series of regularly scheduled seminar sessions.

The cycle is designed to build within a school the capacity to create professional development programs that incorporate the five key elements of the center's model, namely, that the seminars are designed and led by teachers, involve collaboration among teachers and with resource people outside K–12 education, are sustained over time, are inquiry based, and are focused on serious ideas and texts.

Collaborative Partner Roles

The Teacher Leadership for Professional Development Program unites three types of institutional partners: the school district where the seminar will take place, the centers of higher education supplying the consulting scholars, and the National Humanities Center. At the seminar level, the initiative requires the collaboration of participating teachers, consulting scholars, and center program trainers. At both the program and seminar levels, each collaborative role entails certain responsibilities for this professional development model to be implemented successfully.

School District Partner

Within this three-way collaboration, the responsibilities of a school district partner are fairly straightforward. It must (a) recognize a need for an alternative approach to professional development, (b) acknowledge the legitimacy and value of this approach, (c) require that district and building administrators support the teacher participants (e.g., by freeing time), and (d) fund the direct program expenses (e.g., consultant honoraria and study materials). Finally, building administrators must signal to teachers that the seminar approach is a legitimate form of professional development, something that is to become part of the regular life of the school, not merely a special, one-time project.

University Partner

Although in many cases a partner university supplies free seminar meeting space, its chief responsibility is to provide consulting scholars. A liaison is needed to assist the professional development seminar coordinators in their search for suitable scholars. An effective liaison should understand the seminar model and possess a good sense of the university's faculty resources. He or she explains the program to department chairs and other university personnel; makes the necessary contacts, inquiries, and introductions; and, in general, directs the seminar coordinators through the university maze to appropriate consulting scholars. For many seminar groups, especially those whose topics had a humanities emphasis, university deans of arts and sciences have filled this role successfully.

National Humanities Center

Within the collaborative, the National Humanities Center provides the training and technical assistance a school needs to implement professional development seminars and serves as a bridge builder between the school district and the university. It is distinctly well suited for this latter role. For decades, its primary mission has been to provide fellowships to scholars from the United States and abroad, who spend a year in residence at the center (located in Research Triangle Park, North Carolina), writing on topics in history, literature and language studies, philosophy, and criticism of the arts. Recognized as one of the most prestigious in the humanities, it provides a "scholarly cachet" that gives the program intellectual legitimacy among arts and sciences faculty, thus affording teachers access to such fields as history, English, philosophy, anthropology, or sociology. These are precisely the resources that some teachers need to deepen subject matter expertise and that all teachers need to grapple with "big picture" issues such as multiculturalism or moral choice.

Teacher Participants

At the session level, the teachers primarily are the designers of the collaborative. Ideally, the group should consist of fifteen to twenty (unpaid) volunteers who are willing to commit two years of seminar development and implementation, with all the study, meeting attendance, and collective grappling with ideas that this entails. Moreover, past seminars have functioned smoothly when the teacher participants have exhibited intellectual curiosity and have been active contributors of ideas and opinions within the group. Frequently, teachers have acted as group facilitators during the Study Year, sharing this role with collaborating scholars.

The professional development seminar coordinator is responsible for facilitating the sessions of the Focus Year. To do so, the coordinator requires skills in leading discussions, keeping the discussions focused, providing guidance and support to others, eliciting opinions, summarizing points of view, and helping teachers reach consensus on topic selection and the development of framing questions. Despite this facilitator role, however, the coordinator is not the primary decision maker for the teacher team but a partner in a collaborative effort. In addition, the coordinator helps educate others in the school community about the value of this approach to professional development and handles all the logistics of planning and scheduling meetings. During the Study Year, the coordinator continues to function as an organizer and communicator but is an equal participant with the rest of the team during the seminar sessions. Nonetheless, the coordinator elicits evaluative feedback from the group after each session and shares with the participants and scholars to address group concerns. Because of the broad responsibilities of the professional development seminar coordinator role, the National Humanities Center recommends that two persons share these responsibilities at each site.

Consulting Scholars

A successful consulting scholar brings subject matter expertise and scholarly credibility to the seminar collaboration. In addition to academic strengths, a consulting scholar needs to respect teachers as professionals and have a true interest in working with them as colleagues. In the Focus Year, the role of the consulting scholar is critical in refining the syllabus and guiding the selection of seminar materials. During the Study Year, the consultant must be willing to work with teachers to find a suitable seminar format. In some cases, consultants were the primary facilitators of the sessions; in other cases, they shared this role with teacher participants; and in others, they relinquished this role altogether. Regardless of the format chosen, the consultant must have facilitator skills to help discussions stay linked to the framing questions and substantive issues raised in the study materials.

Center Trainers

During the focus year, National Humanities Center staff visit a school to educate teacher participants about the program's underlying philosophy of professional development. They also attend the topic selection session and framing question selection sessions. In this role, they must be sensitive to the dynamics of the individual groups and their respective coordinator leaders. They must be able to provide guidance without taking away control of the seminar development process from the teachers. Like the consulting scholars, center personnel need to have professional respect for the teachers and to interact with them as colleagues.

Mechanics of the Collaborative

It is important to note that the sequence of the Focus Year and Study Year constitutes the Teacher Leadership Program's training cycle, which is designed to build capacity in a school to implement the model, demonstrate its value to teachers and administrators, and suggest potential applications for it. The center fully expects a school to adapt the elements of the training cycle to meet its distinctive needs as it develops seminars on its own.

In the first step of the Focus Year, seminar participants individually submit topics to their professional development seminar coordinators. These are documented and shared with center staff who organize them into thematic clusters and pair each cluster with a pertinent reading designed to provoke thought and stimulate discussion. The readings are distributed to the seminar participants for study. Under the leadership of the seminar coordinators, the participants meet to winnow the topics to a consensus choice and develop framing questions to guide their inquiry into it.

The framing questions constitute a broad syllabus outline. Equipped with this document, the seminar coordinators meet with their university liaison, who guides them to scholars, usually a team of two, whose expertise addresses the topic and whose personalities suit them for collaborative work with adults. When the coordinators find consultants they consider appropriate for their group, they invite them to join the project, and if the consultants agree, they arrange an informal meeting during which the consultants and the seminar participants become acquainted and explore the seminar topic.

With a firm sense of what the participants hope to accomplish in the seminar, the consultants develop a "menu of resources," a list of potential texts and media—books, chapters, articles, poems, films, paintings, musical pieces, and so forth—with annotations explaining how each addresses appropriate framing questions. This menu becomes the focal point of the final planning meeting, the syllabus-building session, during which the participants select the texts and media they will study the following year. The participants and consultants also develop a seminar schedule.

Once the syllabus is set, the coordinators assemble the texts and other media and, ideally, distribute them to the consultants and participants before school ends for study over the summer. To illustrate, a recent seminar focused on "Civic Virtue and the American Identity." It inquired into the values that shape our sense of right and wrong and asked if there was ever a widespread moral consensus in the United States. Core texts for this session included The Declaration of Independence, The Constitution of the United States of America, and a number of secondary texts related to these documents and the issues contained therein.

Typically, four or five seminar sessions are held during the Study Year at regular intervals from August through May. Ideally, a school should devote regular in-service time to the sessions to eliminate the need for expensive substitute teachers and to signal that the seminar is a sanctioned school program. In the model's early implementations, center staff believed that daylong sessions, running from 9 A.M. to 3 P.M., were optimal, and indeed they may be appropriate for some schools. Now, after seeing the model at work in twenty-two schools, it appears that sessions running about three hours may be more appropriate. That amount of time is long enough for participants to engage their texts seriously but not so long that the seminar outstrips their energy and enthusiasm. Moreover, without the generous expanse of a daylong session spreading before them, participants tend to focus on profitable exchange and avoid the temptation of mere ventilation. Finally, sessions of such duration are easier to fit into a tight academic calendar. Seminar discussions focus on the syllabus texts and are guided by the framing questions. The participants or consultants, or a mix of both, depending on the preferences of the group, guide seminar discussion.

Why Collaborate?

Catalysts for Involvement

Teacher Participants

Across school sites, teacher participants have described through the evaluation process strikingly similar catalysts for becoming involved in the Teacher Leadership for Professional Development Program. They are particularly drawn by the opportunity to design their own professional development activities. In contrast to workshops over which they have no control and that require generally passive participation, the seminar model allows them to become actively involved in virtually every aspect of planning and implementation. They are also attracted to the prospect of challenging study, in some cases beyond their own areas of specialization, which promises intellectual stimulation and renewal. Finally, they are strongly motivated by the chance to overcome the isolation of classroom teaching by getting to know their colleagues.

Consulting Scholars

The motivations for the involvement of consulting scholars in the seminars tend to vary more widely than those the teacher participants cite. For some scholars, the intellectual appeal of the seminar topic is the primary motivator to become involved. For others, it is the opportunity to connect with teachers of basic and secondary education. For still others, the primary catalyst is that their dean has urged them to do community outreach, an increasingly important element in many university and departmental missions and one recognized in the incentive systems for faculty.

University Partners

For universities, the pressure to engage in general community outreach has been mixed with specific requests to advance K–12 school improvement and, in the case of some state-supported institutions, legislative mandates to do so. Schools and colleges of education have been well positioned to respond, but arts and sciences departments have generally found it more difficult to get fruitfully involved in the schools. The center's model presents these departments a structure that allows them to bring their expertise to the schools, and they have welcomed the opportunity.

District and School Partners

Schools and school districts have chosen to collaborate for a variety of reasons. Some simply wanted to add a new approach to their repertoire of in-service strategies. Others saw the school-centered, teacher-led seminars as a way to bring site-based management to professional development. Still others were attracted by the model's vision of teacher professionalism.

Impacts of the Collaborative

The impacts of this collaborative model have been remarkably similar across implementation sites, as evidenced by the program evaluation findings described below.

Impacts on School Participants

The model provides intellectual stimulation and renewal. The program affords teachers the opportunity to read for intellectual growth, to engage in reflective and critical thinking, and to exchange ideas in a collegial setting. Many participants have commented that they appreciated the "academic" nature of the seminars, as opposed to the typical in-service focus on instructional methods or classroom strategies. Over and over teachers have reported that the model helps to fend off burnout and enables them to bring new energy to their classroom work. One teacher characterized the seminar experience as "a jolt of electricity to a lazy and sluggish mind."

The model enhances professionalism, boosts morale, and changes the image of the teacher. Teachers report that this approach to professional development is one of the few that actually makes them feel like professionals. They speak of being valued as thinkers and lifelong learners who are trusted to take control of their professional growth. They also note that this model encourages them to see themselves less as dispensers of information and more as analyzers of ideas.

The model builds collegiality among teachers. Repeatedly, teachers have reported that they feel closer to their colleagues and know them better as a result of sharing a seminar with them. The seminars themselves give teachers the opportunity to talk to each other at levels that transcend day-to-day, nuts-and-bolts conversations and gripe sessions. Often the subjects of those day-to-day conversations change, too, as participants informally discuss their common readings.

The model gives lifelong learning a more prominent place in school culture. Most schools today spend a great deal of time extolling the value of lifelong learning. This approach gives teachers not only the opportunity to pursue it but also to model it for students. Students inevitably become aware that their teachers are "taking a course" and often express curiosity and even surprise that teachers, who are supposed to know everything already, feel the need for continued study.

The model encourages more active, inquiry-based classroom instruction. For many teachers, the seminar they encounter in this program is the first in which they have ever participated. Having never experienced active, guided discussion in their own schooling, they do not employ it in their classes. After seeing how it is done, many bring the method to their students. Some teachers also have adapted the model's use of framing questions to their classes. At the outset of a lesson, they ask their students what they hope to learn and help them state those goals as questions that then guide inquiry. Teachers using this approach report that it has helped motivate students and invest them more deeply in their coursework.

The model provides some teachers with new material for their classes. Literature and social studies teachers often introduce seminar texts into their classes. A teacher in Texas, for example, used a seminar reading on the influence of television in a media class, and a North Carolina teacher who read a slave narrative in her seminar assigned the text in her honors English course.

The model enables teachers to take responsibility for their own professional development. Not only have teacher participants designed and led program seminars, they have assumed responsibility for designing the structure and content of additional professional development efforts to meet the needs of their school communities.

The model provides substantial job satisfaction for the professional development seminar coordinators. Every coordinator has reported taking deep pride and satisfaction in leading colleagues in a challenging enterprise that enriches both the school and the individual teachers.

Impacts on Consulting Scholars

Although the primary focus of the collaboration in this model is the teacher, it is clear from past implementations that a number of benefits accrue to participating university faculty as well.

University faculty members experience intellectual stimulation and renewal. Like their teacher partners, university faculty have consistently observed that their participation is a source of intellectual renewal and stimulation. The reasons for this vary for each participant. Some consulting scholars find the seminars to be "an intellectual time-out; a retreat." In the words of some scholars, the seminars provide an "opportunity to see one's own intellectual theories played out" or "to examine one's specialty area from a new perspective." The seminars, university faculty have noted, also provide exposure "to fields and literature outside one's specialty area," meaning both the world of basic education practice, and in many instances, the additional opportunity to work with a colleague from another discipline.

University faculty members find increased collegiality with high school teachers. Consulting scholars frequently come away from the experience with a greater appreciation for the world of the teacher and a significantly enhanced sense of collegiality with teachers. This is accomplished when both teachers and university scholars wrestle with the issues and texts that are examined in the seminars. The seminars offer an opportunity to reflect on "matters of the intellect" and are not structured as the traditional "knowledge transfer dyad." As teachers' experiences are integrated into seminar discussions, participating university faculty learn much about current educational practice.

University faculty members gain an enhanced sense of professionalism and common educational purpose. Former consulting scholars indicate that the seminars "reminded one of why they got into education" in the first place. Some describe the experience as "pure education," where participants are able to concentrate on the quality of the exchange, free from the "tyranny of a syllabus."

University faculty members acquire knowledge and experiences that are of instrumental value in their professions. University faculty have noted that the seminars often provide an opportunity to research their own ideas, to learn from teachers about areas of mutual interest, and to learn more about and to practice "effective teaching." Some consultants have viewed the seminars as a mechanism for improving their own teaching and writing. Others have noted that, beyond the many positive seminar effects on teachers and themselves already mentioned, they also fulfill university accountability demands (e.g., demonstration of the relevancy of one's work to precollegiate education). This latter effect has become even more relevant in a state such as North Carolina, where there is an explicit press to find ways to enhance the relevance of higher education institutions to basic education in the state.

Challenges to Collaboration

The National Humanities Center's Teacher Leadership Program has managed to overcome some of the challenges that impede school–university collaborations. First, it has shown that sound, well-conceived topics, presented to scholars in ways that engage their interest, will induce busy university faculty to serve as seminar consultants. Second, the program has redressed the imbalance of power that typically afflicts such collaborations. In most, the school is decidedly the junior partner; the university, with greater resources and prestige, usually calls the shots. In this program's model, the teachers in the seminar invite the university into the project on their terms. They "hire" the consultants and ask them to follow a path they have laid out. Thus, the collaboration is constructed on terms of greater equality between the partners. Finally, in this model, the rigor of the syllabi developed by the teachers and the amount of work a seminar requires have been found to be persuasive arguments for rewarding teacher participation with substantial certificate renewal. In fact, at one school the partner university arranged graduate credit for participating teachers who wanted it.

Even with these successful innovations, however, the collaborations spawned by the Teacher Leadership Program, like most school–university partnerships, face many challenges.

Because the seminars at the heart of the collaboration are teacher designed and led, the impetus to inaugurate them must come from a school's faculty; it cannot be imposed from above. District-level officials charged with professional development must understand the collaboration to be a complement to their work. They must see the seminars that emerge from it as a valuable addition to their professional development repertoire, rather than as threat. And, of course, it is essential that superintendents, principals, and university officials support the collaboration, for without their cooperation, its seminars will not be afforded the time, funding, and scholarly resources they need to flourish.

Another challenge to collaboration is the sheer amount of time it takes to fill the role of seminar coordinator. Is the role too burdensome to combine with classroom teaching? Thus far the answer seems to be no. The center has tried to fashion the seminar coordinator position in such a way that it will not impinge on a teacher's classroom duties or require substantial amounts of release time. Splitting the role between two teachers helps make the workload manageable, and good coordinators quickly learn that some jobs, especially logistical arrangements, can be delegated to seminar participants. Some release time may be unavoidable, however, especially when coordinators have to go off campus to meet university liaisons or consulting scholars.

Participating teachers sometimes express reluctance to take on the burden of study that a seminar requires. This hesitation usually evaporates when they realize they will be able to customize the demands of the seminar to fit their schedules because they, not the consulting scholars, build the syllabus and make the assignments. Moreover, teachers often see the seminar work as something they "do for themselves" and are thus more willing to accept it.

Although the seminars are modest in cost, funding them will always be a challenge. Nonetheless, with growing concern about teacher shortages, more support is likely to flow to professional development. Because the Humanities Center's seminar model addresses many of the complaints that drive teachers out of the profession, it can be seen as a useful teacher-retention tool and as such may attract some of this new money. In addition, outside sources of support, such as local foundations or corporations, may be drawn to an innovative program to upgrade teacher quality that is itself driven by teacher initiative. It is also not beyond the realm of possibility that, in these days of increasing demand for public outreach, the partner university may underwrite such expenses as the consultants' honoraria.

Another challenge to the sort of collaboration described here is the view that its seminars are "mere enrichment." Following this line of argument, some administrators have questioned the appropriateness of a model that explores topics like the changing South, childhood in the United States, and civic virtue at a time when accountability programs demand that every professional development initiative immediately address student performance. Proponents of this model have responded to this criticism by noting that teacher-selected topics often relate directly to class content. Moreover, teachers energized through the study of such topics are likely to perform more strongly in the classroom, regardless of what they teach, than those forced to sit through mind-numbing workshops with narrow emphases. Moreover, the center has sought to shape its model to meet the pressure of accountability programs by encouraging implementations that build seminars around state-mandated standards.

This strategy has implications for the institutionalization and long-term sustainability of collaborations based on the center's model. The more such collaborations address district and state needs, the more likely they are to become a regular part of a school's life. In pursuing this strategy, the challenge will be to take state and district concerns into account while keeping the seminars firmly in the control of the participants and retaining all the other features that make them appealing to teachers. Much of the responsibility for meeting this challenge will fall to the seminar coordinators. Their capacity to envision useful applications of the seminar model, their success in working with administrators, and their ability to marshal their colleagues will, to a great extent, determine how a collaboration will manifest itself in a school. By supporting the coordinators closely with free, ongoing organizational and intellectual advice, the center will do all it can to ensure the institutionalization of the seminars and the maintenance of the relationship between the school at its partner university.

There is one more challenge to consider: higher education's propensity to reward research and publication over service. Andrew Delbanco, a professor of English at Columbia University who served as a consulting scholar in a seminar with teachers from Walter Williams High School in Burlington, North Carolina, addressed this issue in *Ideas*, the National Humanities Center's magazine.

> Some of my colleagues back home made it clear to me that they thought I was wasting my precious research time. So what was I doing? . . . The answer, I think, is the same that accounts for why research scholars devote time to teaching undergraduates: the novelty, the originality, of the insights of our students is more than enough to justify our labor and time. The Walter Williams [High School] teachers may not have read much in John Dewey's works on the theory of education, but they understood the point of teaching and learning precisely as he did, when he wrote in *Democracy and Education* (1916) that thinking is a process of inquiry, of looking into things, of investigating. Acquiring is always secondary, and instrumental to the act of inquiring. It is seeking, a quest, for something that is not at hand. We sometimes talk as if "original research" were a peculiar prerogative of scientists or at least of advanced students. But all thinking is research, and all research is native, original, with him who carries it on, even if everybody else in the world already is sure of what he is still looking for. (Delbanco, 1996, p. 62)

Elements of Successful Collaboration

Goodlad (1988) noted that "the history of school–university collaboration is not so much . . . replete with failure as it is short on [good] examples . . . [having] carefully crafted agreements and programs" with individual and institutional commitment on both sides (p. 12). Goodlad describes substantive school–university partnerships as "symbiotic" in nature, involving "unlike organisms (or institutions) joined . . . for mutually beneficial relationships" (p. 14). Three conditions apply to such relationships: (a) there is a dissimilarity among the partners, (b) the relationship permits the attainment of self-interests, and (c) there is sufficient selflessness on the part of each partner to allow for the accomplishment of the goals of other partners. Schlecty and Whitford (1988) offered a different basis for effective partnerships. These writers suggested an "organic" orientation. While recognizing the potential efficacy of "enlightened self interest" (the essence of a symbiotic relationship), they argued that such arrangements are "inherently fragile" (p. 191). In their view of an organic partnership, the participants are united in a commitment to common goals with each partner fulfilling somewhat unique functions as they work toward these.

The Teacher Leadership for Professional Development Program has aspects of both symbiotic and organic partnerships. For example, the attainment of mutual self-interests is seen at the institutional levels, with each partner taking something away from the collaboration that serves its own self-interests (e.g., a university's increasing need to be relevant to basic education; a district's need to provide stimulating, rigorous professional development to its teachers). Concomitantly, the collaborative goal that "centers" the work at the individual partnership level is intellectual stimulation and enlightenment, with teachers and consulting scholars contributing unique perspectives that work to achieve these common goals.

Figure 10.1 summarizes the essential elements of the Teacher Leadership for Professional Development Program that have characterized past program implementations. "Key players" have been participating teachers, consulting scholars, and National Humanities Center staff, with supportive administrators on the ground in the district where the seminar is implemented. More recently, the "coordination" role in the school has become more formalized, and in future implementations, the role of "university liaison" is likely to be an important addition to the configuration of key players as the program reaches for broader dissemination. Careful, collaborative planning has been the hallmark of successful Teacher Leadership for Professional Development Program collaborations. Planning begins with the coordinators and teachers working with center staff and quickly involves the consultants, as the "essence" of the intellectual exchange to be shared in the seminar is crafted by the collaborative. The seminar's structure has several essential elements with the core being the lively exchange of ideas grounded in the reading of serious texts. Remarkably modest and cost

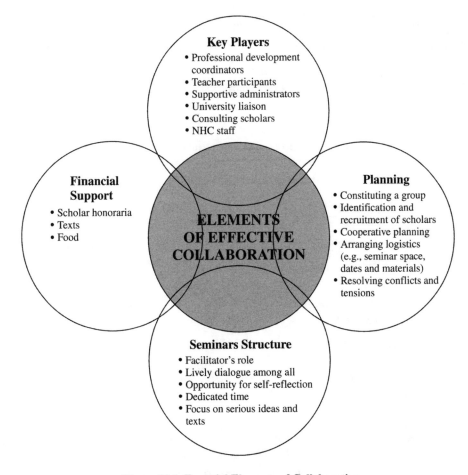

Figure 10.1. Essential Elements of Collaboration.

efficient, there are several cost aspects that are important to successful seminar implementation: scholars' honoraria, the costs of texts, and refreshments. Current implementations that involve university systems and school districts more directly are generating interesting strategies for sharing the already modest costs across collaborating partners.

The Teacher Leadership for Professional Development Program has a strong track record of offering an important example of how teachers and university faculty can work together to achieve significant benefits for participants in the seminar. With its more recent implementations involving the development of a professional development seminar coordinator's role and more formal, institutional collaborative engagement of districts and universities, the program is beginning to develop evidence of beneficial outcomes at institutional levels as well.

References

Bickel, W. E., Hattrup, R. A., & Pine, C. (1994). *The National Humanities Center's Secondary School Faculty Development Project: Year two documentation report.* Research Triangle Park, NC: National Humanities Center.

Delbanco, R. (1996). Converting life into truth: Seminars for high school teachers. *Ideas, 4*(2), 59–62.

Goodlad, J. (1988). School-university partnerships. In K. A. Sirotnik & J. I. Goodlad (Eds.), *School-university partnerships in action* (pp. 3–31). New York: Teachers College Press.

Hawley, W. D., & Valli, L. (1999). The essentials of effective professional development. In L. Darling-Hammond & G. Sykes (Eds.), *Teaching as the learning profession,* (pp. 127–150). San Francisco: Jossey-Bass.

Little, J. W. (1993). Teachers' professional development in a climate of educational reform. *Educational Evaluation and Policy Analysis, 15,* 129–151.

National Board for Professional Teaching Standards. (1998). *About the National Board.* Retrieved from the World Wide Web: *http://www.nbpts.org/nbpts.nbpts.html.*

National Humanities Center. (1999). *National Humanities Center, Teacher Leadership for Professional Development.* Retrieved from the World Wide Web: *http://www. nhc.rtp.nc.us:8080.*

Pine, C. K., Bickel, W. E., & McNelis, R. H. (1998). *The National Humanities Center's Teacher Leadership for Professional Development Program. Documentation report on the program's Focus Year.* Research Triangle Park, NC: National Humanities Center.

Schlecty, P. C., & Whitford, B. L. (1988). Shared problems and shared vision: Organic collaboration. In K. A. Sirotnik & J. I. Goodlad (Eds.), *School-university partnerships in action* (pp. 191–204). New York: Teachers College Press.

Shulman, L. (1999). Foreword. In L. Darling-Hammond & G. Sykes (Eds.), *Teaching as the learning profession.* San Francisco: Jossey-Bass.

Chapter

From Practicum Improvement to School Improvement: A Developing Partnership

Catherine Sinclair and Lil Perre

Traditionally, a limited relationship has existed between schools and teacher preparation institutions (the universities in Australia). Schools perceive their role as the education of school students, and universities see their role in schools as only the professional preparation of student teachers. At its worst, the relationship between school-based and university-based educators can be one of "them" versus "us." In this situation, there is little understanding of the work of schoolteachers because the university professor may only visit the school site on limited occasions during a practicum to talk with the school principal or school coordinator or perhaps to observe a student teacher's lesson.

Schoolteachers, too, may be unaware of the various roles university professors undertake in research, scholarship, teaching, and administration. Often teachers are critical of university professors and the limited occasions they visit the school site for a practicum. Even a recent survey conducted by this university professor (Catherine) found that a number of teachers choose not to supervise student teachers for the practicum because they are too busy. In addition, the teachers consider it the work of university professors, not their own responsibility, to regularly supervise student teachers. They believe it is not a schoolteacher's job to oversee student teachers' lesson plans, observe their lessons, and then provide written feedback (Sinclair & Thistleton-Martin, 1999). There is, then, still little understanding of the collaborative role school and university educators can play in the professional development of student and practicing teachers.

Nonetheless, in recent years there has been growing interest in the importance of developing partnerships between universities and schools for both improved practicum experiences for student teachers and school renewal, with improved outcomes for students, student teachers, practicing teachers, and university professors (Bullough, Kauchak, Crow, Hobbs, & Stokes, 1997; Fraser, 1995; Furlong, Whitty, Barrett, Barton, & Miles, 1994; Gore, 1995; Grundy, 1996; Hooley & Jones, 1997; Howard, 1998; Sinclair & Woodward, 1997; Wilkin & Sankey, 1994). This chapter will outline the development of such a collaborative partnership between one university professor, Catherine Sinclair, and a school. In particular, it focuses on the collaboration between Catherine and the school's principal, Lil Perre. This partnership moved from one of comfortable collaboration, through structured collaboration, to critical collaboration (Hill, n.d., p. 1).

One School, One University

Mount Pritchard East Public School (MPE) is a small, public elementary (primary) school with 320 students. The school attracts funds from the Disadvantaged Schools Program because of the low socioeconomic background of its parent community. It has been part of the program since 1993. There are twelve classroom teachers, half of whom are in their first or second year of permanent employment and three of whom are classified as executive staff. (Executive staff consist of the principal, assistant principals, and executive teachers who have additional authority and responsibility for staff supervision as part of their roles within the school.) There is a nonteaching principal, a part-time learning-support teacher (who works with students who have learning difficulties), as well as English as a second language and reading recovery teachers. There is also a part-time teacher librarian.

Lil was appointed to MPE in January 1995. She had been in the teaching profession in Australia for thirty-two years and had been a principal for eleven years. She brought with her changes in a leadership style that facilitated and promoted the following:

- opportunities for staff and the school community to develop their talents and interests;

- a "have-a-go" approach to innovative practices;

- reviews of all school policies and procedures;

- increased funding support for program implementation;

- flexible staffing and flexible use of time;

- collaborative decision making as the preferred whole school model;

- collegial planning and professional growth through professional debate, teamwork, planned staff development, an expansion of school-based roles for all members of staff, and school-based and external in-service programs;

- an expansion of professional resources;

- parental involvement in whole school planning, evaluations, and classroom support; and

- effective organizational structures to improve student outcomes, student welfare, staff morale, staff professional development, time management, school communication, school image, parent involvement, assessment, and reporting. (Perre, 1999, p. 4)

The school was therefore becoming a learning community. In addition, Lil developed a "Policy/Innovation Model" as outlined in Figure 11.1.

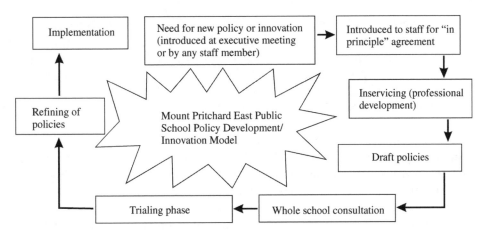

Figure 11.1. Policy Development/Innovation Model (based on Perre, 1999, p. 5).

The University of Western Sydney Macarthur (UWSM) is one of Australia's newer universities, established in 1989. It is one member of a federation of three university members (all originally colleges; in 2000, the three joined to become the University of Western Sydney). By itself, USWM caters to more than nine thousand students in six faculties on two southwestern suburban campuses of Sydney. (Faculties are large groups or schools of academic and general staff responsible for the provision of courses in various areas. The faculties at UWSM include education and languages, law, business, informatics, science and technology, health, and arts and social sciences.)

The university prides itself on its commitment to social justice by providing an opportunity for university education for students from lower socioeconomic backgrounds; by serving the needs of its region, the nation, and the global community; and by the ways in which it "value adds" to the development of its students (University of Western Sydney, 1997). The Faculty of Education and Languages at UWSM, to which Catherine belongs, offers a range of programs, one being a three-year undergraduate elementary (primary) teacher preparation degree program. (The University has recently extended the teacher preparation course to four years.) Throughout this program, practicum (the experiential aspect where firsthand, "site-based" learning takes place) occurs in all semesters.

Catherine, the university professor involved in the MPE collaboration, has had more than ten years of experience as a university educator. She has a strong commitment to the professional development of future teachers. Over this period, her role as a university educator has changed from direct supervision of student teacher lessons (with little time for anything else) to a mentor of student teachers and colleague and consultant to their school-based practicum supervisors. This change in roles has necessitated more frequent, ongoing, and intensive relationships with particular schools rather than a more superficial relationship with a broad range of schools. She also coordinates the university's joint theory–practicum subjects in the first and third year of the elementary teacher education program, teaches in postgraduate programs, and is currently the practicum coordinator for the entire elementary teacher education program.

Beginning a Partnership for Practicum Improvement

Elementary student teachers undertake their first practicum in the first semester of their teacher preparation program to not only help them prepare for the dynamic and demanding teaching profession into which they will enter but to make informed career choices early in this preparation. It and all subsequent practicums are integrated within subjects so that learning to be a teacher occurs simultaneously on campus and in schools (for details of these programs, see Sinclair, 1998; Sinclair-Gaffey, Woodward, & Lowe, 1995).

A school-based coordinator is responsible for the overall conduct of the practicum in the schools, whereas the school-based practicum supervisors at each practicum school supervise the student teachers (one student teacher each) including evaluating the student teacher and awarding a practicum grade. University professors attend schools for up to half a day each week to work with both the student teachers and their practicum supervisors. They do not directly observe or assess a student teacher's teaching unless they consider it necessary or are invited to do so by the student teacher, practicum supervisor, or school coordinator or if the student teacher is "at risk" for failing the practicum. Their roles as mentors to student teachers and consultants to their practicum supervisors means that they are "an integral part of the practicum experience. They are not merely school visitors whose sole responsibility is liaison. Nor are they outside 'experts' whose sole responsibility is assessment of teaching. Their role . . . is one of facilitator and mentor, working in partnership with school-based personnel, to optimize student teachers' learning from the practicum" (Sinclair-Gaffey & Dobbins, 1996, p. 118).

To encourage practicum supervisors to supervise first-year student teachers, it is only possible to supervise a final year student teacher if they have supervised a first-year student teacher earlier in the year. The result of this requirement is that practicum supervisors may be involved in the professional development of student teachers over extensive periods throughout the school year. This situation can also result in university professors who frequently teach both the first year and final year subjects working at the same school for twenty weeks throughout the entire year. Unless a university professor is dissatisfied with a particular school or does not teach both subjects, he or she works with the same school in both semesters and in subsequent years to facilitate the development of a partnership. We believe that building and developing an ongoing, permanent relationship with particular schools can improve the practicum experiences for student teachers, lead to professional development opportunities for school and university educators, and promote school improvement. It was this ongoing relationship with a particular school that led to the creation of a project to evaluate (and possibly improve) a school innovation in the teaching of numeracy at MPE.

Extending the Partnership: From Comfort to Structural Collaboration

The beginnings of the relationship between Catherine (from UWSM) and Lil (the principal at MPE Public School) began in 1997 when Catherine began undertaking practicum visits to the school for both the first- and third-year subjects. She therefore worked in the school over two 10-week periods across the four school terms. Facilitated by Lil's collaborative, open-door leadership and Catherine's commitment to partnership in teacher preparation, the two educators conversed each week during Catherine's visits to the school. Various levels of dialogue developed. Initially, there would be an informal dialogue, an exchange of information, with Lil providing information about the teachers in the school, particular school programs and initiatives, and recent initiatives and documents from the New South Wales government Education Department (Department of Education and Training) and Board of Studies (which generates curriculum documents for use in government schools). They exchanged views on issues related to teaching in general, to MPE in particular, and to the broader issues affecting education. One example involved the evolution of outcomes-based education and assessment in the school. Discussions and the involvement of Catherine's student teachers in the generation of whole school tracking in literacy and numeracy led to the discovery that the MPE students were strong in the "coding" aspect of reading but less strong in other areas. The school then channeled resources into oracy (talking and listening) and reading comprehension, which has since led to student improvements in these areas.

This dialogue between Lil and Catherine was possible because of the frequency of Catherine's visits to the school (i.e., once a week throughout much of the school year), the length of the visits (generally up to half a school day), and the fact that the visits occurred over a substantial period of time (three years). Openness was another feature that facilitated the relationship. As part of her role with the student teachers, Catherine had open access to the school staff and to classrooms; in turn, she was "open" with Lil in discussions about the university's teacher education program. Time was also key to the development of the collaborative relationship. Both Catherine and Lil made time to dialogue and took opportunities as they presented themselves. Through these means, a "relationship of comfort" developed in which mutual trust, respect, and support arose. They considered theirs to be a two-way relationship, one of mutual benefit.

Lil found it beneficial to "bounce ideas" off another person from another sphere, someone who was not from MPE, not school-based, and not employed by the same government department. She valued the fact that Catherine could bring to discussions a knowledge of the research literature on learning and teaching, schools, and school improvement, as well as a wider, less-parochial perspective. Lil believed that schools were more isolated and insular than ever before as they had become self-managing and self-monitoring. Following Education Department restructuring, senior education staff were less available to individual schools for strategic planning and annual management planning. Thus, both educators valued these informal discussions highly. Indeed, Lil believed it was to the school's benefit to have the best possible relationship with the university.

Catherine felt safe asking questions about the MPE's policies and practices and encouraging the staff to look beyond the school's four walls. She also felt safe sharing information about the trials and tribulations of working in the university system. The result was a success in three ways: It built a better practicum for the student teachers, offered a better experience for the MPE's students through better practice by student teachers, and offered the university a practicum partnership whereby school-based and university-based educators worked as a team in guiding the professional development of student teachers, developing commitment and involvement among practicum participants, and promoting a positive image of both school- and university-based teacher education. University professors working in schools do not always enjoy such success. Indeed, there have been occasions of unsatisfactory practicum experiences in other schools, for both Catherine and for the student teachers, when no effective partnership has developed (Sinclair-Gaffey & Dobbins, 1996). Visits to such schools were unpleasant for Catherine because of the lack of cooperation and the overt antagonism of school-based educators who were distant and unapproachable, reluctant to meet with her, or unwilling to take on the additional responsibility of working with student teachers. Furthermore, she believed that in this situation, she had little influence on student teacher learning or on teacher supervision. This example is in marked contrast to the open, trusting, respectful, and welcoming relationship that existed with MPE.

Over subsequent university semesters (and school terms), the informal sharing of ideas and the discussions of pedagogy gave way to more formal levels of dialogue and collaboration as Catherine and Lil's relationship developed. For example, Lil was invited to participate in the university's evaluation of its practicum program, and Catherine was invited to address an International Teachers' Day Assembly at the school, which as organized by the local parent community to recognize and celebrate the work of the teachers in the school and to raise the status of teaching in the community. Catherine arranged to have academic gowns from the university supplied for the occasion to demonstrate to a community generally unfamiliar with tertiary education the level of training that teachers undertake. An additional formal relationship arose when MPE was accepted into an Australian national project documenting and evaluating innovation and best practice in education. It is this relationship that will form the remainder of this chapter.

Critical Collaboration for Innovation Evaluation and School Improvement

The National Innovation and Best Practice Project was funded by the Australian national government and awarded to a consortium of four universities in four states of Australia (none of which were UWS). Initially, Lil spoke to Catherine about the value of applying to be part of the national project. On agreement as to its value, they submitted a proposal to the consortium. Lil became the project leader, and the school counselor and two assistant principals became the project team. After discussion with the school staff, the project team constructed a proposal to study the implementation of school-wide initiatives in outcomes-based education, assessment, and reporting and submitted it to the consortium, where it was duly accepted but refined to focus specifically on mathematics education.

Once the proposal was accepted, each of the 107 participating schools was asked to enlist the assistance of an academic to act as "external" researcher and support them on the project. Lil approached "the university we know best," UWSM, even though it was a different university from those sponsoring the project; and Catherine, who had attended that school each week for the practicum. Initially, Catherine sought out others in her faculty with greater expertise in mathematics education to be involved but eventually accepted the school's invitation to act as external researcher. Both Catherine and Lil thought the school staff would prefer to work with someone they knew and with whom they felt comfortable. Lil believed that to having an external partner who knew MPE school and who had all the necessary skills to undertake the role was a real bonus. Furthermore, this project was considered to be as much about school organization and reform as about mathematics education, and it therefore reflected Catherine's expertise. During this period, Catherine continued to visit the school weekly with her final-year practicum student teachers. She and her student teachers gathered additional data during this time.

The whole school Vertical Mathematics Groups innovation saw the school restructure its classes and school timetable, use all teaching staff within the school to teach mathematics, and purchase textbooks and extensive resources to support outcomes-based teaching programs and reporting (see Perre, 1999, for details of the project). The results of the evaluation demonstrated that the Vertical Mathematics Groups innovation was successful in improving the numeracy outcomes of students. Teachers were also found to have changed their pedagogy and work practices. Collaborative planning improved, school monitoring of student outcomes and indicators inherent in the mathematics syllabus became the norm, and there was a decrease in overall workload for many teachers.

For Lil and Catherine, an additional project outcome included the successful completion of the project (something that had not occurred with all 107 school projects). Lil commented that "you couldn't have a more clear indication of the effectiveness of the partnership than that." Both Catherine and the MPE staff and students received accolades from National Project leaders on both the results and the research methodology. This success led to the consortium's follow-up research on school leadership. Catherine and Lil were also invited to speak about connecting schools and universities at various principals' associations.

Reflections on the Collaboration

There is no doubt that the actual project itself was successful, but what factors made it a successful collaboration and partnership? Day (1998) defined a partnership from the 1980 Partnership Act as "the relationship which subsists between persons carrying on a business in common with a view to profit." The partnership between Lil and Catherine reflected this definition and Day's view that "partnerships are usually formed because each partner has something to offer the joint enterprise, which is different from but complements that which is offered by the other partners" (1998, p. 419). Through reflective discussion on the partners' motivation and expectations; negotiating roles and responsibilities; styles, perspectives, and shared understandings; changing roles; differences between expectation and reality; the dynamics involved;

and sustaining interest and involvement, essential features of this effective school–university collaboration can be outlined.

Motivation and Expectations

For Lil, the motivation to begin the National Innovation and Best Practice Project was that it enabled the school to evaluate a "real thing" that was already happening at the school with funding made available to undertake the task. The school had already analyzed well their literacy practices and student outcomes in literacy, but it had not done the same for numeracy because student literacy standards were such a huge problem for the school.

Catherine's motivation was the opportunity to evaluate school practice and to play a part in school reform, as well as the opportunity to earn additional income. She expected to use and develop her own research expertise in the evaluation of the school's numeracy innovation. It was an opportunity for her to be involved in a large-scale national project. Furthermore, it enabled her to extend her role in the school from practicum consultant to co-researcher. She felt secure enough in the relationship to act at times as a "Devil's Advocate" to challenge the thinking of the school staff. Because she was not an employee of the school nor of the Education Department, her professional future was not dependent on making the school "look good." Her expectations of Lil were that she would manage the project at the school level, be open and honest in their interactions, undertake her responsibilities of the project, and "deliver" the final report according to the necessary time lines. Both Lil and the project met Catherine's expectations.

Lil's expectations of Catherine as an "external researcher" were to play a major part in collating the data the school had already collected, to generate additional data (such as the interviews), and in the to validate the data. She also expected Catherine to write a report outlining her findings because the school staff did not have the expertise, especially with statistics. Even the two MPE staff members with master's degrees would not have been able to undertake the research aspect of the project because they were already overcommitted in school matters and did not have the time to dedicate to the project. Lil knew it would have been impossible to ask them to do the research; had they done it, it would not have been to the depth that Catherine could provide. In fact, the projects at schools that did not enlist the assistance of an "external researcher" failed to reach a successful conclusion, even if their innovations did not fail. Catherine also met Lil's expectations.

Negotiating Roles and Responsibilities

The roles and responsibilities for the project arose from the guidelines provided by the National Consortium. The partners negotiated who would take on what responsibility, based on skill levels, through open, honest, and tactful discussions; roles were not forced on any of the participants. Although the particular roles and responsibilities of the project were different from those of the practicum partnership, they were easily negotiated because of the existing relationship of respect, trust, and comfort. Both Catherine and Lil set deadlines, and both kept them. Both are people who will "deliver," and as each needed information or action from the other, it was delivered on time. In this way, no resentment occurred; no one thought they were doing all the work, and no one was delayed by the other's tardiness or inaction.

There were no hierarchical issues that arose because Lil believed she had chosen the "right person for the job." The communication channels were always open, and although the MPE staff who attended statewide workshops as part of the project noted that some other external researchers had "threatening manners," this could not be said of Catherine.

The roles of all participants were negotiated. For this reason, a participant's role might not be an equal one, but it was "the most appropriate one." Once the roles were negotiated, individuals had "more than an equal voice" in the parts of the project for which they were responsible. For Catherine, her role involved undertaking and reporting on the research itself; for Lil, it was the overview of the project and writing of the final report. Catherine was aware and of the opinion that the school "owned" the project and so made no attempt to take it over or tell the school how it should carry it out. Rather, she considered her role as a consultative one, providing advice through discussion on undertaking the project, asking questions, being a sounding board for Lil's ideas and those of other school personnel, and facilitating the data gathering and analysis so that the school could achieve its purpose of evaluating the Vertical Maths Groups Innovation. School ownership of the project empowered the school as it entered into a new domain, the formal and external (rather than informal and internal) evaluation of their whole school Vertical Mathematics Groups Innovation. Indeed, unbeknownst to Catherine, the National Consortium warned schools that their external researchers might try to take over their projects. Schools were informed that they owned the project but warned that academics as "external researchers" can overshadow, overpower, and eventually overtake a project because of their familiarity with and expertise in the area of research. This situation did not occur because Catherine and Lil's roles were jointly defined early on in the project. Together they formulated a plan to determine what needed to be done, how the task was going to be undertaken, and how the final report would be written. Lil was appreciative that Catherine did not try to take over the project and noted that other schools had not been so fortunate with their external researchers.

The collaboration was symbiotic and synergistic—each needed the other, their roles and findings interwoven like a tapestry into a final report and the results of this collaboration greater than either one could have presented alone.

Styles, Perspectives, and Shared Understanding: Collaboration as Teamwork

There were no great differences in Lil's and Catherine's styles and perspectives. They have similar writing styles and ways of thinking. These similarities have arisen over time. There was also no difference of perspective because Catherine was able to see the project from both the school's and the teachers' points of view. This would not have been the case had a complete stranger been the external researcher. Even if the writing styles and ways of thinking were the same, these would not have been obvious from the outset of the project and may not even have arisen during the course of the project. It takes time to build professional relationships, just as it takes time to build personal ones. Having an existing relationship saved a lot of time and facilitated the conduct, reporting, and success of the project. For any successful collaboration, it is necessary to build the relationship first.

Both Catherine and Lil, and indeed the whole school project team, had a real and shared understanding of what the project involved, what the data were, and where they wanted to go with it. This understanding arose through Catherine's long-term involvement with the school, her understanding of the school context, and the fact that she was seen as a member of the school's team, not an "add on." Catherine "delivered" data, and together she and Lil looked at the information and decided what was appropriate and what was not. Together the team sorted then negotiated where would be the best place to locate data within the final report and which data could be enhanced through graphic representation. For this reason, it wasn't a disjointed project. Also, Catherine received drafts of the report as they were written, thereby assisting her own writing because she was not undertaking her task in isolation. Catherine also linked the conclusions she made from undertaking the research with the sections of Lil and her team's report so that what she wrote fit in with the overall purpose, goals, and outcomes of the project. In these ways, Catherine's findings were integrated into the style of report writing that was the basis of the final report, leading to a seamlessness between authors in their writing styles. Her use of a combination of qualitative and quantitative methodologies was acceptable to Lil and the rest of the team. From the beginning, they considered Catherine a member of the school project team, even though she was contracted as an external researcher. Catherine knew what the school project team was doing, with no surprises, so the communication channels were effective. She attended the workshops with the school team as a part of that team and also continued her weekly involvement in the school through the practicum.

For some schools in the National Project, this was not the case. External researchers were seen as some unknown expert who would flit into the school, undertake the research, write up the findings and conclusions, and then disappear from the scene. They never became a part of the project team and rarely attended the National Project workshops. Lil also believed that some external researchers at the workshops had a threatening manner and so was concerned about their relationship with their project schools. They did not appear to have the rapport that existed between Catherine, Lil, and project team. Indeed, while other external researchers presented the findings of the school projects at a state workshop, Catherine and Lil gave a joint presentation.

The interweaving of voices into the rich tapestry that became the final report was possible because both parties accepted advice from each other that would improve the project and its final written report; neither was inflexible, insisting that the way she did things or presented her sections of the report must remain exactly as it had been written. They discussed all issues, and individual contributions to the final report were complementary.

The only major issue for resolve originated outside the school–university partnership, and that was the National Consortium's time line for project completion. The time line had been decided by deadlines from the funding agency, the Australian government. Unfortunately, that time line crossed over two school years, with projects starting late in one year and needing to be completed by early in the next. The Australian school year ends in December and begins again at the end of January. It is over these six-week school holidays that staff changes occur, and the loss of key school project-team staff, particularly the principal as project leader, could have had severe repercussions for the successful completion of the project. Catherine and Lil discussed this possibility and as a result generated contingency plans in December to complete the project should Lil leave MPE. Fortunately, these contingency plans were not needed, and the project was completed as originally negotiated, although Lil believed the principal thought that more could have been learned if the project had occurred during a single school year. The time line was considered to inhibit rather than hinder moving the project forward.

Changing Roles

There were really no significant changes in team roles during the project because these were well defined in the definitions stated in the National Project guidelines. These guidelines were appropriate to the people involved in the MPE project and their particular skills and experiences. The collaborative relationship was already in existence, and this project was just a different form of collaboration for Lil and Catherine. The project accommodated the collaborative model that had already been developed.

Differences of Roles Between Expectation and Reality in the National Project Experience

That there would be any difference in their roles as collaborators in reality to their expectations was not even considered, particularly because a collaborative "working" relationship for practicum already existed. Nonetheless, collaboration for the purpose of research and evaluation was a new form of collaboration for both Lil and Catherine. Their complementary thinking and similar working styles (i.e., commitment to the task at hand, negotiating tasks to be undertaken, reliability in the completion of those tasks, and a flexibility and openness to the ideas of others) led to the reality and the expectations being synonymous. Once Catherine was contracted to act as an external researcher, she fit well into the planning because, as Lil reported, she was cooperative and helpful.

There were, however, marked differences in reality and expectations for both parties in the level of involvement necessary for the project and in the amount time it would take to complete the project. Both had underestimated these issues by approximately 500 percent, with Catherine completing her part of the project and having it delivered during the school holidays to Lil's home. Lil was able to complete the project only by using a flexibility of school structure and "buying time" to release herself from her normal duties with one assistant principal acting in the role of principal for almost two weeks. Indeed, Lil reported that she was close to "throwing in the towel" as far as the project was concerned, but because she is not a "throwing-in-the-towel type," she and the school rallied and restructured to get the task completed. The project was considered "a big ask" from the National Consortium and one Lil would not enter into again. Nonetheless, having done this sort of project once, both Lil and Catherine believed they had learned a lot. It is interesting to note that in other schools involved in the National Project, there were instances in which the project and the final report were left to the external researcher to complete alone because schools did "throw in the towel." What made the difference in the MPE project was the commitment of both Lil and Catherine to complete a job once it has been undertaken, to think "outside the box" for alternate ways of achieving the desired ends, and a willingness to "go the extra mile" by working longer hours to ensure the completion of the project and its report.

The Dynamics Involved

The dynamics that existed between the collaborators within this partnership centered on a mutual respect between Catherine and Lil and her team. Important facilitating factors included the comfort of the existing practicum partnership, Catherine's knowledge of the school context, Catherine's integrity as a researcher and academic and Lil's as a school manager and educative leader, and both parties' viewing MPE as "our school." They were "task focused" as well as "people focused." They knew that neither would fall short of the other's expectations. The relationship between Lil and Catherine has evolved from the personal to the institutional, breaking down the uncomfortable barriers that can exist between school and university. The school staff also is more at ease in dealing with university personnel, as was demonstrated in the follow-up interviews conducted by the one of the leaders of National Consortium with members of the original project team and other teachers. As Lil commented about this interview, "We're used to having a Ph.D. [i.e., Catherine] in our office talking to us . . . so it was just another Ph.D. talking to us as opposed to our own Ph.D."

The dynamics within the school also supported moving the project forward. There is an excellent relationship between Lil and her staff. Furthermore, MPE is a learning community in which members of the staff are comfortable with suggesting innovations and making constructive criticisms. They also know others listen to their views and that everyone on the staff and in the parent community is part of what is happening at the school. In fact, the chief education officer (School Improvement) from the Education Department commented on MPE and its principal, saying, "There are lots of schools which move and shake and nothing happens but at MPE it's moving and shaking and something does happens." Lil further added to this statement that "Everyone's part of the something and sometimes they're the ones doing the moving and shaking."

The leadership style at MPE is not "top down," and there has been the development of a shared pedagogy based on student outcomes that the staff has developed and that is then used to plan and program for student learning, assessment, and reporting. The children and their learning outcomes are at the center of pedagogy, the driving force behind teaching and learning in mathematics, and everybody in the school shares this approach.

Catherine added that the school is used to evaluating its practice, and this project was just another form of evaluation, a normal school task except more detailed in its undertaking. Lil also believes this was why the project was so easy to "sell" to staff; the only difference was that an external researcher was conducting the evaluation. The staff became more involved in project through the interviews. As a precursor, Lil suggested to the staff that she wanted to know their personal views on the innovation without any inhibitions so it would be more appropriate for an the external person (Catherine) to conduct the interviews. Lil doesn't know what happened in the interviews and doesn't want to know, except on a wider "whole system" basis. Lil obviously trusted her staff, and her staff trusted Catherine. The school staff did not see her as a threat during the interviews, and they trusted her to treat information in a highly confidential manner. She would not make public the information that individual teachers provided because it was unethical to do so and was not really relevant to her own work at the university. Lil was concerned that if she had been the interviewer, the teachers would have watched their words more carefully. If Catherine had divulged that information, not only would she contravene ethical guidelines, but she would have lost both her credibility with the school staff and possible practicum placements for her student teachers.

Thus Lil believed that a certain integrity could be achieved by using an external person. It was not compulsory for teachers to participate in the interviews, but 100 percent of staff chose to do so. The interview questions were made available to teachers before the interviews, and time was made for the interview to occur, at times through release from class. Catherine explained that all information would be treated confidentially, that anonymity would be assured, and that she would not be reporting the views of individuals to Lil or project leaders (or anyone else). It was an indication of the level of trust and the existing relationship with Catherine that all teachers took the opportunity to be interviewed, even teachers with whom Catherine had had little previous contact. Lil knew she had taken a risk by allowing Catherine "to look in our cupboard" because it might reveal some "skeletons." She wondered if she and Catherine hadn't already had a trusting relationship whether she should have been quite as comfortable in doing so.

A further dynamic that contributed to the success of the project was that as a learning community, Lil knew there was no one on the MPE school staff that would say that he or she "knew it all." Indeed, other members of the staff would look at anyone who said they knew it with great suspicion. Every person at MPE is on a learning curve—and proud of it. The idea of "I'm the expert and I know everything" is considered the most damning statement one could make. Lil considers those who say they know everything to have a problem. In her own way, Catherine is aligned to this learning community model because she does not purport to be the "expert" but rather a colleague, co-investigator, and co-researcher who is helping the school study school practice to better it.

Given the climate of MPE and the existing practicum partnership, teachers accepted both Lil and Catherine and the roles they undertook in the project. The teachers were part of the learning journey of school reform as part of a whole school learning community. Both Lil and Catherine considered the external researcher a real partner in the project rather than a consultant contracted to undertake research, deliver the results to the project leader, and then move on. Catherine was one of the team. Because her name was on the final report, her reputation was involved in the quality of the project and the report. In other words, she, too, had a major stake in the project and the way its findings were presented, even if she did not have a stake in what those findings actually said about the effectiveness of the school innovation.

Sustaining Interest and Involvement in the Project

The elements contributing to Catherine and Lil's sustained involvement and interest in the project was a commitment to it, to the existing relationship that both partners valued, and to the school's trust in Catherine. Both Lil and Catherine learned much from this collaborative research partnership. They did not undertake the project solely for the financial reward. Indeed, Lil considered that undertaking the project was goodwill on the part of Catherine and doubted if Catherine would have undertaken such a large project for such little money for another school. That Catherine did undertake the project was testimony to the professional relationship that exists between the two of them. They both believed there were other "in-kind" payments from the project. These included professional development, collaborative writing opportunities, further research and networking opportunities, and a continuation of a practicum partnership. Furthermore, Catherine was intrinsically interested in the project because of its school reform potential: changing pedagogy and school organization to make a difference in the education of children.

The role of colleagues and supervisors in sustaining involvement in the project was minimal for Catherine. Her supervisor was aware of the project only in so far that it was recorded as part of her yearly work productivity report. Other university colleagues had not been informed except those in mathematics education, and they had not taken up the opportunity to collaborate on the project. For Lil, the project provided opportunities to share the results of the project with senior Education Department personnel and so build her credibility and reputation and that of MPE with these officers. Lil believes that from this project, MPE can become a school known for its innovative programs. In general, however, both Lil and Catherine were predominantly self-motivated to undertake the project for the reasons already outlined, such as financing the project, extending normal school-based evaluations of its practices, furthering their own professional development in research and scholarship, facilitating school reform, and making a difference in the education of children.

Key Features of a Successful Partnership: Conclusions from Experience

From the practicum to the Vertical Maths Groups Innovation and Best Practice Project there have been changes in the partnership between this school principal and university professor. From the initial stages to the present, Catherine and Lil's relationship has grown and developed. These changes can be seen in Figure 11.2.

The initial conversations of Figure 11.2 were those described as common to most of the "safe" discussions between school and university personnel during the practicum, the public relations exercise in which university professors are fearful of upsetting school personnel and so limit conversations to providing information about the university's requirements of the practicum, superficial questions about how the student teacher is progressing, and even the weather. Many traditional relationships between schools and universities stop at this stage. The relationship moved quickly to one of sharing in which Lil brought to the Catherine's attention any new Education Department policy or document. On one occasion, Catherine pointed out particular aspects of department policy on "Teacher Efficiency" that Lil had been unaware of, and these aspects then became stimulus reading for all school staff during the school's re-writing of its teacher professional development policy. Catherine's understanding of current changes in school education grew through such informal dialogue, and Lil's knowledge of "cutting edge" or "fresh" approaches in education was enhanced through student teachers working in her school each semester for their practicums. This growing understanding led to "Informed and Structural Collaboration" where specific issues related to practicum and school issues were discussed each week, such as the philosophy of the university's teacher education program, "best practice" of practicum experiences for student teachers, the changing nature of initial teacher education and the practicum, the changing roles of university professors and practicum supervisors in a "partnership" approach to teacher professional preparation, financial constraints on initial teacher education and its practicum, and outcomes-based programming and reporting. From these discussions a "personal partnership" developed in which information sharing was replaced by a more genuine two-way dialogue between two colleagues who were open to ideas and opportunities; willing to share perspectives, policies, and practice; respected each other's views; and gave positive feedback when necessary. Lil was particularly delighted with positive feedback from Catherine because this was not forthcoming from school staff, who could be quick to criticize but not to praise her efforts.

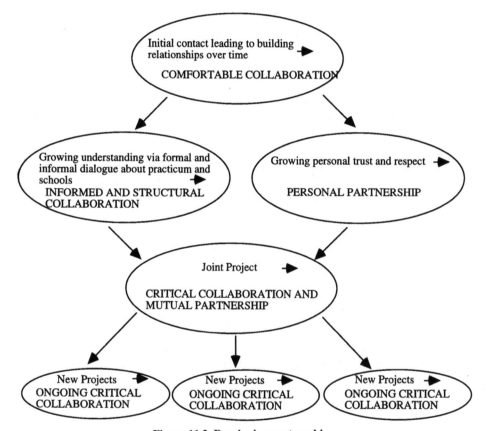

Figure 11.2. Developing partnerships.

In time, these forms of collaboration and a personal partnership between the university professor and Lil gave way to more formal collaborations. This developing partnership meant that as soon as the school was accepted into the National Innovation and Best Practice Project, Lil immediately thought of involving Catherine, whom she considered a "critical friend." Participation in this project then enabled the relationship to evolve to where collaboration could become more critical than just comfortable, and a greater mutuality of relationship and benefit resulted. Once the partnership has reached this stage, it is possible to continue critical collaboration on new projects, and both Catherine and Lil are on the look out for further opportunities.

From their experience and reflection on that experience, the key features of Catherine and Lil's partnership throughout its evolution were the following:

- *Time* to develop a personal and a professional relationship. Long-term involvement is also necessary because it brings knowledge of each partner's particular context and shared understandings.

- Ongoing, frequent *contact* and involvement of all key personnel for a particular purpose. It is also necessary for each contact to last as long as required for the particular purpose that brings partners together to collaborate.

- *Commitment to lifelong learning* and to the acceptance, development, and evolution of *different perspectives and practices*.

- *Creativity* to think "outside the box" in the generation of strategies to undertake the required tasks and to solve problems that arise.

- *Commitment* to the relationship, the particular purpose that brings partners together and for the successful completion of that purpose.

- A *relationship* that is seen as *nonthreatening* to both partners, is *valued*, and exhibits and values trust, safety, integrity, respect, comfort, and reliability.

- Open, honest, and tactful *communication*.

- *Joint ownership* of and *responsibility* for the relationship and the particular purpose that brings partners together. Each partner has a "stake" in the success of the task or project and of the collaboration.

- *Integrity and professionalism* of participants.

- *Mutuality* where each partner gains something from the collaboration (and this does not necessarily mean financial rewards).

- *Self-motivation* to make a change, to make a difference, or to merely undertake the particular task.

- *Shared beliefs* in the value of the task or project that brings partners together. For example, the project team of which Catherine was a vital and valued member shared a belief in child-focused education; clear goals based on student outcomes; the value of collaboration, professionalism, and a commitment to lifelong learning for all educators; and the need to push the perimeters and "have a go."

The MPE Innovation and Best Practice Project was a collaboration that cemented Catherine and Lil's relationship and enhanced their mutual understanding and respect. They look forward to future collaborations for the benefit of both school and university students.

References

Bullough, R. V. Jr., Kauchak, D., Crow, N. A., Hobbs, S., & Stokes, D. (1997). Professional development schools: Catalysts for teacher and school change. *Teaching and Teacher Education, 13*(2), 153–170.

Day, C. W. (1998). The role of higher education in fostering lifelong learning partnerships with teachers. *European Journal of Education, 33*(4), 419–432.

Fraser, D. (1995, February). *Pain and pleasure in partnership: The state of the partnership between teachers, students and lecturers.* Paper presented at the Second National Conference on Practical Experiences in Professional Education, Gold Coast, Australia.

Furlong, J., Whitty, G., Barrett, E., Barton, L., & Miles, S. (1994). Integration and partnership in initial teacher education—dilemmas and possibilities. *Research Papers in Education, 9*(3), 281–301.

Gore, J. M. (1995). *Emerging issues in teacher education.* Innovative Links Project Report. Canberra: Australia Government Publishing Service.

Grundy, S. (1996). Building professional research partnerships: Possibilities and perplexities. *AER. The Australian Education Researcher, 23*(1), 1–15.

Hill, S. (n.d.). *New forms of collaboration.* Paper presented at the University of South Australia, Magill, South Australia.

Hooley, N., & Jones, D. (1997). Development of school-university partnerships in undergraduate and postgraduate teacher preparation courses. In A. Yarrow, J. Millwater, S. DeVries, & D. Creedy (Eds.), *Practical experiences in professional education* (Research Monograph 2, pp. 33–51). Brisbane, Australia: Queensland University of Technology.

Howard, P. (1998). *Quality student teachers through quality practicums. Quality management review 1996–1997.* North Sydney: Australian Catholic University.

Perre, L. (1999). *Improving outcomes for students in Years 2–6 through Vertical Math Groups.* Unpublished report for Innovations and Best Practice Project. Mount Pritchard East Public School, New South Wales, Australia.

Sinclair, C. (1998). From student to teacher: An Australian approach to early career decision making. *Journal of Professional Studies, 6*(1), 31–48.

Sinclair, C., & Thistleton-Martin, J. (1999, January–February). *School–University Tensions in the Practicum: Partnership or Imposition?* Paper presented at the Fourth National Conference on Practical Experiences in Professional Education, Christchurch, New Zealand.

Sinclair, C., & Woodward, H. (1997). Exploring collaborative ventures for improved teacher education and school reform in Australia. *Brock Education, 7*(1), 59–75.

Sinclair-Gaffey, C., & Dobbins, R. (1996). Tertiary teacher educators: Do they make a difference in the practicum? In A. Yarrow, J. Millwater, S. DeVries, & D. Creedy (Eds.), *Practical experiences in professional education research* (Research Monograph 1). Brisbane, Australia: Queensland University of Technology Publications.

Sinclair Gaffey, C., Woodward, H., & Lowe, K. (1995). Improving school experience: An Australian perspective. *Action in Teacher Education, 17*(2), 7–17.

University of Western Sydney. (1997). Vision 2020. Sydney: Author.

Wilkin, M., & Sankey, D. (Eds.). (1994). *Collaboration and transition in initial teacher training*. London: Kogan Page.

Chapter

12

Finding Keys to Educational Improvement Through Collaborative Work

Karin M. Wiburg and Yvonne Lozano

This chapter describes three years of a university–public school collaboration intended to integrate technology with literacy teaching in a Southwest border school district. It analyzes the growing collaboration between the university and the district as the players increase their focus on systemic school reform. The story of this collaboration is told through the voices and experiences of the primary leaders in this effort, the authors of this chapter.

Yvonne Lozano is the associate superintendent for instruction of the 13,000-student, low-income district described in this chapter in which the majority of the students are learning English as well as academic content. Before coming to the district, she spent forty years as a science teacher and administrator of curriculum and instruction programs in a neighboring state. Five years ago, she retired from this large district and crossed the state border to teach chemistry at the high school in a small, rural border community. Soon she was drafted by the new district's superintendent to help with a myriad of problems, including potential loss of accreditation, low-performing schools, poor test scores, and the need for teacher professional development. It was at this time, in the fall of 1997, when Lozano had become a new assistant superintendent of the struggling district, that the authors of this chapter met.

Karin Wiburg is an associate professor and coordinator of the learning technologies graduate program in the nearby college of education and has a long history of collaborative work and research with local school districts in New Mexico and previously in California. She has worked in education for more than twenty-five years, fourteen years as a K–12 teacher and administrator and then in higher education as a teacher educator. Her work has focused on the design and implementation of technology-based learning environments in K–12 schools. Over time she has become increasingly interested in what system-wide factors facilitate or limit positive change in learning environments in schools (Ritchie & Wiburg, 1994; Stafford-Levy & Wiburg, 2000; Wiburg, 1997). She recruited two other faculty members from the university to assist with this project, Dr. Verlinda Thompson, a reading professor, and Dr. Ana Huerta-Macías, who coordinates the TESOL (Teaching English to Speakers of Other Languages) program.

A Technology Literacy Challenge Fund (TLCF) grant from the state funded the project. These grants are intended to assist K–12 districts, along with community, business, and university consortia, to better use technology to improve student learning. The project, which is now in its third year, is called La Clave para Mejorar (The Key to Improvement). *La clave* in Spanish refers to a foundation stone or a conceptual key, a stronger word that *la llave* or house key, and was thus used as a name for this project. Other members of the district team include an instructional technology coordinator and a group of ten teacher leaders serving as curriculum alignment facilitators in the schools.

The collaboration began as a consultative relationship in which university faculty worked with the district to provide continuous professional development in technology and literacy integration to teams of teachers from each of seventeen schools and their principals. Opportunities were also provided for district teachers to enroll in university graduate coursework at their district site. Thus, this collaboration began as a combination of a consultative model with site-based graduate study opportunities.

The following chapter describes the evolving nature of the collaboration between the university professor and the school district associate superintendent, Wiburg and Lozano, respectively. It also describes the rather unique sociocultural context of the district. A number of key questions regarding collaboration were used to organize our writing. At times, each of the authors offered their own perspectives on answers to these questions.

Getting Started

What, If Any, Were Our Expectations before Starting the Project? What Motivated Us to Start?

Wiburg: Collaborative efforts with school districts to use technology to improve teaching and learning have been at the heart of my university work for many years. I had been working with our closest school district as a consultant for the previous four years, and when an opportunity came to write a consortium grant, I asked Albert Campos, instructional technology coordinator and master's student in our technology graduate program, if his district would like to participate in a consortium for professional development using technology. The two districts shared the challenge of having a large number of students for whom English was not their native language. Research (Wetzel & Chisholm, 1998; Wiburg, 1998; and Wiburg, Sandin, & Montoya, 1999) suggests that technology can help with language learning, and the consortium grant would provide an opportunity to connect theory and practice in the university's two neighboring school districts.

Lozano: I was motivated to get involved in this project by my students, whom I had just returned to the classroom to teach. These students were quite different from those I had taught eighteen years earlier in my career. They preferred a more hands-on approach and were attracted to the use of media and tools. I suspected that integrating technology tools, and especially computers, into the classroom might be helpful in increasing student achievement.

Expectations and Roles

How Different Were Our Roles as Collaborators in Reality from Our Expectations?

Wiburg: I'll never forget the first time I met Yvonne Lozano. We had recently received the consortium grant, and I had traveled to the district to meet with the new assistant superintendent for the first time. The first question she asked me was, "What's in this grant for the district?" This was followed up with, "What do you expect teachers to look like at the end of the project?" I was taken aback for only a few minutes while my respect for this spunky administrator grew. Universities have in many cases simply used districts, coming in and gathering data and then disappearing. I also had enough curriculum background to know that the second question was essential. What were we trying to change with this intervention? And what would the teachers gain? I had not expected a high-level district administrator to be so forthright. I was used to a more formal level of communication with top administration. The potential for a much deeper collaboration than I had expected emerged in this initial meeting.

Lozano: Because the district in which I work has a 95 percent Hispanic population and is a 100-percent free-lunch district, educational researchers frequently approach me asking to use the district demographics for testing products or determining test validity and reliability. Over the course of my career, I have become used to university personnel flying in, gathering the data they want for their research, and then leaving. I didn't see the benefit of this type of collaboration, especially for the teachers in this struggling district.

What I liked about Dr. Wiburg's proposal was her intention to build expertise in the district. Although the first year of the grant involved only a collaboration of middle schools with the university and a second district, by the second year we had begun designing in-depth interventions together for the Gadsden district. We had written and received additional grants to support sustainable professional development for teachers and administrators and were involved in the collaborative development of goals and implementation strategies. Our collaboration took on its own character, one that was neither university nor district. This was not without problems, especially from the district's perspective, but it made possible a deep change effort.

The Sociocultural Context of the District

It was essential to understand the nature of the district in which we worked for our reform initiative to work. The district is located in a southwest border area of New Mexico, with Texas to the east and Mexico to the south. It is forty miles from one end to the other and consists of eleven distinct small communities, all of which have their own elementary school. Problems with decreased achievement and increased dropout rates occur when students must leave the elementary schools for the district's three middle and two high schools. Economic development is minimal, and the area lacks a tax base for adequate school funding. The district itself is the largest employer in the area, employing people from the valley in support staff positions, such as secretaries, janitors, and instructional assistants. The school board is also made up of citizens in the valley who have a vested interest in maintaining the rural character of their community. In contrast, many of the teachers and administrators come from neighboring urban areas and do not live in the community. Their children don't often go to the schools in which they serve as administrators and teachers. In addition, turnover of professional staff has historically been high, with 100 percent turnover in the teaching population in the last three years. Seven superintendents, coming from outside the community, have served the district in the last twenty years, many staying only a year or two. The current superintendent has remained in place over the last six years and has brought needed stability.

From the perspective of the board and the district workers who live in the community, many of the teachers and administrators are seen as outsiders. Because of high mobility, these professionals who come and go may be seen as interchangeable parts of the system who can be easily replaced. In addition, those who live in this rural valley are anxious to maintain their lifestyles and may be suspicious of reforms that come from outsiders. Within this difficult context, we decided that any work we did together must be for the purpose of building sustainable change in teaching and learning in valley schools.

Keys to Our Successful Collaboration

One of the advantages to our collaboration was that neither of us had much to lose by taking the risks required to create sustainable change. Lozano was retired from another district, and aside from a personal commitment to improving the teaching and learning environment in the district for kids, she wanted to retire again within the next few years. Wiburg had a full-time tenured position at the university and many additional projects that required her time. In sum, we were both interested in building sustainable systemic change for the sake of student learning and had little vested interest in our own long-term ownership of the process.

In addition, we discovered that we had shared beliefs about how to create positive changes in teacher practices and student learning environments. We knew that change had to be both top-down and bottom-up (Fullan, 1995) and that teacher change required a careful balance, which we came to call "structure without prescription." We both believe that teachers won't change as the result of a top-down prescriptive intervention. Teachers will change when they have opportunities to engage with colleagues in thoughtful reflections on their own practice (Darling-Hammond, 1997; Eisner, 1998).

We also wanted to carefully consider the many variables that influence successful restructuring in schools. Darling-Hammond (1998) reported on a growing field of research on restructured schools, many from the 1980s, that are beginning to show remarkable success in providing students with rich learning opportunities. She suggested twelve principles that were followed by the restructured New York high schools that she studied. (The first two columns in Table 12.1 refer to these principles). All of the factors these schools had in common were important to one or the other of us. It may be interesting to note that if we had not been a university–public school team, some of the factors might not have been of interest. Lozano, as someone deeply involved in school purposes, had been working for many years to create high academic standards and had already worked on a district project to develop, with the help of teachers, performance assessments that could strengthen classroom instruction and student achievement. Wiburg came from the university and knew about research-based practice, particularly as it related to student-centered, multicultural, and technology-enhanced curricula. Both of us had a certain attitude and belief in the possibility of reform in spite of obstacles that might be encountered and had successful experience in creating positive change. As we wrote this chapter and reflected back on our collaboration, we decided to add to this restructured principles table our own principles of successful collaboration. These can be seen in last two columns of the table and will be discussed more fully later in the article.

Table 12.1. The Principles of Restructured Schools with Value Added by the Principles of Successful Collaboration

Restructured Schools Principles (Darling-Hammond, 1997)	Comments	Successful Collaboration Principles	Collaborators Comments
1. School purposes	Helping all students use their minds well	Shared vision	Sustainable systemic change that enables students to achieve their own visions of who they want to become
2. Academic standards	High and universal for all students	Commitment to high quality	High-quality standards for professional development and learning
3. Interdisciplinary, multicultural curriculum	Focused on powerful ideas	Inclusive political style	Ability to get diverse groups working together by organizing around powerful ideas

Table 12.1. (*continued*)

Restructured Schools Principles (Darling-Hammond, 1997)	Comments	Successful Collaboration Principles	Collaborators Comments
4. Small size and personalization	Schools of 30, teams of 75–100, and 5–6 teachers	Person-to-person interactions	Ability to work together without interference of layers of bureaucracy
5. Student as worker, student as citizen	Commitment to this goal	Student and teacher orientation	Central focus on importance of student learning and the crucial role of the teacher
6. Performance-based assessment	Tied to clearly stated competencies	Reform effort driven by Performance-based assessment	Professional development connected to standards and performance assessment
7. Respectful tone and values	Emphasized nonanxious expectation and decency	Human values and credibility	Integrity of collaborators—*doing what you say you will do*; credibility within respective institutions
8. Family involvement	Shared responsibility for student	Community Outreach	Extending commitment to include parents and community
9. Shared decision making	Increased teacher control of areas for which they are responsible	Collaborative leadership and decision making	Agreed-upon goals that were bigger than the two institutions and a "quixotic" notion that the goals could be met

Table 12.1. (*continued*)

Restructured Schools Principles (Darling-Hammond, 1997)	Comments	Successful Collaboration Principles	Collaborators Comments
10. Commitment to diversity	Among students and staff	Structure without prescription	Flexible organization of professional development to meet diverse needs
11. Student choice in school selection		Teacher empowerment	Teacher–peer development at core of project
12. Budget targets aimed at reduced student load and shared planning time	At no more cost than regular school budgets; not as many administrators; different structures	Leverage diverse resources to meet the reform goals	An attitude that a project can be done no matter the obstacles
13. Personal attributes		Personal attributes	Extensive experience at all levels of education (20–40 years); ability to share load

Our Design

We followed several important principles of successful staff development (Norton & Gonzales, 1987) including providing training for teachers as close as possible to their classrooms, supporting monthly workshops, and providing continuous mentoring. We used the same software and hardware in the workshops that teachers and principals would be using in the schools. In fact, during this last year, all 125 La Clave teachers received their own computer for use in their classroom. Our design centered around building strong teacher and principal instructional technology teams in all seventeen schools. On each team, there were six teachers, a district curriculum facilitator, who was a teacher based at the school site, and a technology teacher. We also required all seventeen principals to attend monthly workshops in which they learned the same technology applications their teachers were learning only in the context of school administration.

In designing the model for the project, the technology needs of the district had to be balanced with the research orientation of the university toward technology-integrated instruction. The design and communication of the model was critical to receive support from district administrators and school board members. The involvement of teachers and principals simultaneously in learning technology integration established a campus culture of common knowledge and expertise. All principals, as well as other district administrators, were also brought together as a group to learn about specific applications of technology to administrative problems.

Another key to the reform was the use of curriculum facilitators who had already been working in the buildings on curriculum reform involving performance assessments and curriculum alignment. These instructional leaders were asked to become technology leaders. They embraced the use of technology and were an essential part of successful integration at the schools.

A well-developed professional development model in technology was used to provide technology workshops that built confidence and skill in the use of the tools while requiring all projects to be done within the district curriculum, which emphasized performance evaluation and the use of high standards. The workshops were designed to help teachers move from users of computers to producers and designers of classroom learning using technology. The monthly workshops and materials are available on the La Clave Web site (www.mathstar.nmsu.edu/gisd).

From Collaborators to Friends

Were There Any Changes in Our Roles over Time as Perceived by Each of Us?

Wiburg: We both enjoyed this collaborative project, and as we spent more and more time together, we became friends. During the second year of the project, I spent one day a week in the district working closely with teachers, principals, the superintendent, and the students. Joining me were a talented graduate student and Dr. Ana Huerta-Macías, the university colleague who helped design and implement the workshops.

Together with the Gadsden School District team, we built assessment tools for evaluating the impact of the project, including a pre– and post–self-assessment instrument and a hands-on performance assessment (which required a day in the fall and spring to complete). Interested in research that connects teacher change to student learning, we also connected items on the teacher performance assessment to student scores related to higher-level thinking on the district-mandated Tierra Nova standardized test. We are currently compiling these results.

When I went on sabbatical for a semester in 1999, Dr. Huerta-Macías took over much of my role for a few months. Huerta-Macías and I had worked together at the university for six years, developing courses that combined technology and methods of teaching English as a second language, and we had a similar commitment to working in the field.

At present, our collaborative leadership team has expanded in scope and depth to involve more players and more projects. As we began to build an educational reform effort involving technology, we needed human resources and additional financial support to complete the many and varied steps along the way. Early in the project, we collaborated with the RETA (Regional Educational Technology Assistance) Federal Challenge grant. A RETA teacher came to the district and worked with our student team, and RETA funding provided additional computers for all the teachers in the project. We are now partnering in two new university-initiated grants, a Preparing Tomorrow's Teachers to use Technology (PT3) grant and a Department of Education Star School's grant focusing on improving mathematics achievement in the middle school.

The university teacher education program recently committed to placing more student teachers in the district's schools and working with the district to build professional development schools. Both of us are playing on a larger stage, with Lozano working more and more at the state level and my own work with the university expanding into deeper involvement in more than one project with the district.

Although this is a success story in many ways, there are also potential problems when more players become involved in a change effort. Our concern is that we will forget our original goal of using technology to help teachers expand their instructional strategies and create rich learning environments for children and that ours will become a math or a teacher prep project. In addition, there are times when we miss working together on a smaller scale as we did when the project began. There was more time to plan and design than we have now.

Lozano: In this collaboration, we created a third role that was neither district nor university. Instead, our role was as a collaborative leadership team. We jointly developed goals and action plans for the La Clave grant initiatives. We asked questions together, such as, How will the classroom change if new technology and pedagogy are used well? We didn't spend a lot of time worrying about our respective roles as members of our institutions. At the same time, we soon discovered that it was important to understand what each of our institutions needed from the collaboration.

Problems with Our Institutions

Because we were so focused on what the teachers and kids needed and the excitement of the changes we were seeing, we sometimes forgot to communicate our actions to our respective institutions. When problems arose, it was usually because we temporarily forgot to keep in mind the different cultures of a university and a school district. School districts tend to work on the basis of what is working and what has worked based on experience and effort over time. Universities operate more on research-based practices and theories. A district is a much more hierarchical structure than the university, especially as it relates to the role of the professor, and it is important to go through all necessary channels and get buy-in from all layers of the school district organization. At the university, getting stakeholder buy-in is only necessary for large change efforts affecting the university as a whole, not for experimental work with teaching and learning. Professors are given more leeway in making their own instructional decisions than teachers are.

One time we simply forgot to ask the principals about a graduate class we planned to offer the teachers. This should have gone to principals and district officials before we passed out flyers to the teachers. Since then, we learned to meet with principals and the superintendent whenever we planned professional development opportunities.

At the same time tension increased with the school board as the technology initiative gained support. During the second year of the collaboration, the school board membership dramatically changed, and the members who had worked so hard to obtain funds to support the hardware acquisition and technology training were not reelected. The incoming board members questioned the expensive project when there were crucial needs for additional classrooms all over the district. Classrooms were so short that when the opportunity came to have full-day kindergarten, the district could not commit to the opportunity because of insufficient classroom space. This problem is common in poor districts in which the need for buildings, books, and other basic supplies make the acquisition of technology increasingly difficult, contributing to a growing digital divide. As Damarin (1998) reported, " inner city and poor rural districts can not provide *both . . . and* but must settle for *either . . . or.*" Yet our project somehow weathered this problem, perhaps because teachers were provided with personal computers and software and parents were invited to attend computer classes with their students. Or perhaps the project was already well in place before the change in the school board. Whatever the reason, the school board recently voted to continue with the use of teacher instructional leaders and the professional development work with teachers.

Negotiating Differences

How Did We Negotiate Roles and Responsibilities? How Did We Resolve Any Differences in Our Styles and Perspectives?

Wiburg: Lozano and I spent a lot of time talking and found the time to do this by engaging in shared activities, such as attending professional conferences together. I remember our spending three hours together one evening at a conference, examining in detail what would be the next step in moving professional development for teachers from the district level deeper into their classrooms. That night we developed an exemplary classroom model. In spring 2000, additional computers were given to those teachers who were recommended by their team as ready to integrate what they had learned about technology into their daily teaching.

We also learned to recognize our special strengths. I was good at conceptualizing the big picture and providing a research base for our work. Lozano was good at planning the detailed work required to accomplish our goals. She would often say that the power was in the details. She had a reputations for always following through on her intentions and for not being willing to *just go away*. The district had become used to administrators coming and going, and she was a new kind of leader for many of the district staff. Teachers began to trust Lozano and count on that fact that she would do what she said she would. Teachers received well-organized and sequential training over two years and received personal computers and software. At the same time, some school board members and administrators who wanted to keep things the way they always had been became uncomfortable.

Lozano: We became increasingly sensitive to the culture and constraints of each other's institutions. We solved challenges to our reform effort by focusing on the state mandate given to the district that we improve our test scores and by pointing to the agreements we had made with the state in accepting the technology grants. The focus was the improvement of learning for district students through the use of technology and professional development. We focused our institutions and our critics on the problem we were trying to solve (poor achievement in a poor district) and the need for the district and the university to work together to help solve these challenges.

What was really important was that this collaboration became a person-to-person effort rather than a district-to-university collaboration. One of the factors in successful collaboration is being able to have a person-to-person relationship. Another has to do with human values and credibility, specifically integrity and the ability to trust that each partner would do what we said we would do. We respected each other and were respected within our own institutions. As we worked together doing what we said we would do, people from both institutions supported our work.

Additional Dynamics

What Dynamics Did We Identify That Existed within Our Partnership and within Others Involved in the Project That Either Supported or Hindered Moving the Project Forward?

As mentioned previously, we were fortunate to have strong support among colleagues at both the university and in the district. The district instructional technology coordinator had completed a master's degree in learning technologies at the university, and many of the district teachers, especially those in instructional leader positions, had taken the master's classes offered on-site. Some also had enrolled in the masters program at the university. All of the players on both teams were committed to the project and to hard work. They all had a sense of humor and a high level of persistence. In addition, we just plain enjoyed working together.

Lozano: The primary hindrance to the relationship came more from the district than from the university in this project. It was necessary for us to take a larger systems perspective to understand and deal with much of the resistance to the change we were implementing. The resistance we encountered needs to be understood within the unique sociocultural context described earlier in this chapter. The university and administrators from outside had come and gone over the years, leaving little impact. As we began to build sustainable teacher teams and provide those teachers with personal computers and resources, things began to change. Some worried that we did too much technology and didn't provide enough support for academics or bilingual education. At different times, we both grew discouraged with some of the criticisms. One school board member suggested we should spend as much money teaching about reading as we spent on teaching technology. What these people didn't realize was that technology had always been a tool to improve teaching and learning. We used technology as a catalyst to help teachers think differently about their practice as they redesigned instruction to include more projects and culturally responsive teaching (González, Macías, & Tinajero, 1998).

It was our friendship and our extensive experience that helped during these times (factor 13 in our list of factors for successful collaboration). We took turns sometimes carrying on, with one person doing most of the work for a period and then the other doing the major part of the work in another period. In this way, one of us always kept the project going. We took turns writing reports and planning workshops. We talked when we were discouraged and looked at things from a system perspective, not from a personal one.

In Conclusion

What Elements Contributed to Our Sustained Involvement and Interest in the Project? What Was the Role of Our Colleagues and Supervisors in Sustaining Our Involvement in This Work?

Our collaboration has continued to grow. As of this writing, we are working together with a third faculty member, Dr. Cathy Zozakiewicz, who directs student teaching at the university. Next year, preservice teachers will begin to work in the classrooms of the La Clave technology team teachers. For the first time, we are now talking about ensuring that the same strategies taught in methods classes could be collaboratively developed by both institutions and used by the cooperating teacher and student teacher to design learning together. We are offering workshops on mentoring new teachers in the district and inviting master teachers from the district to come teach with us at the university. As to the La Clave technology initiative, we think that by the end of next year, this change effort will be well enough in place that teachers will continue to use technology for teaching and learning long after we are gone.

What were the most important variables in the success of this collaboration? The following are the key factors: a school district under a state mandate to improve test scores; a high-level district administrator who has been given authority by the superintendent to reform the instructional; a university professor with public school experience as a teacher and administrator who comes from a university department committed to field-based change research in a border area; a grant from the state technology fund to help the district use technology as part of solving learning problems; and a project located in a rural valley that wants to keep things how they've always been, at least to some extent.

This is the context in which we successfully developed an expanding university–public school collaborative leadership team. As we reflected on leadership within the context of restructuring schools, we were excited to find that many of the principles of successful collaboration aligned remarkably well with the principles of restructuring, as can be seen in the last two columns of Table 12.1. Our collaboration was based on (a) a shared vision of systemic change; (b) an commitment to high-quality standards; (c) an ability to work with diverse players; (d) a person-to-person relationship possible in a smaller district; (d) a focus on teachers and students; (e) an orientation toward performance-based assessment; (f) respect and credibility with each other and in our institutions; (g) a view of education as community based; (h) agreed-upon goals and shared decision making; (i) a commitment to valuing diversity; (j) teacher empowerment as key to student learning; and (k) an ability to leverage budgets and resources to meet reform goals. The final factor we listed in the table was our personal attributes. We became friends who shared the work of implementing a change project, and together we had more than sixty years of experience at all levels of education from K-12 through the university.

All of these factors need to be considered, but we think it is also the collaborative nature of the leadership that mattered. Although this leadership was founded in shared beliefs about how teachers and students learn and how one can facilitate systemic change, it may also have been influenced by the institutions from which each of us came. The professor provided a research-based perspective on schooling and learning, and the experienced administrator could take our shared vision and operationalize it all the way down to the smallest necessary details.

References

Damarin, S. (1998). Technology and multicultural education: The question of convergence. In A. DeVancey (Ed.), *Technology and the Culture of Classrooms. Theory into Practice* [special issue], *37*(1).

Darling-Hammond, L. (1997). *The right to learn.* San Francisco: Jossey-Bass.

Eisner, E. (1998). *The kind of schools we need.* Portsmouth, NH: Heinemann

Fullan, M. (1995). *The new meaning of educational change.* New York: Teachers College Press.

González, M. L., Huerta-Macías, A., Tinajero, J. V. (1998). *Educating Latino students: A guide to successful practice.* Lancaster, PA: Technomics.

Norton, P., & González, C. (1998). Regional Educational Technology Assistance Initiative—Phase II: Evaluating a model for statewide professional development. *Journal of Research on Computing in Education, 31*, 25–48.

Ritchie, D., & Wiburg, K. (1994). Factors influencing successful integration of technology in schools. *Journal of Technology and Teacher Education, 2*(2), 143–153.

Stafford-Levy, M., & Wiburg, K. (2000). Multicultural technology integration: The winds of change amid the sands of time. *Computers in the Schools, 6*, 121–134.

Wetzel, K., & Chisholm, I. (1998). An evaluation of technology integration in teacher education for bilingual and English as a second language education majors. *Journal of Research on Computing in Education, 30*(4), 379–397

Wiburg, K. (1997). The dance of change: Integrating technology in the classrooms. *Computers in the Schools, 13*, 171–183.

Wiburg, K. (1998). Literacy instruction for middle school for Latinos. In González, L., Huerta-Marcía, A., & Tinajero, J. V. *Educating Latino students: A guide to successful practice* (pp. 269–287). Lancaster, PA: Technomics.

Wilburg, K., Montaya, N., and Sandin, J. (1999). *Nuestra Tierra: A University/Public School Technology Integration Project, 21*, pp. 183-219.

Model III

One-to-One Collaborations

A university faculty member works as equal partner with a school-based practitioner in this model. Both partners plan and carry out the research project.

Chapter

The Dialectic Nature of Research Collaborations: The Relational Literacy Curriculum

Ruth Freedman and Diane Salmon

Individual researchers form collaborations for a variety of reasons, and then these collaborative relationships may take on a life of their own. In this chapter, we share the story of how one collaborative research partnership evolved. The Relational Literacy Curriculum (Salmon & Freedman, in press) was developed through the collaboration of a school-based practitioner and a university faculty member, each with different areas of interest and expertise, one in literacy and one in the psychology of relationships. Through our shared and equal partnership, we developed, implemented, and evaluated this curriculum during a six-year professional and personal relationship. In assuming this collaboration, we began a simple professional partnership, yet more than six years later the collaboration has grown beyond its original definition, and the professional and personal relationship continues.

A Collaborative Relationship

As collaborators, we have always seen ourselves as equal, and we place value on this important equality in our partnership. Our collaboration is based on two knowledgeable individuals with distinct, primary expertise in two domains, one academic (literacy) and one less so ("relationships"). In addition, our collaboration is based on the notion that as educators, although we have different expertise, we share a conceptual model and a value system with respect to our assumptions about thinking and learning. The combination of our diverse domain knowledge and our shared assumptions is the basis for our research project and collaboration. As with any healthy relationship, we have an appreciation and understanding of different expertise while sharing a strong conceptual framework. Our accomplishment was greater than either individual could have achieved on her own. We have developed a curriculum that blends a traditional academic domain (literacy) with efforts to foster greater relational competence.

Similar to the one-to-one partnerships developed through centers such as National-Louis University's Center for Collaborative Research, we spent six years working together to develop our curriculum. Our collaboration follows the model of Goodlad (1988), in which practitioner and researcher have a symbiotic relationship and information flows in a two-directional pattern. We had shared values and a shared framework, as well as complementary expertise and goals. Ruth, the classroom teacher and researcher, had the context and the situated problems and knowledge with respect to friendship, whereas Diane, the university-based researcher, had the process and the abstract principles with respect to friendship. The bonus has become the curriculum, which we collaboratively developed, as well as a very special friendship. This curriculum is a link between relationships and literacy, and it is powerful because of our shared, collaborative relationship nurtured over time.

Ruth's Initial Motivation

As a teacher with more than seven years of teaching experience, a master's degree, and some further postgraduate educational work, I found myself, in the spring of 1993, with a group of third-grade girls struggling through a wide range of complex social issues. Parents of the children in my classroom were making requests in relation to this group. After extensive work, I had exhausted my personal expertise to deal with this challenging situation. I began to seek outside support to facilitate a resolution to the conflicts in my classroom, just as I might with any curriculum concern. Being a member of a university community, I turned to a colleague within the college who, I was aware, had expertise in the area of "relationships." After consultation with Dr. Diane Salmon, she began to work with my students, implementing a social problem-solving process during lunchtime with minimal teacher involvement.

After observing the work Diane completed with my children and through shared discourse, we determined that a process working with my students about relationship issues could best be implemented through a collaborative process involving Diane and myself. In our collaboration, Diane could bring her considerable expertise in the area of relationships, human development, and learning, whereas I could bring my understanding of curriculum theory, daily classroom life, and contextual information about my students. Although my primary motivation was to resolve the social issues present in my classroom, I did sense other possibilities. As part of my commitments at the University Lab School, I felt that involvement in a collaborative research project would be a good undertaking to pursue, and Diane's interests were appealing to me as a classroom teacher. I knew my colleagues and administrators at the university would fully support my activities.

Diane's Initial Motivation

As a school psychology professor, I had been involved in a clinic-based program for children with difficult friendships for several years. The program focused on social problem-solving skills through discussion, role play, and goal setting. I had become dissatisfied with the decontextualized nature of the clinic work, however. Although the children in these "friendship groups" had learned skills and experienced themselves in a positive social group, I knew they returned to complex classroom and playground dynamics in their school lives. I knew that to have real change, I would need to involve their classmates in an ongoing way. I had also come to believe that a child's ability to make and keep friends didn't reside solely within the child, but was also distributed throughout his or her social context and depended on the social processes encouraged there. I believed it was important to involve teachers in supporting children's relational understanding and growth.

I wanted to further develop the principles I believed to be important in supporting children's relational growth and contextualize these principles in a useful and flexible classroom curricular process. I hoped to find a teacher with needs and an interest in experimenting with the possibilities. In my initial contacts with Ruth, I felt the potential for a generative collaboration. She was a master teacher, whose classroom exemplified many of the principles I valued and taught to graduate students. Ruth quickly understood the significance of the theory and research on friendship and the development of children's friendships for classroom community life. As we explored our shared and complementary frameworks, a powerful cycle of experimentation and learning began.

The Collaboration Becomes a True, Shared Partnership

Following the consultation period, we formed a more formal research collaboration and began our exploration into the social problem-solving process and the subsequent development of the Relational Literacy Curriculum (Salmon & Freedman, in press). We realized that we wanted to take a proactive stance toward social relationships and place them into the foreground of the classroom curriculum thus providing students with experiences in working through social problems. In such a process, they would gain access to multiple perspectives about relationships and elaborate their constructs about friendships. Ruth's implicit knowledge was woven together with Diane's explicit knowledge, and new expertise emerged for both of us.

Our six-year research process involved a multilayered sequence of events. Along the way, we have both gained many insights about relational literacy, about friendship, about ourselves, and about the students with whom we worked. When this process began, we were two individuals with a shared interest in developing and implementing a classroom social problem-solving curriculum. We both knew that we would learn from each other about children's friendships and the classroom social problem-solving process. We began with Diane as the prominent leader during the process, moved to a more shared model, and finally to a place where Ruth took ownership of the process. Each of us has grown professionally and personally and has developed a broader perspective about classroom curriculum through sharing with one another. Together we have shared a range of educational theories through reading, writing, and discourse. Ruth has influenced the process with her background in language and literacy; Diane has contributed her expertise in cognitive theories and social psychology. Finally, we learned a great deal about children's friendships and about a true collaboration.

What is unusual about our story of collaboration are the things we did not expect to happen. As two educational professionals, we created an incredible opportunity to share in a mutual learning process over a six-year period. Each of us has been an expert, and each of us has been a novice. At different times along the way, one of us has taken the lead within the work, and the other has been a follower. We have brought our own strengths in our own discipline and worked to honor one another. Throughout our research process, we have had incredible mutual respect for our individual domains of expertise. The research process has been a supportive project in which we each carry the strengths and challenges of the other. In this way, we have created and developed a balanced team that is based on our mutual areas of expertise and personal strengths and weaknesses. Over the past six years, we have become a team and totally interdependent.

As researchers, we have worked hard to explore and discover new ideas about children's friendships, specifically as the children constructed meaning during the social problem-solving process. At the same time, we have learned about friendship through a sharing of our own personal lives. Our work has been enriched by a true collaboration on both a personal and a professional level. We each hold the other in high esteem as both an educational professional and as a personal friend.

The Relational Literacy Curriculum

Through our research project, we have developed the Relational Literacy Curriculum. The goals of the curriculum address both individual and classroom social developmental needs. The goals are

- to help individual children elaborate and refine their understanding of friendship and other classroom relationships,

- to help children develop a language with which to share and clarify their social experiences,

- to provide a process through which children can articulate, explore, and critique group norms, and

- to foster independent problem-solving strategies.

The basic process involves a two-week cycle of problem solving and role playing around stories of social problems familiar to students. Stories are constructed that reflect events likely to occur between friends in the classroom and that represent tensions associated with the maintenance of friendships (Rawlins, 1992). Rawlins identified four dialectic tensions that characterize interactional challenges between close friends. Independence–dependence highlights the voluntary nature of friendship in this culture. In middle childhood, problem situations involving this tension are often about one friend's shifting interests or a friend's concern for the incorporation of new children within the play. Expressiveness–protectiveness refers to the delicate balance between openly communicating one's feelings and needs and strategically protecting oneself or the feelings of the other. Problem scenarios depicting "bossy" or overly aggressive friends are typical examples of this tension. Judgment–acceptance refers to the tension between being evaluated and held to some standard by a friend versus being largely accepted for who one is. Situations among middle-childhood students that reflect this tension usually involve exclusion, rejection, and teasing. Instrumentality–affection describes the tension between spending time with friends because we like them and spending time with friends because of their usefulness to us. An example of a dilemma reflecting this tension for middle-childhood students would involve one friend playing with another only for his or her toys or valued skills. These four tensions serve as the background framework for enriching children's understanding of relationships.

Goals of the Chapter

The goals of this chapter are to tell our story as constructed through this unique interdisciplinary collaboration. We attempt to share a description of how we collaboratively evolved the curriculum over the past six years and how each of us took on particular roles during this time period. Our story reflects the evolution of a curriculum through shared episodes and dual interpretation. We describe the important phases we see in our relationship and work over this time period. Through the use of Rawlins's (1992) four tensions, we highlight the different dimensions of our collaborative relationship and our research process. The reader will understand how each of our thinking processes, educational perspectives, learning styles, and personalities have complemented the other and made the curriculum and the research more thoughtful and rigorous. Thus, a research partnership and close friendship has been born through more than six years of professional and personal collaboration.

Research Phases and Rawlins's Tensions

As we reflected over the course of our collaborative relationship, it became clear to us that during the course of the research, we seemed to move through particular phases with respect to our individual roles within the research. These had unique phases, which could be related to one of Rawlins's (1992) dialectic tensions. We saw the use of these tensions as a powerful framework for exploring the evolution of our research collaboration.

One way of characterizing relationships for both children and adults is in terms of the tensions that tend to arise. Conflict is a natural part of any relationship or collaboration. Through in-depth interviews with adults, Rawlins identified four dialectic tensions that characterize communications among friends and potential sources of conflict in these relationships. Rawlins provided a particularly useful framework for understanding the challenges inherent in maintaining friendships or other kinds of relationships. Our six-year collaboration or any research collaboration is a relationship that must maintain itself through a varied set of events and conflicts. Keeping in mind the nature of all relationships, we use these tensions to frame our six-year collaboration to give the reader a sense of our evolution.

Table 13.1 provides an overview of the phases of our collaboration. We first defined these phases in terms of the primary research tasks: initiating contact, beginning research, consolidating research, and expanding and disseminating research. We further describe them in terms of the primary contexts, our roles, and the nature of our goals in each phase. As we branch out from the initial classroom research context, our roles and goals in relation to each other converge. Finally, we characterize each phase as a relational process in which one of the four dialectic tensions described by Rawlins summarizes the nature of our interactions. The primary tension we negotiated in each phase was different, illustrating the relational process our collaboration involved. The final column of our table elaborates on each relational tension by indicating the more specific issues we had to negotiate. We more fully describe these in the subsequent sections of the chapter.

Table 13.1. Overview of Our Collaboration as a Relational Process

Primary Research Tasks	Primary Context of Relationship	Primary Roles within the Relationship	Goal Structure within the Relationship	Primary Relational Tension	Primary Relational Issues Negotiated
Initiating contact	Teacher's classroom	Classroom teacher/ university researcher	Distinct but complementary goals	Instrumentality –Affection	Determining how our individual goals and needs can be met
Beginning research efforts	Teacher's classroom	Classroom teacher/ university researcher	Distinct but complementary goals	Judgment –Acceptance	Exploring standards for and constraints on the relationship; evolving sense of mutual trust
Consolidating research program	Teacher's classroom to home offices	Coresearchers/ Coteachers	Evolving shared goals	Independence– Dependence	Renegotiating roles; evolving greater interdependency
Expanding and disseminating research	University and other teachers' classrooms	Coresearchers	Elaborating shared goals	Expressive– Protective	Negotiating new personal boundaries; redefining quality of relational space

The Initiation of the Collaboration: Understanding Instrumentality and Affection

As we reflect across our six years of collaboration, the story begins and ends with a reflection on the dialectic tension of instrumentality and affection. The dialectic of instrumentality–affection describes the tension between spending time with another because of his or her usefulness versus spending time with another because it was enjoyable to do so. Although this tension was not particularly salient for the children in the classrooms with which we conducted our research, it is probably the central tension for this and many other collaborative relationships.

For both of us as researchers, this relationship was initially based on a professional need or goal: One of us needed to resolve classroom social conflicts, and the other one was looking to expand her work in the area of classroom friendships and relationships. There was clearly an instrumental quality to the collaboration at this point. Ruth was very much interested in the research process for the purpose of resolving social problems in her classroom and eliminating some of the stress she was feeling within the social domain of her curriculum. She believed a partnership with Diane would resolve this and improve and elaborate her teaching. Diane, on the other hand, had a stronger research agenda and really wanted to elaborate her work and intellectually develop the theories behind her "friendship groups." At the initiation of the project, each of us, in our own way, was using the instrument of the project and collaboration to achieve our own goals.

Phase I of the Collaboration—Classroom Teacher and Educational Researcher Collaborate: Negotiating the Dialectic Tension of Judgment and Acceptance

We describe the first and second year of our collaboration as the time in the relationship in which two distinct roles were played by each of us in the collaboration. Ruth saw herself as a classroom teacher, and Diane saw herself as an educational researcher. The period represented a time when Diane was looking for a good and successful research collaboration, whereas Ruth was looking for the value of the curriculum. In addition, each of us was interested in the relationship that was evolving as part of the collaboration. The dominant tension was the dialectic of judgment–acceptance, which refers to the tension between evaluating and holding the other to some standard versus largely accepting the other for whom he or she is. This dialectic articulates the tension involved in building trust within a relationship.

During the early stages of the research process, Diane took a leading role. She obviously had the expertise when it came to all of the theoretical knowledge and how this would influence the development of the Relational Literacy Curriculum. In addition, Diane seemed to be the one conducting most of the research. She developed much of the research design we used at this point in the research, from selecting the research to the collection of data. She did all of the writing during this first phase. Diane was dominant in collecting the data, transcribing the data, and organizing the structure of the research project. For each week, she would prepare the materials for the students, including the stories. It seemed that Diane devoted far more time and resources to the project in these early years. She had a student researcher and spent far more time debriefing the first year with this student. Although she was orchestrating the research, she was very careful to respect the needs and expertise of her partner. Ruth felt that her contributions were more related to the context of her classroom and, specifically, what she knew about second- and third-grade children and their learning.

Early on in any relationship, the tension of acceptance–judgment can play a key role in the developing relationship. This was very much the case for us. As Diane took the lead in so much of the work, Ruth often felt as if she were not carrying her weight and that Diane was judging her for contributing less to the work. For Diane, there seemed to be a considerable concern for her about judging the value of each person's contribution. Ruth was concerned that her commitment was being judged and that her style of writing was less effective because it was different from Diane's. As the first phase evolved, Ruth became more comfortable with the roles both partners took and the contributions and their relative importance. Ruth also felt judged in relationship to her teaching about whether Diane was making judgments about her perceived domain of expertise, the classroom. Diane would spend time in Ruth's classroom observing and learning about her teaching. Deep down, Ruth wanted Diane to judge her teaching and expertise very positively and in an approving manner.

For Diane there were different issues associated with the dialectic challenge of judgment–acceptance. A dominant struggle for Diane was the struggle for resources and an equal sharing of those resources. She felt particularly troubled by the sharing of time, which often manifested in a feeling that Ruth wasn't sharing an equal commitment to the project. This feeling emerged when Ruth would cancel sessions in her classroom or change a meeting time. Diane judged this as a lack of interest on Ruth's part rather than Ruth's efforts to balance the needs she had as a classroom teacher to those as an emerging researcher. Diane felt judged herself in different ways that Ruth didn't value. Diane's time and energy were also important, but she did not feel valued. She gradually began to be less judging and understood that there were different demands on Ruth as a classroom teacher; Ruth's issues with her own time and the classroom time were part of differing roles. Gradually, Diane grew toward a greater acceptance of the limitations of Ruth's role while she was also teaching. A second set of struggles for Diane centered on how she felt judged in small ways around the "teacher role" she played in the classroom while implementing the relational curriculum. For example, she was not used to printing for second and third graders, and they were sometimes not able to read her writing. At other times, she needed support in managing the children's behavior.

Throughout the first phase, we gradually began to accept each other's strengths and weaknesses and not be so judgmental or feel so judged. We learned to balance each other in important ways. Each of us found balanced roles within the curriculum and research processes, such as Ruth managing children and the pacing of the curriculum, and Diane drawing on the principles of the curriculum to prompt deeper discussions. As the phase evolved, Ruth began to feel more empowered by the curriculum because she felt she was beginning to understand it and was able to implement it more successfully. As Ruth took more ownership of the research collaboration, Diane became more comfortable with her role as the lead researcher and writer.

Over the past six years, we have had to learn to accept our differences in the work mode and accept that each of us works differently. As we learned about the different ways we work, we negotiated the meanings of these differences. There were times of judging or feeling judged and other times of accepting and honoring the differences. It is our belief that as a relationship grows, as the tension of instrumentality–affection becomes more of a balance, it is easier to balance the judgment–acceptance tension. There is more safety in the interactions, and therefore a judging statement is more accepted. Collaborators can share their struggles with the other person so that both people grow in the relationship.

Phase II of the Collaboration—Coresearchers/Coteachers: Negotiating Independence–Dependence: Evolving a Set of Shared Goals

As we reflected on our third and fourth year of the collaboration, our relationship changed and developed. During this two-year period, we found ourselves sharing one another's roles and therefore taking on the roles of coresearcher/coteacher. In taking on one another's roles, we eventually felt more confident and internalized these new roles. Diane developed expert knowledge about being the teacher during the process and its critical features, and Ruth took on more responsibilities as a researcher and a partner.

Where the dialectic tension of judgment–acceptance dominated years one and two, the dialectic tension of independence–dependence dominated the next phase of the research, years three and four. The dialectic of independence–dependence highlights the voluntary nature of friendship. It refers to ones' needs to feel free to pursue his or her individual interests and simultaneously to remain available to each other to sustain the relationship. As the two of us assumed one another's roles, there was a natural growth and focus in the relationship with respect to the independence–dependence tension.

Although there were challenges related to this tension during the first few years of our work together, specifically trying to understand the needs and roles of one another, it played a major role during the second phase of our work. In the beginning, we had clear realms of control and decision making as well. Diane tended to call the shots from the research point of view and Ruth from the classroom context vantage point. We seemed to operate independently in those realms, coming together to address our separate goals. Diane was dependent on Ruth's willingness and openness with her classroom for the research. Ruth needed to share or give up some of her independence in running her classroom. She felt many demands within the classroom. Over time, Diane grew to understand the needs and challenges that anyone teaching a classroom of children faces, as well as the needs of multiple curriculum demands. At the same time, Ruth felt very dependent on the expertise Diane brought to the project and her writing and research; this made her feel overly dependent on Diane. Over time, she began to take on more responsibilities and feel more independent in the research domain.

This tension also can be illustrated in the shifting responsibilities, which occurred throughout the length of the project. Diane began as the dominate leader with the process, but over time Ruth took on far more leadership with the process when working with the children in the classroom. Diane later found a different role to play in the process component of our work together. Initially, Diane took far more leadership with respect to the research process, but then at a later point, Ruth played a stronger leadership role in the research process. As Ruth began to engage in other research independent of this project, she felt more empowered in the research domain.

There was ultimately a renegotiating of our roles. Over time, our individual goals became less distinct. We developed a new set of shared goals that created a healthy interdependence. Together we knew the curriculum we had cocreated, and we knew what and why we were doing in the classroom. We had developed new and shared expertise. We knew what we wanted to happen with other teachers. There had been a shifting of roles and responsibilities that we had been able to successfully negotiate.

That is not to say that over time there were not conflicts over who had primary responsibilities for what. As we worked through issues of judgment and acceptance, we more
confidently negotiated tensions related to our interdependence. There were clearly
times when Diane felt a heavier burden as the primary researcher when Ruth felt con-
sumed by the elements of her teaching job. Ruth always felt that she contributed her
knowledge and intellectual expertise to the collaboration and that Diane accepted this.
Diane valued the teacher's contribution and recognized the differing nature of a professor's life and that of a classroom teacher. There were many reasons why we were
able to make this work so effectively. Diane's ability to acknowledge and honor the insights and thoughts of Ruth as the classroom teacher was critical at this time. She truly
valued the unique insights that teachers bring to the research collaboration, and this
was a great strength. In addition, we began to recognize the different strengths we each
brought to the process and use them as a benefit rather than as a challenge.

This is possibly the most successful tension we negotiated. It links our shared and
complementary expertise and goals and was where we really developed in our collaborative relationship. Over time, we were able to appropriate expertise from one another
and create a new hybrid. In addition, we also appropriated each other's goals and developed shared goals. So those aspects of our distinctness became truly shared, and a
healthy interdependence grew. Thus, the critical element here is that each of us came to
the research relationship with strong independent expertise. This allowed for a healthy
interdependent collaborative research relationship to develop. We were confident in
our own areas of expertise and could allow the other to state strong opinions and beliefs
and then negotiate them.

We began this two-year period with some distinctive independent roles and a
strong dependence on one another. At the end of four years of collaboration, we had
truly developed an interdependence in which each of us contributed important elements critical to the project. But it was the nature of each of our distinct roles and expertise that proved to nurture the reliance we felt for each other's expertise. We had
developed a strong interdependence, and we knew that the strength of the project and
all the collaborative activities were in our interconnectedness.

Phase III of the Collaboration—Coresearchers: Negotiating the Tension of Expressive and Protective

As we entered into the fifth and sixth year of our research collaboration, many
elements of our work and our roles shifted. Each of us took on new and different projects, which had a profound effect on our work together. During this period, Ruth left
her classroom for a year of sabbatical, as did Diane. For Ruth, spending her first year in
more than fourteen away from children presented many new and profound shifts. As
she truly became a co-researcher without a classroom to fall back on, she tried to understand her new role. Diane was also spending her year in a different context and exploring new opportunities. For the two of us together, there were no longer any
identifiable separate roles as we got involved in writing during our sabbatical year and
a grant proposal to take our collaborative work to other classroom teachers.

As the distinction in our roles was eliminated, we also began to spend considerably more time together involved in tasks such as analyzing our data, grant writing, and
research, and new challenges emerged within the relationship. This two-year period
was dominated by the tension of expressiveness–protectiveness as we tried to work

much more closely together without distinct spheres of control. The dialectic of expressiveness–protectiveness refers to the delicate balance between communicating one's feelings and needs and strategically protecting oneself or the feelings of others. As relationships grow, there becomes a greater need to express one's feelings, yet the need to protect the other grows as well.

The next two years presented many different challenges for both of us. During our sabbatical year, we attempted to work through many changes in our own research and our personal and professional lives. We attempted to find a publisher to publish our work and determine exactly the type of book we wanted to publish. Tensions arose as we explored our differing needs in respect to the publishing task. The expression of these needs presented new challenges. During the sixth year, we applied for and received funding for a grant and began to implement the Relational Literacy Curriculum with three new teachers in a new school context. During this phase, we took on new roles, which continued to involve the evolution of our relationship together.

Challenges within the expressive–protective tension were evident from the time when we started to work together. From the onset of our research collaboration, this was the tension that presented us with the greatest challenges. The way in which things were communicated between us was often complicated. Ruth found it a great struggle to be protective when she was feeling the need to express her feelings. On the other hand, Diane felt overwhelmed with the directness of Ruth's communications. She was less comfortable with asserting her thoughts and frustrations directly to Ruth. Ruth's nature is to be more expressive, whereas Diane had the tendency for protectiveness, and this presented many challenges for us. These challenges were particularly highlighted during these two years of intense research and writing. During the first four years, we worked together on a weekly basis for one to two hours; during these two years, we often spent entire days together analyzing our research and discussing the work in general. As Ruth left the classroom, she spent far more time writing and doing research. As a researcher, the changing role in her own life and with respect to the work challenged her. For Diane, there were shifts as she worked more intensely with Ruth, and they tried to negotiate their respective roles.

Even at the end of six years, although Ruth is still more expressive and less protective of Diane, she has learned to be more sensitive to this. As the relationship–friendship grew and there was true affection between them, Ruth found being protective of Diane to be more natural. She learned to hear Diane's voice and temper her own. Over time, Diane has developed and changed in respect to this tension. In the process of negotiating what we have been doing, she has learned that she needed to be more direct, and that this was all right. She learned to feel less threatened with the direct feedback from Ruth. For Diane, what might have felt like a confrontation in the past now felt less so.

Although we have made tremendous progress working through this dialectic tension, challenges continue to exist. As we continue to add new dimensions within our personal life and our work together, there are inevitably new challenges to face. As we work to meet new concerns, we work through elements of this dialectic tension. The complexity of a growing relationship highlights the tension of expressiveness–protectiveness for the two of us.

Instrumentality–Affection Revisited

As we reflect on where the collaboration is today, we realize the collaboration has taken on a life of its own, and the tension of instrumentality–affection again is a central theme. A relationship has formed that will remain long after the research questions have been exhausted. The ending of the story is quite different from the beginning in terms of instrumentality–affection. Clearly, as we negotiated the other tensions in the course of this collaboration, we redefined the nature of our relationship. It is now more heavily based on affection rather than the instrumental goals , which is reflected in the ways we work. We meet and sometimes spend very little time on work. The need to process our personal lives and to support each other with whatever is going on take center stage. This has become primary, and the work gets done second. Often, the research discussion comes after a period of update about our personal lives.

At the end of six years, the research remains, and the usefulness of our relationship is intertwined with true affection and a new friendship. There could be many aspects of our friendship shared as we become balanced in this tension. As with any relationship, we continue to struggle with aspects of each of the four tensions. That is an ongoing, ever-evolving part of any true friendship. Because we have developed a strong friendship, we continue to reflect on our collaboration, and we think we have often been deliberate about using the tensions to explore our collaborative struggles. Through our work, we have extended our lives and shared our research and personal beginnings and endings.

Summary of Our Collaborative Process

We explored our research collaboration as a relational process using Rawlins's dialectic tensions framework. As we reflected on our experience and the evolution of our work, we noted that each of these tensions dominated our relationship at different times. They seemed associated with our primary research tasks, the nature of our roles, the context, and our goals.

In initiating the research, it was significant to have distinct but complementary goals and expertise. This resulted in a strong motivation for both of us to pursue the collaboration. Clearly our professional collaboration began as instrumental to elaborating each of our individual professional pursuits.

As we began the research, additional issues arose. We needed to negotiate the standards to which we held one another and to learn to accept each other's limitations. This was one of the most sensitive times in the evolution of our collaboration. Had we not resolved the judgment–acceptance tension successfully, we may not have pursued the research to the same degree. As it turned out, this phase of our collaboration resulted in a strong sense of mutual trust.

We moved on to consolidate our work and conceptualize a research program by defining additional writing projects and exploring other contexts in which to work. In doing so, we needed to renegotiate our roles and evolve a shared set of goals. We no longer had distinct spheres of influence but worked interdependently within the same spheres. In renegotiating the independence–dependence tension, we each, to some degree, appropriated the other's goals and expertise.

As we worked interdependently in the final phase of expanding and disseminating our work, we became faced with negotiating more personal tensions in our relationship. For us, achieving a mutual balance with the expressive–protective tension was key. Our styles of disclosure were quite different. We had to make these differences explicit to one another and consciously achieve a comfortable balance for each of us. In successfully negotiating these more personal tensions, we deepened our relationship. Indeed, our research collaboration was transformed into a true friendship.

Implications for Practice and Research

We found the dialectic tension framework extremely useful in defining the nature of our collaboration. The tensions provided a tool for characterizing the quality and focus of the interactions within our relationship. In this regard, they helped us to "see" the relationship as a whole. Such a framework may prove useful in exploring and understanding other collaborations for different purposes.

On a practical note, the tensions framework may prove useful in helping professionals in collaboration to "diagnose" problems or conflicts they are experiencing in their working relationships. Specifically, we found this framework to help prevent instances of "blaming the other." The dialectic tension orientation allows a focus on the dynamics involved encouraging one to a focus on the interactions and how each contributes to them. At the same time this orientation discourages a focus on either the self or the other in isolation. If partners can step back and look at the dominant tension in their interactions, they gain a broader, more dynamic perspective in resolving and moving forward with the issues in their collaboration.

A second recommendation from our experience would be for potential collaborators to attend to issues of judgment and acceptance within their relationship. Collaborators may want to discuss and clarify several questions before they start their work together. For example: What expectations does each collaborator hold for the other? What does each collaborator expect of himself or herself? What kind of standards for working do collaborators wish to hold? How might each collaborator need to adjust these expectations and standards as he or she learns about his or her own and the other's limitations? In our work, these issues were extremely important to address in a timely and sensitive fashion. They are likely to surface early in a collaboration and must be successfully negotiated for the collaboration to proceed and deepen.

The dialectic tension framework may be useful in defining future research questions regarding collaborative work. For example, we found our collaboration to have a distinct evolution. Is it possible that other professional collaborations have a similar evolution? Would it be useful to describe collaboration as having a developmental phase structure? From our experience, we speculated that professional collaborations are likely to begin with an instrumental quality and to require the negotiation of acceptance–judgment issues. Moreover, successful negotiation of the judgment–acceptance tension may be crucial to establish more long-term collaborations. We further speculated that negotiating the independence–dependence tension would be necessary to deepening and expanding the collaboration and the work that is generated from it. In negotiating this tension, there is a true interchange of the professional selves and a new hybrid created.

Further research might also explore the unique qualities of various collaborative relationships. That is, the tensions could provide a framework for capturing variations in collaboration. How are issues of judgment–acceptance and independence–dependence experienced in other collaborative relationships? How are they negotiated and resolved? What happens when a balance is not achieved? What implications would this have for mentoring others in collaborative work?

Clearly the dialectic tensions framework provides a vehicle for examining relationships (Baxter, 1993; Baxter & Montgomery, 1996; Rawlins, 1992). Moreover, the tensions offer a promising conceptual tool to enhance our understanding of the nature of collaboration. They suggest a way of capturing complex relational dynamics and the shared meaning systems they spawn (Dixon & Duck, 1993). In this way, the dialectic tension framework can help us study collaborative professional relationships—both their variations and their similarities.

References

Baxter, L. (1993). The social side of personal relationships: A dialectic perspective. In S. Duck (Ed.), *Social context and relationships* (pp. 139–165). Newbury Park, CA: Sage.

Baxter, L., & Montgomery, B. (1996). *Relating. Dialogues and dialectics.* New York: Guilford Press.

Dixson, M., & Duck, S. (1993). Understanding relationship processes: Uncovering the human search for meaning. In S. Duck (Ed.), *Individuals in relationships.* Newbury, CA: Sage.

Goodlad, J. (1988). *School-university partnerships for educational renewal: Rational and concepts.* In K. Sirotnik & J. Goodlad (Eds.), *School-university partnerships in action: Concepts, cases, and concerns* (pp. 3–31). New York: Teachers College Press.

Rawlins, W. K. (1992). *Friendship matters.* New York: Aldine DeGruyter.

Salmon, D., & Freedman, R. A. (in press). *The relational literacy curriculum.* Mahwah, NJ: Lawrence Erlbaum.

Chapter

14

Working Together:
A Successful One-to-One
Collaboration

John Kornfeld and Georgia Leyden

Implementing totally new curriculum can be an exhilarating experience—enlightening for students, exciting for parents, and rejuvenating for the teacher. Nonetheless, for many classroom teachers, who are busy enough teaching curriculum familiar to them, experimenting with new content and pedagogy can be a daunting endeavor. There's the added time needed for preparation, the added stress of trying something new, and, of course, the fear that the new curriculum may fail altogether. When a classroom teacher and university professor face these concerns together, however, such a project can seem much less formidable; moreover, the different spheres of knowledge and types of experience that each person brings to the project can greatly enhance the likelihood of success.

This chapter describes and examines a successful one-to-one partnership between an elementary school teacher and a university professor. For five months, we worked together, planning new curriculum and team teaching it in Georgia's first-grade classroom. While examining and reflecting on the instructional impact of our collaboration, we were also analyzing the nature of this mutually satisfying association. Would it be possible, we asked, to distill the key features of this relationship to create a model that other school–university partners could emulate? In this chapter, after providing an overview of our project, we will discuss our collaborative process and its impact on each of us. We conclude with a discussion of what we learned from this project about fostering successful one-to-one collaborations and the potential for such partnerships to stimulate curriculum development on a broader scale.

Project Overview

We first met in the fall of 1995 when John's son was a student in Georgia's first-grade class. With John acting as a parent helper in the classroom, we worked together on a number of projects, including a writers' workshop and a science inquiry unit. During the 1997–1998 school year, we resolved to collaborate on a more challenging multi-disciplinary project: to plan and implement an integrated social studies curriculum centered around historical plays that the first graders would write, stage, and perform for the rest of the school.

This project grew out of our ongoing conversations about literacy (Georgia's area of expertise), social studies and drama (John's areas of expertise), and our mutual interest in African American history and literature. For nearly two years, we discussed the feasibility of children learning reading and language through the content areas, with John encouraging Georgia to experiment using drama as a way to help students connect with historical events.

Early in the school year, we met over a period of weeks for the initial planning of our project. When we were ready to implement our plans, John began team teaching with Georgia two or three mornings a week. We read aloud to the students several pieces of literature related to African American history and engaged them in discussions and activities designed to deepen their understanding of the stories. After the students chose the books they would make into plays, they dictated the dialogue for each play by acting out the story as they remembered it; made backdrops, props, and costumes; and practiced, practiced, practiced.

Originally we had planned to perform all three plays together, but as productions grew more elaborate, the first graders had difficulty keeping track of them. We decided it would be best to create, practice, and perform one play at a time before moving on to the next one. As a result, our two-month project extended into a five-month one, with a series of performances in February, April, and June.

As we lived through the project, we continued to meet after school, and occasionally on weekends, for extended conversations and planning. Our talk focused on both the curriculum project and the nature of our collaborative relationship. We took field notes and kept journals to document our experiences, impressions, and conversations as we worked with the children and each other. Occasionally, as part of our meetings, we conducted formal interviews with one another in which we explored the nature of our collaborative process.

The Collaborative Process: Georgia's Voice

At the time that we met, John was completing his doctorate, and I was working on a master's degree in education in the Reading and Language Program at Sonoma State University, where John had just been hired. During the time John volunteered in my classroom, we had spirited conversations about language and learning. Our decision to enter into a collaborative relationship grew out of these conversations; our talents and interests complemented one another's well, and, because we had already established a working relationship, we knew that we were compatible and would be able to work well together.

We began our first collaboration after attending a seminar featuring Jerome Harste from Indiana University. His keynote speech focused on inquiry-based learning. John and I, excited about what we had seen and heard, decided to begin an inquiry project that would enrich my first-grade geology curriculum. Our collaborative project was an extremely satisfying experience for me. In working with John, I found a partner with whom I could try out new ideas, someone to share the successes and failures of the inquiry process, and someone who could offer different insights on our common experience.

The inquiry project was a complete success. Students were motivated in their learning, parents were pleased with their children's enthusiasm and the enriched curriculum, and the administration was impressed that an innovative approach to learning was being developed on the school site with the cooperation of a university educator. In some ways, it put our school "on the map" in the minds of the superintendent and principal. I teach in a small, rural district, and we are often overlooked by the county office of education and the university in favor of the larger districts of neighboring cities.

Whereas our first project was based on an approach we were both interested in examining, we embarked on our second project with divergent agendas in mind. John was most interested in studying our collaborative process. I was interested in the plays we would produce and the impact they would have on my students. For me, this undertaking was inspired by my desire to put on a classroom play, my anxiety about doing so, and John's expertise in drama. John had been encouraging me to use social studies to help my students in their literacy development, so, once again, we decided to bring together our interests and expertise and use drama as the vehicle to help my students learn about African American experiences and perspectives.

My personal motivation for continuing our collaborative relationship was multifaceted. I wanted to grow as an educator, to try out those theories and methods I had been learning about. I wanted to provide my students with an enriched curriculum that would increase motivation and excitement for learning. I knew that plays could be particularly motivating for students, yet I was reluctant to attempt them on my own. I also wanted to work with John because we shared an enthusiasm for our profession and a delight in student learning.

During our project, our collaborative roles evolved as I had anticipated. John listened to my ideas and provided other perspectives, which we incorporated or not depending on the weight of my own perspective; his intention in this relationship was not to prove that he was the expert but to work with me on equal terms. Before this project, I had never had experience with drama and felt thoroughly intimidated by the idea of creating a play. In the early stages, I depended extensively on John, who planned and directed the rehearsals. Gradually, however, John stepped back as my feelings of inadequacy subsided, and I took the lead. Eventually I led rehearsals completely on my own and felt quite comfortable doing so.

A major reason for the success of our collaboration is the way we began it. Neither of us brought a specific agenda to the process, and neither brought a preconceived notion as to how the project should evolve. Fortunately for me, John did not try to lead me to his way of thinking. He asked me what I would like to work on with my students, and we developed the project together based on the area of study that I wanted to address. We began with a "Let's see . . . what will we do first?" attitude that served us well in developing our project; and as we worked toward producing the play, we both had ideas and offered them to one another as colleagues and fellow researchers.

John and I worked well together. Perhaps because we had begun our relationship as parent and teacher rather than university professor and teacher, I was not intimidated by John's position as university professor. I respected him as an educator and listened eagerly to his ideas about the project and to theories, new to me, that expanded my way of thinking. I felt comfortable telling him my ideas as well and disagreeing when I believed an approach would not work well with the developmental phase of my first-grade students. We worked together through all of the planning and implementation stages. John helped as the students wrote the plays by role playing the stories, and he came to school consistently throughout the project, not just as a university researcher, but as a participant in the process.

This "equality of voice" in our relationship is one reason our partnership has been successful. Generally, I feel very comfortable in my role as a first-grade teacher, especially in the area of language arts. I did not begin our collaboration as a struggling teacher looking for help to improve a deficient program. Consequently, I assumed from the beginning that I would function as an equal partner with John. He appreciated my input about early language learners, and I valued his knowledge and ideas in the areas of social studies, drama, and the collaborative process itself. We negotiated our roles and responsibilities as peer collaborators do: We gave more weight to my ideas in those areas where I had the expertise, such as early language learning and ways to work with the individuals in my classroom; we gave greater weight to John's ideas in those areas where he had greater expertise.

Collaborative partners must be open to one another's ideas and feel free to make suggestions. Equality of voice gave each of us a sense of ownership in the process and in the product. Each of the plays was a huge success, enjoyed by the larger school community and the students' families. John and I took great pride in our students' work. Our labors had been tremendous, but the plays and the students' pride in their work—and our own sense of accomplishment—made it well worth the effort.

The Collaborative Process: John's Voice

As Georgia indicates, our collaboration began in a rather unusual way: with informal conversation. After school on the days that I helped in Georgia's class, we'd chat about what had gone on in class, what Georgia was hoping to accomplish, and ways that I, as a parent helper, could assist. At first, the conversation took on an almost surreal quality as we were finding out how much we had in common: "Oh, you're new at Sonoma State? We'll I'm working on my MA there." "Oh, you were reading Harste yesterday? I took a class from him at Indiana last year." The more we talked, the more interested we became in picking one another's brains and trying out new ideas in Georgia's classroom.

During the years that we worked and talked together, our conversations ranged over a wide variety of topics and issues, shifting continually between the personal and the professional, between the practical and philosophical. Gehrke (1988) likened the optimal mentor–protégé relationship to Buber's (1970) "I–Thou" relationship, in which two people transcend the manipulative, utilitarian "I–It" relationship that characterizes most human interaction and enter—at least for a few moments at a time—into an authentic relationship in which the parties see one another for what they really are. I was not a "mentor," nor was Georgia a "protégé," but our evolving conversations certainly took on this I–Thou quality. We learned about each other's families, personal histories, and hopes for the future. And when discussion turned to Georgia's curriculum, we didn't just talk about what we wanted to do with the students; we discussed what we believed about kids and school and knowledge and literacy. Mayer (1977, p. 12) could have been describing our conversations when he wrote that meaningful dialogue "is necessarily patient, persistent, and painstaking, endlessly backing and filling." In our conversations, we established the trust and respect we needed to work together, and the consequent I–Thou bond that cemented our commitment to working together. This deeper shared understanding helped keep alive our hope and vision even during times when the plays were not going well, when Georgia was feeling harried by conflicts within her school community, or when my university duties prevented me from working with Georgia and her students as often as I would have liked.

As Georgia noted above, our evolution from parent–teacher to professor–teacher was a gradual one. I had previously participated in school–university curriculum projects (Kornfeld, 1993, 1996), and when Georgia suggested that we experiment with Harste's inquiry curriculum, I began taking notes to document the process. The more we worked together, the more intrigued I became with the ease of our communication and the intensity of the curriculum we were developing. What was it about our relationship that fostered this rewarding process and extraordinary product? The more notes I took, the more it became clear to me that my perspectives, by themselves, could only provide part of the answers to my questions. So I asked Georgia to join me in a formal examination of the collaborative process itself. Georgia said sure—as long as I was willing to embark on an even more ambitious inquiry: the plays.

A commonality in our beliefs about children and education initially convinced us that we could work together to plan and implement powerful curriculum. Much to my surprise, however, it was the differences in our visions and styles that often helped propel and sustain the curriculum development process. As the project unfolded, Georgia revealed strengths that ultimately moved the collaboration in unexpected—and exciting—directions. For example, as stated above, I was the partner who, we both acknowledged, was contributing the expertise in drama. Having had considerable experience directing elementary school kids in theatrical productions, I felt I knew what we needed to do to make my visions a reality. But Georgia did not start with my vision and did not conduct her class as I would have. She wanted to elicit more student input in creating the plays than I would have; she spent weeks with the students creating backdrops and props, which I had always considered of minor importance; and she was adamant about providing the students with a context for these plays by reading related works of fiction and conducting activities connected to the books. These alterations to my approach, which I at first would have preferred not to do, made the whole project substantially more time-consuming and complex, and I worried that they would undermine the process as I had conceived it.

Of course, the plays that resulted from this process turned out to be far better and more elaborate, and the students' understanding and commitment far deeper, than anything I could have imagined. Georgia is a master at preparing and juggling many things at once, including the brainstorming sessions, art activities, book discussions, and rehearsals that she conducted on a daily basis in preparation for the plays. I realized that I needed to let go of preconceived notions of how the class should look or how it should be run and replace those ideas with an ever-evolving vision reflecting the strengths— as well as the personality, attitudes, and outlook—of both parties.

I agree completely with Georgia that equality of voice was key to our successful collaboration. Each of us occupied our own area of curricular expertise and our own realm of power. Theoretically, Georgia held the ultimate power in our relationship be- cause she could have vetoed any suggestion I made or even asked me to leave if she wished. In practice, we acted as equals in the planning and implementation process, as- suring us each an equal voice in our negotiations.

This dynamic became increasingly more complex as our relationship evolved. Whereas Georgia at first felt dependent on my expertise in drama, I counted on her knowledge of and experience with first graders. Gradually, our respective feelings of angst subsided. Even as our mutual dependence diminished over time, we continued to rely on each other in other ways: for sharing ideas, for advice and encouragement, for having another educator with whom to talk on a regular basis. Thus, throughout our as- sociation, we weren't merely equals; we were *interdependent* equals. Each of us pro- vided nurture, insight, and support for the other, while planning and implementing curriculum that was more exciting than anything either of us could have developed on our own

Attributes and Complexities of the Teacher–Professor Relationship

In a school–university partnership such as ours, each party plays a unique and in- tegral role in the research and curriculum development process. Professor and teacher become "mutually dependent colleagues" (Gomez, 1990, p. 49), working together to make school a better place for teacher and students. As Johnston and Kirschner (1996, p. 146) explained, "Collaboration is not an end in itself, but a way of relating and work- ing together."

In examining the way we related and worked together, we identified several dis- tinct attributes of our relationship that proved to be invaluable to the success of our as- sociation. These features include making time for meaningful conversation, not just structured planning time, but time simply to talk informally, to connect on a variety of levels and foster a sense of trust and shared vision; being willing to negotiate and com- promise; maintaining reciprocity, not just by helping each other, but by attending to both partners' goals for the project; learning one another's strengths to make the best use of them; recognizing that our relationships, our visions, and our plans will undergo continual evolution throughout the process; establishing equality of voice and interde- pendence, with each partner holding power and knowledge of equivalent worth but de- pending on one another's areas of expertise throughout the process; and moving toward independence, so that when the university partner leaves the scene, the teacher will continue to use what was learned through the collaboration. Finally, and perhaps most important, commitment to the process throughout the collaboration is a crucial factor.

There is a danger, however, in deconstructing a phenomenon as complex as the relationship of two people. Such deconstruction implies that the important features of collaboration, once identified, render the process intelligible and replicable. Certainly teachers and professors working together would benefit from applying these attributes to their relationships, but the way these attributes manifest themselves will vary tremendously in each case. In fact, the more thoroughly we examined the successful qualities of our collaboration, the more difficult it became to define, quantify, systematize, or prescribe the means for duplicating it.

Consider, for example, the notion of commitment. Certainly we shared a deep commitment to our project, both of us throwing ourselves into it wholeheartedly. "Wholeheartedly" can mean different things to different people at different times, however, and there were many instances when we noted minor differences in our respective levels of commitment to the task at hand. For example, during certain periods, John could only spend a few hour per week in Georgia's class, increasing Georgia's burden of responsibility and anxiety about the process. On the other hand, sometimes when John arrived in Georgia's class at a predetermined hour, Georgia and her class would be preoccupied with other school work or unexpected problems that would use up precious time for work on the plays. In addition, although our mutual commitment included many of the same goals for the project, some goals were more important to one party than to the other. For example, sharing our findings with the research community has always been much higher on John's agenda than on Georgia's. Fortunately for John, Georgia took seriously John's desires to publish our findings and took the time needed to write this chapter. The key to maintaining the relationship, we found, was not sharing the same level of commitment all the time but making an effort at all times to recognize and respect the other person's level.

The same can be said about reciprocity. Certainly we were each "getting" something from our collaboration: new curriculum for Georgia and scholarly research for John. Yet at many points, each of us was aware of an imbalance in the reciprocity. For example, even though we worked together to plan the curriculum, almost all of the logistical preparation (gathering of voluminous amounts of materials, organizing parent helpers, etc.) fell on Georgia's shoulders, resulting in many of hours of extra work for her each week. Reciprocity should involve a balance of favors, services, communication, and understanding between parties; without that balance, there is a danger of resentment and dissolution of the partnership. In this case, who was responsible for "violating" the covenants we had established? Was it John, contributing so much less than Georgia, or was it Georgia, always doing more than we had originally agreed upon?

Fortunately, by making time to discuss this and other issues, we were able to overcome the discrepancies in reciprocity that troubled us at times. As each party became aware of the limitations of our time and the boundaries of our commitment, we modified our aspirations and adjusted our expectations. In a word, we compromised.

Compromise drives the collaborative process. It makes negotiating and creating curriculum possible, it allows the teacher to try ideas that the professor recommends, it encourages the professor to modify plans to accommodate teacher strengths, and it permits the process to evolve in exciting and unpredictable ways. What seems most important for maintaining a productive and successful relationship is that the two parties agree on a set of basic principles and continually touch base with one another about what is working and what is not working. We staked out this common ground in early meetings, negotiating the goals we would strive to attain in the classroom. Beyond that common ground, there was much to negotiate over the succeeding months, but we continued to compromise as long as the compromise remained consistent with that overarching goal.

The complexities of personal investment, reciprocity, negotiation, and compromise in the teacher–professor relationship are all related to issues of power and equality. If there was a key to the success of our collaboration, it was that we began with and maintained an equality of voice, with each of us respecting the other's sovereignty while the same time holding a certain amount of power. Preserving that essential balance of power was not a struggle for us, but what if, rather than being generally confident in herself, Georgia had been insecure about her teaching or her relationships with her students? How might this insecurity have upset the balance of power and hindered the collaborative process? Finding strengths in Georgia's teaching and encouraging her to capitalize on them (thereby helping her to establish her own realms of power) might have been even more essential to our success than it actually proved to be for us. Or consider what effect our both being white or our being approximately the same age had on the ease with which we established an equal relationship. Whatever the scenario, establishing equality in the relationship must be a prerequisite to undergoing fruitful discussions about curriculum.

The equality of voice that we maintained throughout our collaboration was essential to our communication with each other and to our ultimate satisfaction with the relationship. To remain interdependent when the balance of power is more tentative than it was with us, both teacher and professor would have to devote considerably more time and effort than we did toward maintaining an atmosphere of equality in daily conversation and negotiation. It takes skill and dedication to maintain equality—especially because the very essence of the relationship involves negotiation and often a clash of agendas and vision—but preserving that balance of power should indeed be a priority of both parties.

Clearly, the attributes that we identified do not constitute a definitive model on which to base other school–university partnerships; indeed, our experience illuminated complexities in the process far greater than any model could possibly control. Our "formula" for fostering successful one-to-one partnerships rests on something far too elusive to quantify—the evolution of a complex relationship between two people. Still, although these characteristics of our relationship cannot provide a blueprint for future endeavors, they do illuminate important considerations for teachers and university partners seeking to build and maintain fruitful collaborative relationships.

Impact on the Teacher: Georgia's Voice

The impact this project had on me as a teacher was broad, evoking a spectrum of feelings from overwhelmed to euphoric. I had always wanted to work on a play with my students, but I'd been fearful of attempting one. With John as a support, a scaffold for the process, and a model for the strategies and techniques I would need to produce a play, I felt confident I would be able to try it out without the worry of complete failure.

Nevertheless, one of the outcomes of collaborating with John was a high level of stress on my part. When John and I initially planned the curriculum, we fed off one another's enthusiasm, and our combined perspectives gave our project a grander scale than either one of us would have attempted alone. We were so excited by the literature and so determined to convey the broad scope of African American history that we decided to produce three plays instead of one. In hindsight, I realize the notion of three plays was both brilliant and foolhardy. Even though I was enthusiastic and excited about our project, I experienced an intense energy drain on a daily basis because play production was unfamiliar to me and I felt vulnerable and out of my league. Had I been on my own, I would probably have abandoned the project, or at least scaled it down, as the stress increased. But because I was working with John, I didn't want to let him down, so I proceeded ahead despite the tremendous work and intensity involved in successfully completing the project.

With practically the entire curriculum revolving around the plays, the daily schedule and pace of the lessons was disconcerting to say the least. This was a whole new way of teaching for me. My days felt much less structured than was customary in my classroom. There were occasional moments of chaos, or so it seemed to me, as children were doing many different things at once and coming up with ideas on the spot that required new materials and someone (generally me) on whom to try out their ideas. Although John managed to come to the classroom several times per week, I was left to fend for myself the vast majority of the time.

When I think back on the experience, I realize that what seemed like chaos was actually the energy of eighteen creative minds working at a feverish pitch to reach their personal and communal goals. Unfortunately, however, one consequence of this period of intense ingenuity and high energy was that I became ill after our first play and was out of school for two weeks.

While there were some negative consequences of my collaboration with John, the favorable results far outweighed the unfavorable. As I watched my students grow in confidence and enthusiasm, I was growing as well. Primarily, of course, I was acquiring new skills in how to work with children in drama and play production. As I took on more of the rehearsal responsibility, my confidence grew, and I began to see that producing a play with my first-grade students was something I could accomplish on my own.

Going through the process of producing these plays was a real journey for me. It added a whole new dimension to my work with first graders. In many ways, this project has changed my approach to teaching, and somehow I now feel different about who I am as a teacher. I feel "solid" in my practice in a way I never did before. Although I've been teaching for quite a few years and I've always tried to be helpful to other teachers, I now feel different about the role I should take with them. Performing these plays for the rest of the school was a very public experience. I felt "out there" in the school community in a way I never had before. Now I feel that I can and should offer assistance to other teachers whenever possible.

Perhaps most important, collaborating with John helped me to understand what doing a play with my students could mean for them as learners. Initially, I had thought it would just be fun to present a play. It *was* fun (although not always!), but it was also educationally profound. I watched my students' enthusiasm and confidence grow, and I saw the curriculum come alive and become real for them.

I learned that through the study of interesting and authentic content, literacy learning takes place. I had always thought that reading was the most important thing that students could do in my class: If they learned to read and write, they would carry that with them for the rest of their lives. Then when John and I began our conversations about curriculum, John talked about the notion that literacy could grow out of engagement in such content areas as science and social studies. That sounded interesting, and it lay there in my mind. Then we did the plays. I saw that through planning and practicing the plays, my students were experiencing literacy in a way I had never seen before. They were not just learning about Rosa Parks, they were living her experiences—and living them at a level they never had before with other lessons in my class.

That is what has happened to me: I, too, was living my literacy experience. Before, John and I had just talked about ways that social studies content can be integrated with reading, writing, art, and music. Now that I was finally living this literacy experience, I *got* it. One day, in the middle of class, I suddenly said to myself, "Oh, this is what John and I have been talking about all this time!" Our conversations and collaboration gave me the opportunity to live it and have the vision unfold before me.

Impact on the Professor: John's Voice

Like Georgia, I was deeply affected by our collaboration. I, too, experienced intense stress and energy drain but for different reasons: The university was providing no funding or release time for engaging in this collaboration, and the time I spent with Georgia and her students made that spring semester the busiest I had ever experienced. I didn't get sick like Georgia, but I felt torn in two. Although I needed (and wanted) to spend more time with Georgia and her class, I was having difficulty keeping up with my teaching and committee responsibilities at the university.

Still, our collaboration has had a powerful and lasting impact on my work as a university professor. In the first place, our collaboration enhanced my conception of literacy. I had read a considerable amount (e.g., Harste, 1994) about the role that various ways of knowing play in enhancing students' literacy, but until Georgia brought this theory to life in our project, insisting that the students create elaborate sets and props to complement the dialogue they wrote, I had never truly understood what I had read. Like Georgia, I had to live the experience to understand it.

My work with Georgia also had an immediate impact on my teaching at the university. At the time, I was teaching a course called "Integrated Curriculum in Elementary Schools," in which students plan and then implement (in their student teaching placements) thematic curriculum. One day in class, I began telling these students about my work with Georgia. I brought in detailed outlines of our overall plan and the daily activities we were conducting with the students, and I told them how the kids were responding to these plans. Each week thereafter, I gave the class updates on our progress. We discussed the rationale for producing the plays and my evolving revelations about literacy, we brainstormed solutions to management and logistical issues that continually arose in Georgia's class, and we considered ways Georgia and I might revise our plans for the following year. In short, my students lived (vicariously) the project; in so doing, they came to understand what truly integrated curriculum can look like.

Another unexpected benefit arose from sharing my experiences with my students: My stories actually enhanced my credibility with these preservice teachers. Students realized that I wasn't just a university egghead who could rattle off educational theory but had no connection to the real world of the classroom. Instead, they could see that I was living it just as they were—putting my ideas into practice in the classroom, worrying at night about the next day's teaching, reflecting on my mistakes, and celebrating my successes—and that I really understood what it took to be an elementary school teacher. Many students (some of whom ended up attending performances of the plays) later told me that it was those firsthand stories of ongoing trial, error, setbacks, and success that helped them to apply to their own teaching the theory and methods they were learning in the course.

Clearly, my work with Georgia affected me in ways that reached far beyond the world of her classroom—ways that I could not have predicted before our collaboration. It reminded me how vital this type of endeavor is to my professional growth. As a graduate student, I had engaged in a number of research projects in elementary and secondary schools (e.g., Kornfeld, 1993, 1996), but upon attaining a tenure-track position, I became so busy that I found it difficult to spend time away from the university. Working with Georgia in her classroom continually reminded me how challenging and exhilarating teaching kids can be. Moreover, it is not enough simply to hang out in the back of the classroom, taking field notes or marking checklists, nor is it enough to interview teachers in the teachers' room. I need to conduct research that allows me to regularly reexperience the act of working with kids, putting to the test the theories, curricula, and pedagogies that I advocate at the university.

What We Learned from Our One-to-One Partnership

Beyond the Classroom

We began this project with no grand plans for school reform. Just producing the three plays seemed challenge enough for both of us. We sought to make changes in Georgia's curriculum, not her entire school; consequently, we gave little thought to the students and teachers outside Georgia's classroom. Clearly our collaboration more than met our goals. Yet much to our surprise, the effects of our project were felt beyond the walls of our classroom, throughout Georgia's school.

The most immediate affect of the project was the way the plays stimulated conversation in classrooms throughout the school. For example, a kindergarten teacher reported to us that after watching our second play, her students returned to their classroom and spontaneously acted out the story for several afternoons. After we performed *I Am Rosa Parks* (our third play), a third-grade class carried on a lengthy discussion about discrimination, resistance, and the Civil Rights Movement. They questioned why African Americans had not gained total freedom since the conclusion of the Civil War. Throughout the school, students were responding to our plays with interest, concern, and, in some cases, outrage.

They were also responding with a heightened interest in drama. Throughout the primary grades, students begged, pressured, and eventually succeeded in convincing many of their teachers to put on plays as well. During the final weeks of the school year, the campus was alive with theater. Student audiences moved from classroom to classroom watching a variety of plays, while teachers and administrators marveled at this unexpected end-of-the-year drama festival.

This interest in drama has continued to this day. By now, seven out of nine primary teachers, including a few who had sworn they would never attempt drama in their classrooms, produce plays with their students. A new focus on drama is emerging at Georgia's school, and a number of the teachers seek out Georgia to discuss a variety of technical, procedural, and content-related concerns. Buoyed by a new sense of confidence and responsibility, Georgia makes a point of connecting with and involving teachers in conversations about drama.

These developments illustrate how one-to-one collaboration can stimulate substantive curricular change far beyond the one classroom where the partnership takes place. Who knows how far it will go? We can easily imagine how this confederation of committed teachers could continue to grow and gradually change the way teachers and their students create curriculum throughout the school and beyond. Beginning with just a few committed participants, a collaborative endeavor such as ours could grow inexorably, as Wood (1992, p. 253) wrote, "classroom by classroom, school by school."

The Importance of Support

No matter how intense the commitment of the two partners in this kind of collaboration, a one-to-one partnership relies on more individuals than simply the teacher and professor. The interest and support of Georgia's school community were critical to the success of our project. Parents were delighted to help students make costumes, props, and backgrounds; the custodian was always available to help us convert the classroom to a performance hall; and the principal provided modest funding for wire, bulbs, and other necessary lighting equipment. Even more important was the tacit support of Georgia's colleagues and the administration. Throughout the project, Georgia's colleagues would ask her about the plays: How are they going? What's it like working with John? When will the performances take place? The principal proudly announced in monthly newsletters that Sonoma State University had "chosen" Guerneville school for important research; recently, she even suggested that the school try to establish a new reputation for an emphasis on theater arts. Our chances for success would have been seriously compromised if, for example, administration had not been cordial to John or if Georgia's colleagues had reacted to our collaboration with annoyance or jealousy. Direct support, in the form of release time or funding for the teacher, can certainly facilitate a partnership, but they are far less vital to its success than the school community's acceptance of this collaborative relationship.

A similar degree of acceptance is necessary at the university level. Certainly, active support in the form of university funding or release time would have greatly reduced the stress that John experienced during the semester that we produced the plays; but more important was the fact that John's colleagues in the Sonoma State University School of Education regarded the work we were doing as legitimate research. We knew, from the outset of this project, that the dean and tenure committees would take our work seriously and that our collaboration and the presentations and papers that would result from our work would satisfy School of Education expectations for scholarly achievement. As long as we both maintained our commitment to the project, we could manage without university funding, but we could not have managed without the recognition necessary to facilitate John's progress through the university's reappointment-tenure-promotion process.

Collaboration: A Special Kind of Relationship

Although the friendship we developed before initiating this project certainly enhanced our commitment to and vision of the project, such a friendship is by no means a prerequisite for success. The prerequisite is that both partners, from the outset, be committed to the project and to making time for meaningful conversation throughout the process. Even after we had begun our work in earnest, we self-consciously carved out time to talk so that conversation would transcend the utilitarian I–It relationship that characterizes conversations when time is severely limited. It was critically important that neither party arrived with an immutable agenda; we needed the time to let the agenda evolve. Friendship is not a prerequisite to collaboration, but, given the time necessary to engage in meaningful conversations, friendship will probably result.

Nonetheless, friendship is not the focus of our collaboration. Our partnership was a purposeful relationship established with professional goals in mind, and, like all such arrangements, it needed constant maintenance. Collaborative relationships cannot be treated as "natural" and left to evolve entirely on their own. We began this inquiry believing that we could step back from the collaborative process—regard ourselves and the relationship from a distance—to understand it better; but it turned out that the more we "stepped back," the more we realized self-examination was itself an integral part of the collaborative process and a key to our continued success as partners. Teacher and professor need to "check in" with one another on a regular basis, not only to ask each other how the curriculum is proceeding but also to ask, "How are we getting along?" In a school–university partnership, the two questions are inextricably linked.

The attributes that formed the basis of our collaboration should help guide researchers and practitioners seeking ways to foster successful teacher–professor relationships. Indeed, each of the features is vital to a fruitful collaboration. Considered together, they provide valuable insight into the success of our partnership; considered one-by-one, they offer a framework for partners engaging in ongoing self-examination. They remind us that throughout the collaboration, each party should be ever mindful of the ultimate goals that they have established together, as well as the infinite complexities and potential pitfalls in the relationship. Each successful relationship, depending on the personalities, abilities, experiences, and aspirations of the persons involved, will attain these goals in unique and intriguing ways.

References

Buber, M. (1970). *I and thou* (W. Kaufmann, trans.). New York: Charles Scribner's Sons.

Gehrke, N. J. (1988). On preserving the essence of mentoring as one form of teacher leadership. *Journal of Teacher Education, 3,* 43–45.

Gomez, M. L. (1990). Reflections on research for teaching: Collaborative inquiry with a novice teacher. *Journal of Education for Teaching, 16,* 45–56.

Harste, J. C. (1994). Literacy as curricular conversations about knowledge, inquiry, and morality. In R. B. Ruddell, M. R. Ruddell, & H. Singer (Eds.), *Theoretical models and processes of reading* (4th ed., pp. 1220–1242). Newark, DE: International Reading Association.

Johnston, M., & Kirschner, B. (1996). This issue: The challenges of school/university collaboration. *Theory into Practice, 35,* 146–148.

Kornfeld, J. (1993, June). Grass roots restructuring and the curriculum consultant: A personal reflection. Paper presented at the Democracy and Education Annual Conference, Athens, OH.

Kornfeld, John. 1996. *Connecting worlds: Revitalizing the curriculum through teacher/consultant collaboration.* Doctoral dissertation, Department of Curriculum and Instruction, Indiana University, Bloomington.

Mayer, M. (1977, January/February). Demise of dialogue. *The Center Magazine,* 12–15.

Wood, G. (1992). *Schools that work: America's most innovative public education programs.* New York: Dutton.

Chapter

The Angst, Ecstasy, and Opportunities of Collaborative Inquiry

Clay Lafleur and Jack MacFadden

This chapter documents the evolution of our collaborative working relationship over time. We explore our passion for doing collaborative inquiry by deliberately browsing some of the nooks and crannies of our life as long-term collaborative action researchers. In addition to sharing some practical tips that we have discovered in our journey together, we also describe the struggles, challenges, and rewards that come from such an enduring and enriching collaboration.

Our collaborative work together, for more than fifteen years, has been an extended junket that involves the sharing of knowledge, skills and values, as well as nonoverlapping competencies, beliefs, and experiences. To understand our story is to understand our commitment to the learning and well-being of students, parents, colleagues, and of each other.

Placing the child at the center of learning has been our beacon for pursuing and continuing our journey. As a result of our experiences, we have come to know and understand better our craft as educators. Our ongoing conversations, reflections, and writings have helped us to develop a better insight into what collaboration and a culture of inquiry truly means.

It is our belief that a culture of inquiry can help each of us embrace different ways of knowing resulting in educators becoming increasingly more collaborative and participatory in an environment where planning, acting, analyzing, interpreting, and reflecting are shared responsibilities. As one of us has indicated elsewhere (Lafleur, 1995, p. 19), in such a context, "We will be able to critically reflect on our own assumptions and practices, meaningfully and openly engage in dialogue and participate as responsible members of a community of learners."

Collaboration does not occur without struggle and commitment. Through collaboration, each person's contribution results in recognition of the whole; this means that all parts belong together, and all parts participate (Skolimowski, 1994). The recognition of each person's contribution comes from a blending of beliefs, values, experiences, and knowledge that enhance the process and products of the collaboration. Through conversation and hard work, each person's own voice becomes clearer and more articulated. Meaning emerges and is socially constructed. In this sense, collaboration is an educative activity that contributes to personal and professional development and more informed action.

Here we want to explore the messiness as well as the exhilaration of the complex and empowering nature of collaboration. In particular, we will emphasize several key tenets of collaboration. A few of these include

- An agreement on a shared vision

- A mutual respect based on the recognition of shared and differentiated responsibilities and expertise

- The acceptance of each person's need and capacity for continued growth and development

- The acceptance of conversation as a form of accountability and growth

- A willingness to find time, especially when our own lives seem so hurried and hectic

- A commitment to action based on a team effort

- The use of communication that enhances team-oriented activities

- A focus on developing and maintaining organizational structures that support collaboration

- A willingness to take risks

- A recognition that collaboration is a process that occurs over time

To understand better the ideas and feelings about our collaborative journey over time, we would like to offer a brief introduction of ourselves.

A Brief Statement about Who We Are

In this chapter we share the process of collaborative inquiry that we have undertaken for the past fifteen years. Although we have collaborated with several other colleagues over the years, the data for our comments come primarily from our work together as colleagues rather than as members of a larger team.

The School District Researcher

My name is Clay Lafleur. In the early 1980s, I accepted a position as a researcher and curriculum consultant in a large Canadian school district. During one of my first system-wide program evaluation projects, I quickly befriended Jack, an elementary school teacher and member of the project steering committee. I arranged to visit his seventh-grade classroom to do research "on" his students related to the project I was evaluating. During the course of my research, Jack expressed interest in what I was doing and increasingly began to participate in the planning and conduct of "my" research into his practice.

Subsequently, we continued to do action research together and started to mutually investigate issues and "troubling difficulties" in his classroom. Our work quickly extended to inquiry with his students about the classroom learning environment, as well as student learning and achievement. Our collaborative inquiry continues today, after more than fifteen years, and has evolved over time into newer and more public forms of collaboration.

In my capacity as a school district researcher, I am keen to establish a culture of participatory inquiry. Working with Jack was an opportunity to support teacher research and to learn how to build the capacity of schools and the district to do inquiry. My partnership with Jack grew over time into a meaningful and collaborative alliance that made a difference—not only as a way to enhance student learning and achievement but also as a deliberate strategy to nurture our own personal and professional growth.

My own career as a school district researcher emerged after several years as an educator having taught in both Canada and Australia, in elementary and secondary schools as well as at the college and university level. I am particularly fascinated with investigating the daily concerns encountered in the workplace and then critically examining the evidence that can lead to change and improvement.

The Teacher

My name is Jack MacFadden. I am an elementary school teacher, and I have been teaching students in the sixth and seventh grades for the last several years. I initially embraced teacher research more than fifteen years ago with my friend and colleague, Clay Lafleur. Initially, teacher research was my entry point to classroom change and improvement. Along the way, the resulting empowerment and professionalism that occurred became a complementary and important feature of the process. While the journey was often difficult and challenging, the discoveries and reaffirmation along the way gave dignity to my teaching and inspired me to continually examine how best to improve student learning.

I am the first to acknowledge that I am neither an extraordinary individual nor an outstanding teacher. It is my belief that collaborative teacher research is something that most teachers are capable of undertaking. I do, however, have boundless energy, persistence, and passion for what I do. In my own way, I am a dedicated teacher who views teaching and learning as hard work. I believe in the worth of all children and in their ability to learn. Putting the child at the center of learning is one of my never-ending pursuits as a teacher. I firmly believe that the school does make a difference. As a classroom teacher, I have found that teacher action research is a critical way to expose invisible knowledge. Reflecting in action and on my own practice enables me to understand and to develop my own theories of teaching and learning. As a result, I am better able to develop a positive learning environment by controlling the conditions that lead to successful student learning.

My efforts as a teacher–researcher have constantly renewed my professional growth and bolstered my self-esteem. Although my job as a classroom teacher has not changed, my knowledge, experiences, expertise, and commitment to my students have been greatly enhanced. Clay has increased his practical knowledge of classroom-based learning by working on various projects with me. He has kept in touch with the reality of the classroom teacher yet has been able to guide me through my attempts to learn new skills.

A Collaborative Partnership

Classroom-based action research has kept both of us on the leading edge of educational change in our province. We are still learning how to collaborate, and we constantly seek ways to share a great deal of "good stuff" that has resulted from our work together. Where possible we participate in public conversations about the value of collaborative inquiry as a strategy for making sense of educational reform and providing direction for improvement. We continually strive to share the experience of learning new skills and honing the old ones. At the present time, for example, we are working with several other colleagues to develop an interactive Web site to support teachers who want to conduct collaborative action research. We delight in each other's successes and regularly act as critical friends.

What Do We Mean by Collaboration?

We believe that collaboration is the ability to work cooperatively together on a task over time so as to achieve mutually agreed upon goals. From our perspective, collaboration reduces isolation and is integrally connected to the sharing of power and affection. It basically means learning how to get along while working on a mutually agreed upon task. Collaboration relies on the successful and everyday demonstration of mutual respect and trust, risk taking, tolerance, acceptance, commitment, courage, sharing, communication, and so on. In many ways, it is a collegial, caring, and professional partnership.

A collaborative working relationship thrives when there are shared purpose and commitment to achieve those purposes. In other words, there is a collective responsibility for attaining mutual goals. A shared distribution of power and affection demonstrates respect for the diversity of experience and expertise that each person brings to the task. Mutual respect and trust, for example, come from the recognition and acceptance of shared and differentiated responsibilities, experiences, and expertise. In our relationship, it meant building on Jack's instructional expertise and daily efforts to improve the learning and achievement of students while at the same time using Clay's research expertise to make classroom-based inquiry systematic and rigorous.

Collaboration thrives when it is robust. In other words, the individuals have a modicum of stamina for persisting with the task, and patience and determination are blended with goal-oriented and respectful behavior. Tolerance comes from accepting and constructively challenging our different values, backgrounds, perceptions, and interpretations of reality. In most circumstances, for example, we viewed problems as opportunities to explore and wonder about what could be. In those instances where problems seemed insurmountable, we had to make time to care, actively listen, and provide support. Although our partnership has been mostly trouble free, there have been "ups and downs" and some of the angst and frustration that characterize most regular problem-solving situations. Missing deadlines, unequal sharing of workload, and feeling overwhelmed, for example, are some of the "nuts-and-bolts" issues that seem to be our constant companions.

Sometimes courage and risk taking are necessary in challenging, influencing, and expressing disagreement without seeking control. As with any relationship that becomes a partnership, it is important to clarify misunderstandings. Communication skills, particularly active listening and creative problem solving, have been critical for us in getting along and getting on with the action research tasks.

Stages of Collaborative Inquiry

We have described our work together as progressing through stages of development (see Appendix 15.1) that are much like the stages of individual development (see, for example, Erikson, 1950) and group development (see, for example, Tuckman, 1965; Schmuck and Schmuck, 1975). In our model, we refer to five stages of development. Much like the stages of group development that have commonly been referred to as "forming, storming, norming, and performing," we have identified five stages of development to describe our collaborative action research. These five stages of development are initiating, dependence, rebellion, cohesion, and interdependence. As a way of explaining how our collaborative partnership has progressed, we describe key issues in five areas for each stage of development. These five areas are teacher's role (Jack), researcher's role (Clay), kind of motivation, type of learning, and optimum environment for progression. We have actually developed scenarios, based on our action research, of learning styles to illustrate our progression through the five stages of development (Lafleur, 1992).

Our Reflections about the Meaning of Collaborative Inquiry

We have been particularly fortunate in what we have learned and internalized as a result of our work together. The following statements, for example, represent a number of ideas that have either emerged during the action research process or have been rediscovered and articulated as a result of our collaboration together. They are offered here without discussion and are presented in no particular order.

- Collaborative teacher research should begin with a practical concern that is personally meaningful and relevant for all participants.
- Think big and start small so that success is guaranteed.
- Ensure that the method is manageable and an integral part of the teaching and learning process.
- There are distinct stages in the collaborative research process with key issues that need to be resolved.

- As with any innovation, collaboration and action research take time.

- The collaborative inquiry process is the antithesis of de-skilling; it supports the development of a sense of efficacy and confidence.

- The classroom teacher and researcher must come to terms with how best to equitably distribute power and affection relationships.

- Teacher research is a renewal activity that contributes to a teacher's sense of confidence and efficacy.

- Working collaboratively with an outsider helps to break the private barriers that result from individualism and isolation that often occur in schools that do not actively support a culture of collaboration and a culture of inquiry.

- Professionalism is much more than professionalization, that is, behaving according to professional standards.

- Mutual respect, trust, and open communication have underscored all of our work together.

- There are real tasks and responsibilities that must be sorted out on a regular basis.

- Regular perception checks are required throughout the process so as to continually negotiate expectations and to use each other's strengths efficiently and effectively.

- Collaborative inquiry supports conversations as valued forums of accountability and encourages participants to be informed critically reflective practitioners.

- Classroom-based inquiry provides results that are practical evidence to demonstrate what is happening in classrooms.

It is not our wish to explore or investigate all of these concepts. Rather, by opening the door to the wide range of possibilities, we want to demonstrate how we responded to those difficult and vulnerable moments in our shared inquiry. The fact that we were able to sustain our collaborative partnership over such a long period of time is something that we frequently ponder and discuss. What did we do that enabled us to work so well together? How did we manage to support and nurture our passion for and commitment to inquiry, change, and action?

Sustaining Collaboration over Time

Sometimes we make sense of events by allowing the past and future to collide in the present. By systematically reflecting on what has happened and anticipating what is likely going to happen, we are better able to describe what is occurring at the present moment. We have identified seven key concepts that explain our staying power and commitment to doing collaborative inquiry. These are shared vision, evidence for decision making, professional learning and efficacy, overcoming complex organizational conditions, resolving temporal issues, dealing with uncertainty, and communicating the results of our research.

Shared Vision

One of the most important features of our work together is our belief in putting students at the center of learning. Having a shared vision of our collaborative research efforts helped us see the big picture while enabling us to be content with small successes. One of our mottoes that we came to truly believe and act upon was, "Think big and start small." Treasure the small successes that contribute to completing the more substantive and important goals.

All of our efforts have been devoted to collecting evidence that can be used to improve student learning and achievement. Our very first project, for example, examined the effect of identifying and responding to the learning styles of students. This led to a natural examination of how small cooperative groups and authentic assessments were used in Jack's classroom. Student-led conferencing was another focus of our inquiry. Our research was continually extended to involve students more actively in their own learning. The action research process continued in a recursive and evolving manner that resulted in deliberate efforts to design student projects so that a total inquiry process was a feature of students' work.

We have attempted to involve students in every phase of our own inquiry process. A natural connection between student inquiry and our own investigations, for example, led to a landmark event for us sharing our work at an international conference. In one of our papers (MacFadden et al., 1998), we jointly presented the findings of our inquiry with five sixth-grade students as coauthors. In our conclusion, we indicated how important students were to our research efforts:

We must find ways for students to participate in crafting quality learning environments. Blending the student voice with our own professional knowledge and expertise can only result in more meaningful learning opportunities. While parents too want to be seen as equal partners in the learning process, they also support the development of the student voice as an important vehicle for students to shape their own learning....

Quality communication is the corner stone of the student voice. Whether it is through conferencing, journals, the use of portfolios and literacy binders, or regular conversations, clear and timely communication is essential. Students and parents must have ongoing forums—both formal and informal—to share their ideas and opinions. Truly successful learning experiences result when the voices of all partners are blended and focused to the benefit of student achievement and learning.

Knowing where we were heading also helped us deal with the bumps along the way. Having a shared vision enabled us to deal with the small stuff that got in the way. It allowed us to problem solve and move around obstacles so that we could get on with what we valued and believed.

Evidence for Decision Making

Obtaining immediate feedback about our own practice was exhilarating and meaningful to practice. We got results that were directly based on what was happening in Jack's classroom. These results enabled us to make design and delivery decisions that made a difference to student learning. What was most exciting was the fact that we had evidence about student learning to show parents and colleagues. We had data to demonstrate how well policies were being implemented at the classroom level.

The recursive and cyclical nature of our inquiry means that we are constantly acting, reflecting, and revising—we are in a continuous improvement mode. We are gathering evidence about classroom practice and using those data to make a difference to student learning, instruction, assessment, communication, learning environment, and so on. The adrenaline rush that comes from being able to make many of the taken-for-granted and everyday activities visible so that improvement can occur is as refreshing as frolicking in a rapidly running mountain stream.

Professional Learning and Efficacy

Working together with another educator, particularly someone else connected to promoting student learning in a different context than your own, is stimulating and rejuvenating. Being involved in our kind of collaborative research is an empowering and practical form of professional development. As we have written elsewhere (Lafleur & MacFadden, 1998),

We believe that collaborative action research fosters self-directed learning. It is one of the most meaningful ways of supporting the efforts of all practitioners. Habits of inquiry are nurtured and thoughtful questioning about everyday experiences is promoted. Collaborative action research is a vital way to provide continuous professional growth opportunities for teachers. It is a superb way to develop and refine key components of professional practice related to planning, instruction, and professional responsibilities. Engaging in collaborative action research helps to promote a culture of inquiry where systematically collected data is used as practical feedback in the solving (and posing) of problems. This form of inquiry positively influences the learning of children and contributes to increased student achievement.

Overcoming Complex Organizational Conditions

We found that working collaboratively requires a modicum of fortitude and determination. Although we encountered a range of obstacles, we were able to resolve most of these without too much difficulty. One obstacle had to do with the very nature of schools. While we were able to work around the prevailing organizational structures in Jack's school, we were saddened by the fact that we were not able to involve more teachers in our inquiry activities. Except for the occasional conversation and questions, teachers were mostly reluctant to get involved.

Not everyone understood what we were doing. Doing research on your own practice has gained more acceptance over the past several years. When we first began working together, however, action research was viewed cautiously and somewhat skeptically. Clearly this kind of activity was viewed as an "add on" that required energy, time, and a modicum of expertise. Uncertainty and reticence were common responses. So, unless this was a credential requirement, others in the school were reluctant to consider it as something that might benefit students and teachers.

Without the support and understanding of the principal and one's colleagues, it is difficult to garnish in-school support. Acknowledgment and recognition are so important. In addition, concessions in the form of planning time or conference attendance, for example, were not easy to come by during school hours. Although the absence of a collaborative culture was never a barrier, it did cause numerous frustrations. We frequently needed to regroup and carefully consider how best to continue our work together.

The way schools are structured frequently mitigates against teachers working collaboratively. For example, timetables and daily routines reduce flexibility and often make it difficult to meet and plan without some strategic leadership. In our school setting, the large number of portables also constrained teachers and limited their opportunities to work together. As a result, teachers often found it easier to work in isolation within their own classroom.

We also found that the preferred way of working in the school was as an individual teacher who was responsible for her or his own class group of students. Teachers coped with the demands of school reforms and other people's expectations by running highly classroom-centered learning activities. This extended to private use of planning time and other activities where cooperative expenditure of effort and sharing of expertise would benefit everyone.

Resolving Temporal Issues

Time is a lens for examining what we do (Lafleur, 2000). Knowing how we spend time and how we experience it help us to understand our lives. Time is basically tragic. We have a limited amount of it. The reality for most of us is that time is a precious and limited resource. As a result, we have to set priorities and strategically abandon certain activities. In our case, it was important to give our project a special status in our lives. We made a commitment to make that extra special effort. Our priorities included our collaborative inquiry.

When we could, we met at Jack's school. This gave Clay an opportunity to meet the students and to participate in classroom activities. Most often, however, we would meet either after school or on weekends, usually at Jack's home. Our meetings normally lasted about one to two hours. Because Clay had more flexibility in scheduling his time, he was the person who usually traveled to our meetings.

When it came to working collaboratively together, we would always "go the extra mile." Because we lived and worked in two different communities that were about thirty miles apart, going the extra mile was something that we literally had to do, and it meant we had to plan our meetings carefully. Planning time often occurred after school and in the evenings, and this usually meant that time was stolen from our family and personal lives.

Dealing with Uncertainty

It is our belief that in these unsettling times of profound educational reform, teachers must find ways to make change their friend. Teaching now occurs in a context of turbulence, ambiguity, political change, market-driven principles, increased demands for accountability, and evolving governance structures. All of these changes make it imperative that teachers find efficient and effective strategies for supporting their own learning. It is our belief that collaborative teacher research is a proactive way for teachers to take charge of their own learning. When the pace of change is so intense and hurried, it is easy to retreat into our classrooms and raise defensive walls. This, however, represents a serious form of malpractice, one that works to the detriment of improving student learning and the professional development of teachers.

Communicating the Results of Our Research

It is important for us to share the results of our collaborative research. We believe that what we are doing can help others initiate their own inquiry and improve their own practice. Having the opportunity to communicate with others is also a way to validate and celebrate our work. We have found that collaborative inquiry is an integral part of good teaching. Consequently, it is important for us to be part of public conversations about teaching and learning based on the evidence we gather. Such conversations are forums for true accountability.

Making our research available, however, means preparing and writing the results of our efforts. In our partnership, the writing always became Clay's responsibility. Because Jack was much more comfortable talking about the outcomes of our research, his involvement in the actual writing was nominal at best. As much as we would have liked to use a systematic process and, for example, taped all of our conversations, this was rarely the case. Most often we had long conversations, each of us making our own notes. Clay would then write a first draft based on his own notes and ideas. Jack would respond to a first draft, and the process would alternate until a final product was ready.

Given that time is a scarce commodity, it was often difficult to produce a written product that was truly collaborative and satisfactory to both of us. What we write is always a work in progress. Writing is still something that consumes a great deal of our time and effort. It is a process that requires respectful negotiation and care in our working together.

Conclusion

We believe that our collaborative inquiry has made a difference for student learning and achievement. Over the years, we have documented feedback from parents as testimonials to the changes in student behavior resulting from the learning experiences in Jack's classroom. In addition, students, including those once deemed "at risk," have been able to demonstrate their ability to achieve curriculum outcomes through classroom demonstrations, portfolios, and scores on large-scale tests. Because our action research has been underway for a number of years now, Jack has had numerous conversations with past students who have specifically recalled the impact of the inquiry process on their own subsequent learning. If asked, "Where's your evidence?" we have data to demonstrate that our action research activities have resulted in improved instruction and student learning. Systems undergoing curriculum management audits (Frase, English, & Poston, 1995), for example, would be well advised to support collaborative teacher research as a way of gathering a variety of data "to evaluate continuously the school district's program" (p. 185).

Our collaborative research has also greatly enhanced our own professional learning. We have developed a sense of confidence and efficacy. We believe our teacher–researcher partnership is a special form of collaboration that is worth sharing. We hope that some of the ideas presented here will complement the other chapters in this book so that a rich and meaningful conversation about collaboration will occur.

Collaboration is not a scary and academic exercise. The very fact that our collaborative inquiry is not undertaken for university accreditation and that it has been sustained for such a long period of time is a testimony that there is more to collaboration than external recognition. It is also an intrinsic and personally meaningful process. Furthermore, collaboration of the kind we have described has tremendous payoff for students. It provides a foundation for improvement.

We do realize that collaborative teacher research takes time. Making your own practice problematic, gathering data about your own practice, and analyzing those data so that improvement can occur is demanding, time-consuming, and focused work. Teachers who work in isolation are rarely able to undertake and really benefit from classroom inquiry in a sustainable way. Because such results-oriented inquiry is so critical to improvement, we strongly advocate the deliberate development of communities of learners where a culture of inquiry and collaboration are actively supported. Where access to a school district researcher or university researchers is not available, we would encourage the development of teacher leaders in schools and school districts who have responsibility for research (see, for example, Hargreaves, 1997).

It is our belief that teachers have a professional responsibility and obligation to be collaborative and critical learners (Smyth, 1991). The teachers' workplace can benefit tremendously by nurturing a culture of collaboration and inquiry. As Rosenholtz (1989, p. 205) said, "the social organization of schools renders meaning to the nature of teaching." Collaboration is an educative enterprise that contributes to school improvement. It empowers those doing the collaboration and helps them come to a deeper, broader, and richer understanding of what they do and how they can do it better. Collaboration has the potential to transform individuals into active agents of change.

References

Erikson, E. H. (1950). *Childhood and society*. New York: Norton.

Frase, L. E., English, F. W., & Poston, W. K. (Eds.). (1995). The curriculum management audit: Improving school quality. Lancaster, PA: Technomic.

Hargreaves, A. (1997). From reform to renewal: A new deal for a new age. In A. Hargreaves & R. Evans (Eds.), *Beyond educational reform: Bringing teachers back in*. Buckingham, UK: Open University Press.

Lafleur, C. (1992, April). *The evolution and value of teacher research in the change process: From learning styles to conferencing.* Paper presented at the annual meeting of the American Educational Research Association, San Francisco.

Lafleur, C. D. (1995). Towards a culture of inquiry. *Orbit, 26*(4), 16–19.

Lafleur, C. (2000, April). *Time as a lens for evaluating educational reform.* Paper Presented at the annual meeting of the American Educational Research Association, New Orleans.

Lafleur, C. D., & MacFadden, J. (1998). Collaborative action research: Increasing standards of practice in a culture of inquiry. In J. Delong & R. Wideman (Eds.), *Action research: School improvement through research-based professionalism.* Toronto: Ontario Public School Teachers' Federation.

MacFadden, J., Lafleur, C. D., Rouhani, A., Geddes, A., Pickles, M., Hofmann, A., & Hodgon, K. (1998, April). *Student voice: Struggling to place students at the centre of learning.* Paper presented at the International Conference on Teacher Research. University of California, San Diego.

Rosenholtz, S. J. (1989). *Teachers' workplace: The social organization of schools.* New York: Longman.

Schmuck, R. A., & Schmuck, P. A. (1975). *Group processes in the classroom* (2nd ed.). Dubuque: Wm. C. Brown.

Skolimowski, T. J. (1994). *The participatory mind.* London: Penguin.

Smyth, J. (1991). *Teachers as collaborative learners.* Milton Keynes, UK: Open University Press.

Tuckman, B. W. (1965). Developmental sequences in small groups. *Psychological Bulletin, 63,* 384–399.

APPENDIX 15.1. Stages of Collaborative Action Research

Stage	Focus	Teacher's Role	Researcher's Role
0	Initiating	Teacher decides to participate, communicates expectations, and negotiates terms of the action research.	Researcher decides to participate, communicates expectations, and negotiates terms of the action research.
1	Dependence	Teacher relies on the researcher for direction and advice. Teacher facilitates researcher activities.	Researcher provides structure. Researcher is "in" authority and "an" authority.
2	Rebellion	Teacher challenges researcher for more control of classroom-based inquiry and becomes teacher-as-researcher in own right. The teacher is prepared to take risks in the teacher–researcher relationship and is more assertive in meeting own needs.	Researcher provides medium to high structure and helps to reestablish expectations and norms. Researcher actively listens to and supports the teacher in becoming more involved in the research process. The researcher comes to terms with "letting go" and begins to share more responsibilities.
3	Cohesion	Teacher and researcher work through each phase of the action research cycle in a cooperative and collaborative manner. Teacher accepts more responsibility for each phase of action research. Teacher provides suggestions about the action research process to the researcher. Teacher becomes an equal partner in the action research process.	Researcher works cooperatively and collaboratively with the teacher. Researcher continues to provide some structure and encourages the teacher to accept more responsibility for each phase of the action research.
4	Interdependence	Teacher continues to do action research as a regular part of classroom instruction. The teacher is a researcher. Consultation and collaboration with researcher continues as required.	Researcher provides little structure and participates in the action research process on a mutually negotiated basis. Researcher continues to creatively extend the action research in a truly recursive way.

Appendix 15.1 (*continued*)

Stage	Kind of Motivation	Type of Learning	Optimum Environment for Progression
0	Motivation is usually extrinsic (e.g., fulfilling course work or thesis requirements, part of a project, research study, or publication effort). The intent is often that of pleasing others, and issues of control tend to acknowledge the status quo. Participation is often of a compliant nature.	Learning tends to be tentative and largely convergent, focused on specific tasks related to launching the action research activities. Learning also relates to how best to negotiate the parameters of the action research task.	Identify an area of mutual concern, one that is both meaningful and practical. Agree on a mutual vision. Negotiate and communicate with respect and openness. Begin in a manageable way.
1	Motivation remains primarily extrinsic and may involve pleasing others, being compliant, and fulfilling external requirements.	Learning tends to be largely convergent— getting the individual research tasks completed. There is a focus on doing the research as planned and coping with the new working conditions.	Keep the research procedure simple and manageable with clearly identified structure and boundaries. Provide opportunities for regular feedback and conversations that feature active listening. Provide opportunities for related staff development.
2	Motivation is both extrinsic and intrinsic. In addition to pleasing others, there is a sense of excitement and a desire to meet one's own needs and to have some control of the research. There is a willingness to take risks and be more assertive about own interests.	Learning still tends to be convergent, although there are concerns about how to do the research more efficiently and effectively. Concerns about roles, respon-sibilities, and relation-ships appear.	Provide consistent structure, direction, and support to the action research process. Continue conversations and focus on building trust and a sense of confidence about the research. Respect individual needs and support risk taking. Continue staff development.

Appendix 15.1 (*continued*)

Stage	Kind of Motivation	Type Of Learning	Optimum Environment for Progression
3	Motivation is more intrinsic than extrinsic. There is now a concern to share affection mutually and to work cooperatively and collaboratively. There is also a need to develop a sense of competence with regard to the social environment and the research process. Mutual respect becomes an issue, and there is a commitment to achieve joint recognition for the collaborative effort.	Real learning about the action research process begins to appear. Learning about the content of the research is still mostly convergent. In addition, there is discussion and reflection, although relatively uncritical, about the research.	Continue building a sense of competence and confidence about the action research process. Extend the repertoire of inquiry skills. Encourage networking and the sharing of the action research experiences. Celebrate surprises, frustrations, and personal learning. Consolidate collaboration skills and work on constructively critical communication.
4	Motivation is mainly intrinsic. Individuals have a sense of competence and confidence about their social environment and are able to work individually and collaboratively with an equitable distribution of power and control.	Conversation is the norm, and issues are critically debated. Learning focuses on how to agree within a context of disagreement. Both convergent and divergent learning related to the research process are practiced.	Focus on new adventures and personal goals beyond the current action research. Consider disengagement issues and negotiate constructive ways to work in different relationships.

Chapter

16

A School–University Partnership: A Commitment to Collaboration and Professional Renewal

Les Vozzo and Barbara Bober

This chapter outlines how two practitioners collaborated on a project to develop a school-based professional development program. Barbara was the leading teacher (equivalent to assistant principal) from a comprehensive girl's high school in Sydney, Australia, and Les was the university colleague from a neighboring university. The project encouraged teachers to critically reflect on their teaching and learning practice and enabled us to understand and cultivate our collaborative partnership over five years. Our focus in this chapter is to describe how our collaborative partnership developed and demonstrate how other educators can facilitate collaboration and professional renewal in their schools or institutions. The first section of this chapter briefly describes the impetus for the project and outlines our roles within the project. The next section describes a model for collaboration between school and university colleagues. The final section examines some of the issues and concerns we faced in developing our collaborative partnership and how we resolved them.

The Impetus for Collaboration

It takes time and the right conditions before a truly collaborative partnership between school and university personnel can take root and flourish. In this section, we would like to emphasize the historical background that led to the development of our partnership and our support of teachers in their professional development. In 1993–1994, there was a significant groundswell of opinion at the school in support of longer periods of teaching time; at the same time the school moved to mixed-ability classes. Teachers, students, and parents participated in a survey that Barbara conducted on "Best Practices for Teaching and Learning for Quality Assurance." These occurrences—together with many teachers attending training courses on a variety of issues such as negotiating the curriculum, addressing individual learning styles, and cooperative learning—resulted in much debate about pedagogy and facilitated a climate for change and collaboration.

In December 1993, the Teaching–Learning Committee made up of voluntary representatives from the faculty of the high school was formed. Its aim was to draw up the Teaching–Learning Charter, which would embody teacher beliefs about good teaching–learning practice. This charter, completed in February of 1994 and ratified by teachers in March of the same year, was to act as a framework for future directions of the school. During this period, Barbara on behalf of the Teaching–Learning Committee applied for funding to the University of Western Sydney Macarthur. These funds were made available as an initiative of the Innovative Links project. The proposal was successful, and this provided the necessary impetus to develop a school-based professional development program that would enable teachers to reflect on and extend their teaching–learning practice.

The Innovative Links Project was an initiative funded under the Commonwealth Government's National Professional Development Program. At a national level, the Innovative Links Project consisted of sixteen roundtables between schools and universities in Australia. The aim of the roundtables was to provide support for ongoing professional development programs that examined the work organization structures and practices of schools in partnership with academic associates (university colleagues) from a university (Sachs, 1997).

Each school in the Innovative Links project had developed its own unique school-based professional development program and met regularly as a roundtable to share what they were doing in their school. In our case, the program aimed to address the individual needs of the participating teachers and explore aspects of the school's learning charter. The program used action or teacher research, conversation, and case writing as processes to help teachers research and critically reflect on their classroom practice. As our partnership unfolded, it also became important for us to research and critically reflect on our individual roles within the program.

The Collaborative Process As It Emerged

At the same time the teachers were carrying out action research on their practice, we were grappling with our own research in how best to support the teachers involved in the school-based professional development program. Initially, our focus in phase one was on developing a possible structure that would best facilitate teachers' use of action research. The focus later shifted in phase two to identifying best ways of reporting teachers' action research projects. This change of focus was a result of what we had learned from the first phase of the project. We adopted an action research approach because it enabled us to reflect on our actions and bring about change to our practice. Carr and Kemmis (1986, p. 165) clearly defined the purpose of action research as "aiming to improve practice, improve the understanding of that practice, and improve the situation in which the practice takes place." This definition was applied to our research. There are areas where the same process is known as teacher research.

In 1996, we wrote and presented two papers about the project. In these papers, we summarized and elaborated on a set of recommendations about school-based professional development. These recommendations were to

- establish a common vision and support structure for teachers within the school,

- encourage teachers to take ownership of their professional development by focusing on their teaching,

- structure time for reflection and collaboration,

- establish the practice of having a professional friend or colleague for each teacher,

- gain access to a university colleague as an associate to the school, and

- encourage case writing for enhancing critical reflection.

Mutual Minds at Work

We worked together for five years on this project and as a result have grown closer professionally. This growth has enabled us to understand how our personal qualities have contributed to our respective roles and to the overall success of the project. As initiators of the project, we placed high value on the importance of building strong relationships with the teachers involved and responding to their needs. The teachers in turn influenced our thinking and the scope of the project.

Les as the university colleague or "professional friend" (Vozzo & Bober, in press) provided advice and encouragement to assist teachers in their investigations. This role provided the impetus for the teams to come together and discuss classroom research. He supported the teachers in three ways: first, by being the "external" person to listen to their ideas; second, by providing knowledge about action research; and third, by guiding and supporting the research process.

We believe this role has the potential to bridge the gap between academic and teacher research and greatly enhance the professional growth of practitioners from both settings. We didn't want to present Les's role as being that of a critic because of his position as the university colleague; rather, we wished to present him as an advocate of praise and professional support. We believed that schools and universities must work together in classroom research and together generate knowledge about practitioner research. Such collaboration would ultimately lead to the production of various publications about practitioner research and contribute to improvements to practice in education settings.

Les explained why he continued to work at the school for five years in the following comments:

> Firstly, I had built up a number of strong friendships with staff from the school. I also enjoyed working in the school and felt that I could contribute to the growth of various educational programs offered by the school. Secondly, it provided a context for my doctoral studies. In this study I could explore structures that could foster an effective professional development for teachers and investigate conditions that would enhance collaboration between university and school colleagues. I used affirmation and encouragement in supporting my colleagues in their research. Thirdly, it gave me an opportunity to focus on my skills in facilitating other people's professional development and giving me the impetus to extend my professional work to other schools. (July 1999)

We both feel that the project allowed us to develop a set of guidelines for establishing an effective professional development program that led to school improvement. We have already a considerable amount of trust with each other; we know that we can work together because we share similar values and have a proven record of working together.

Although it was important to have a university colleague to facilitate the program, it was equally important to have a school-based individual to coordinate and motivate staff in their professional development. Barbara's role as coordinator was to negotiate a research framework with teachers, to liaise with the university colleague, to schedule team meetings, to coordinate funds and training courses for individuals or groups that address teacher research focus areas, and to be a teacher researcher herself. Following are Barbara's comments:

> As the school coordinator I have undertaken my own research project as a way of promoting professional dialogue with colleagues. I have felt a great deal of satisfaction in motivating teacher teams to share their experiences and plan further aspects of their research. I also wanted to have an empathetic understanding of the process . . . to guide and assist teachers, not necessarily to show teachers how to do action research but rather to demonstrate that it could be done. I have always believed that in order to gain a commitment from others you need to demonstrate that commitment yourself particularly through your own words and actions. (August 1997)

In the following section, we outline the key conditions that supported our partnership. The partnership grew mutual respect and admiration as we came to agree on common goals associated with the project. This mutual respect solidified as we encouraged and motivated each other to write and present papers together. It was through this experience that we were able to formulate a model for collaborative professional development.

A Model for Successful School–University Partnership

Our model is illustrated in Figures 16.1 and 16.2. Figure 16.1 summarizes the main personal characteristics and actions we found important in our partnership and believe to be necessary for effective collaboration between colleagues. These characteristics and actions are elaborated further in this section. Figure 16.2 illustrates how these characteristics and actions that defined our school–university partnership were linked to teacher professional development and the characteristics of a school. A discussion of the necessary personal characteristics for effective school–university partnership follows.

Mutual Respect and Friendship

Mutual respect and friendship was essential and contributed strongly to our long-lasting partnership. For us this was based on our understanding of and ability to apply best practices in teaching and learning. Our own participation and interaction with the teachers involved in the project strengthened the mutual respect that developed between us. We would meet regularly to discuss aspects of the project and talk freely about our own actions in leading and facilitating the project. These conversations helped us to understand our personal values and beliefs about education. During these meetings, we would encourage and motivate each other. By going public and presenting our story to others, we were assisted in better understanding the roles we had within the project.

Figure 16.1. Personal characteristics and actions for successful school–university collaboration.

Personal Characteristics	Actions
Mutual Respect Enthusiasm for Learning Shared Goals and Commitment Integrity Strong Interpersonal Skills Effective Communications	Participating Affirming Challenging Clarifying Listening Modelling Mentoring Evaluating

University Colleague	School Colleague
• Awareness and support of best practice in learning and teaching • Aware of processes needed to improve student outcomes • Provide knowledge and experience in undertaking action research • Be a professional friend for affirming and supporting teacher reflection	• Promote best practice in learning and teaching • Negotiate a research framework that focuses on learning and teaching • Lead whole school improvement in learning and teaching • Coordinate and motivate staff to be involved in their own development

Enthusiasm for Learning

We saw the teachers and ourselves as lifelong learners and promoted this concept as we worked alongside teachers involved in the project. As facilitators of the learning process, we modeled the need to keep on learning and to have an open mind to new ideas, particularly when we were so focused on trying to improve our practice as leaders and facilitators of teacher professional development.

We continually talked about learning, and we provided each other with opportunities for reflection and sharing our understanding as we struggled to write various papers. This dialogue and our inherent qualities allowed us to be open, honest, and constructive in analyzing our leadership practice. Our partnership enabled us to be learners and helped us to focus on issues that were affecting our practice. By being frank and honest with each other, we were able to generate solutions and take turns in mentoring each other.

Shared Goal and Commitment—Similar Beliefs and Values

We both were determined to make our project a success. We made commitments to the teachers who participated in the project. We also made a commitment to each other to write and present papers together. The writing was in fact a personal challenge to both of us. We also came to realize that the teachers' own enthusiasm and dedication to their individual projects in turn assisted us in clarifying and reshaping our purpose and giving us the necessary motivation and support to keep working with them. There were teachers who completely immersed themselves in their action research. Their enthusiasm and commitment to exploring their practice affected us in several ways. For one thing, our own confidence in our ability to lead change grew and consequently impacted on our further involvement. In addition, our respect for individual practitioners grew and gave us insight into their needs and strengths. This allowed us to support them in more direct and appropriate ways.

Integrity

Integrity sprang from a continuation of our commitment to the people with whom we worked and to ourselves. Les felt it was extremely important to make a long-term commitment with the school by working on the project for a number of years. This demonstrated the value he could offer the project as the university colleague. In the same way, Barbara tried to put in place contingency plans that would allow things to continue. Both of us had developed strong friendships with the participating teachers and did not want the professional development program to disappear. We believed in the value of the program that the teachers had committed so much of their time and energy over the past five years.

Strong Interpersonal Skills

The underlying characteristic this successful collaboration was the ability of the colleagues to work with one another. The relationships and trust that developed fueled the project. It took time and skill to build trust and the feeling of being valued. We both needed time to get to know each other and to build the trust that allowed us to be open and honest with each other. It takes time for colleagues to be satisfied that something new may bring about benefits.

Effective Communication

The ability for us to articulate clearly our roles and changing expectations was a reflection of the degree of mutual respect and trust that had developed through the process of collaboration. We had to express the goals and desired outcomes of the project and explain to colleagues our beliefs concerning best practice in teaching and learning. We shared our thoughts and feelings as our roles expanded. We also wanted to guide and assist the participating teachers to express their beliefs before, during, and at the end of each cycle of action research.

Figure 16.2. A model for successful school–university partnership.

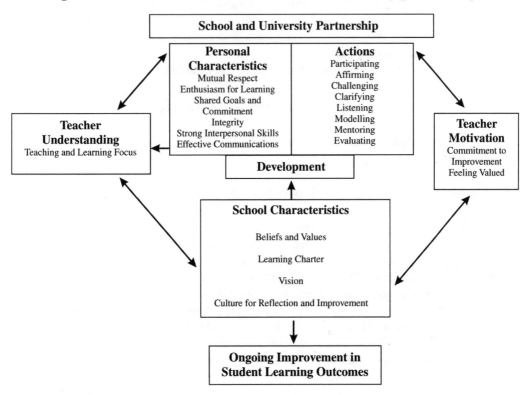

It is important to look at the nature of the collaboration in relation to the context of the project. Barbara's role was to coordinate the professional development program for teachers in her school, and Les's role was to support the initiative and observe changes to work practices of teachers in the school. The project itself became a "playing field" for us to tease out new ideas about practice and understand how learning and teaching was occurring in the classroom.

In terms of how we worked together, Barbara made the following comment during one of our conversations: "We were a good complement. You had the big picture and I was working to understand it and to make sure the school structure could accommodate what you were suggesting. I would often translate and work out what I had to do to put the ideas into action" (December 1999). Les believed that the project was process oriented, saying, "The way I like to operate is to listen to the other person and build on what they have to say. And you are similar in that you like to take on board different people's ideas and merge them with your own to develop something that is quite unique" (December 1999).

In Figure 16.2, we illustrate our collaborative model and show how our personal characteristics and actions associated with our school–university partnership are linked to teacher professional development and the characteristics provided by the school. The interplay resulted in improving teacher motivation and understanding that it contributed to improving the achievement of student learning outcomes.

Some Issues and Resolutions

In this section we discuss the major issues and concerns we encountered and their solutions.

The Role of the University Colleague/Consultant

Initially, the role of the university colleague was undefined. This allowed a range of possible roles, depending on what the school required and what interested Les. During the first phase of the project, the role of the university colleague was that of a consultant or facilitator of the action research process. In the second phase, this role was expanded to include researcher and professional friend.

Les's role was not typical of the traditional role of the consultant or academic coming into a school. He very much wanted to establish a long-term professional partnership with Barbara and the teachers involved in the project. This did not mean his involvement was without its concerns. One tension Les experienced was his need to conduct research to complete a doctorate while honoring the teachers' needs and not exploiting their situation. In other words, his research had to be relevant to them. Les took comfort in what Barbara said on this issue:

The fact that you needed to complete your doctorate did not preclude the benefits to the staff who participated in the project. Quite often the real motivation for schools to work with a university colleague is the mutual benefits that are derived from such collaboration. We discovered that your interest in learning was the real motivation for you to work with the school. It was to our advantage that you could work with us, even though conditions had changed, and the project itself was no longer funded. (October 1999)

Les continued to work on the project for a number of reasons. He said, "I got to know people, and my role was helping them. It gave me a great deal of satisfaction. In the first phase, my role was to facilitate others in using action research. In the second phase, my role was different. I became very much a stakeholder, and I felt an ownership of the program. I was able to suggest groupings amongst the teachers and suggest refinements to various aspects of their research" (October 1999).

Maintain Dialogue and Ensure That Structures Were in Place to Support Such Dialogue

Constant dialogue about practice is vital for all practitioners. In this project, we established a structure that brought colleagues together in teams to talk about their research. This structure enabled cross-faculty teams of three or four teachers, based on trust and mutual respect of each person's expertise, to develop. This led to the teachers experiencing ownership and commitment to the professional development program.

As the project proceeded, the team meetings occurred on a more regular basis and were audio taped so that teacher conversations could be recorded and used by both the teachers and by Les for analysis and writing. This required an extra amount of time from Les to transcribe and return transcripts to the teachers. Les found this task difficult and summarizes his thoughts in the following comment: "I was very slow in transcribing the conversations from the audio-tapes, and this caused me some frustration. This process would take some weeks before the teachers could get back their account" (October 1999).

The team meetings were an integral component to the success of the project. Teachers' discussions across different subject areas and about different teaching strategies resulted in a productive learning environment that contributed to their professional development. Asking them to share their practical knowledge and experiences resulted in the teachers gaining a better understanding of their practice. We also found the conversations were essential to helping us understand what we were doing as leaders and facilitators of the professional development program. We came to realize that the teams and the way they meet must follow a protocol that encourages affirmation and sharing. In developing this protocol, we found that it was important for us to improve our ability to ask questions and critically reflect on our practice.

The Need to Develop Self-Appraisal Strategies and Skills in Writing

Practitioners must know what questions to ask of themselves to guide their research and bring about change to their practice. They also must be supported with appropriate training in how to formulate their research focus, how to carry out action research, and then how to evaluate their practice.

We used the writing of papers and teacher cases (vignettes) as a strategy to encourage critical reflection and gain recognition of personal achievement. The writings served as milestones for indicating professional growth. Initially, we all found writing daunting. One of the greatest difficulties about teacher case writing was the teachers' acceptance of the process. Too many immediate problems got in the way, and it took a special effort on the part of the teachers to allocate time to write. Only when teachers were able to make a link of presenting their research to a wider audience of colleagues with their own changed practice and learning did they find a reason to write. In our case, we found that writing and presenting papers made us realize the value of what we were doing and gave us a purpose for the partnership.

During the first phase of the project, the teachers were encouraged to keep a learning journal on their research. Barbara made the following comment: "The fact that Les collected the journals in the first phase was the main reason why the teachers kept them. In hindsight we should have emphasized the need to keep a journal as a reflective tool to aid their thinking about practice" (January 2000).

In the second phase, we emphasized case writing as an important process to facilitate critical reflection. The teacher cases were collected and compiled in a book for the school library. We believe this was important for the participating teachers because it provided an account of their research to be disseminated to a wider audience. It also gave them some recognition of their achievement. Nonetheless, finding time to write was a hurdle for all of us to overcome.

Teacher Inquiries and Promoting Further Learning As a Way of Professional Life

Over the past few years, we have strongly advocated the importance of recognizing the wealth of practical knowledge that can be generated from practitioner research. In 1998, Les initiated discussion with the New South Whales (NSW) Department of Education and Training (DET) to pilot a new work-based master's program in practitioner research. In 1999, the University of Western Sydney Macarthur and the NSW Department of Education and Training launched the Master of Practitioner Research program. The DET provided sponsorship, and eighteen educators started the pilot program in July 1999. Initiatives such as this are important for acknowledging the value of workplace learning and can provide a vehicle for practitioners to gain recognition for their research.

The Question of Leadership and the Need to Foster Individual Leadership within Teacher Teams

In 1998, Barbara left the school to accept a new appointment at another school. Her departure led to the introduction of team leaders to facilitate teacher action research and support new teachers within the program. The role of team leaders created a new role for some of the experienced teacher–researchers and allowed time for Barbara's successor to settle in to her new role as the school's professional development coordinator.

Conclusion

We have shared how our professional partnership evolved and how it affected the outcomes of the project. Our research has given us an understanding of how to advance possible structures for teacher reflection and identify what personal qualities and actions are important for enhancing the professional growth of educators. We hope ur account will inform policy designers as they make decisions about the future delivery of teacher professional development in schools and the nature of school–university partnerships.

The personal benefits we gained from working together, we believe, may provide educators with incentives to build similar partnerships in their professional lives. For Barbara, the benefits were as follows:

I have a great deal of personal satisfaction from my involvement in the program. I was able to fulfil my role as the leading teacher. I gained respect for colleagues through listening to them, and they respected me as someone who was willing to focus on teacher needs and share ideas. My enduring focus on students and teachers as learners has reinforced the importance of collaboration in improving learning and teaching practice. I have been able to talk from experience and model the process as a classroom teacher and school leader. This has given me a great deal of credibility and the knowledge to implement change elsewhere. I now want to test the school–university partnership model in my new school. [Barbara left East Hills Girls Technology High School at the start of 1998 to take up a position as principal in another school]. (January 1999)

For Les, the benefits were the following:

I gained a real understanding of what problems teachers encounter when they undertake action research and case writing. By listening to the participating teachers, I was able to modify the professional development program that Barbara and I were leading and keep a focus on the practicality of what we were trying to do. I was able to identify questions I should ask to best facilitate teacher talk and writing. I realized how critical this was in improving teacher reflection. I developed an appreciation of the wealth of practical knowledge classroom teachers have and the importance to have that knowledge shared within the teaching fraternity. (January 1999)

We want to emphasize the importance of providing time for practitioners to plan, reflect, and talk to others about research and practice. School leaders need to make sure resources are available to allow this to happen. Funds must be available for curriculum initiatives such as those discussed in this chapter.

We believe that university and school personnel who engage in professional dialogue and writing have the potential to significantly broaden teacher understandings of pedagogy, raise standards of teaching, and enhance ongoing student learning outcomes.

References

Carr, W., & Kemmis, S. (1986). *Becoming critical: Education, knowledge and action research*. Melbourne, Australia: Deakin University.

Sachs, J. (1997). Renewing teacher professionalism through Innovative Links. *Educational Action Research, 5*(3), 449–462.

Vozzo, L., & Bober, B. (In press). School-university collaboration and teacher professional growth. In J. Baird (Ed.), *Reflecting, teaching, learning: Perspectives on educational improvement*. Melbourne, Australia: Hawker Brownlow Education.

Model IV

Multiple Collaboration Projects Under One Umbrella Organization Acting As the Facilitator

In this model, each project team is composed of university-based and school-based educators, as well as other possible stakeholders. Collaboration takes place within each team and across teams.

Chapter

17

The Center for Collaborative Research at National-Louis University

Marianne Handler and Ruth Ravid

In the fall of 1990, we attended a meeting of a group of National-Louis University (NLU) faculty members convened by our dean. The meeting served as an open forum for faculty to share ideas and projects related to the improvement of education in the Chicago public schools. At that meeting, we discovered a shared interest in creating an umbrella organization aimed at bringing together school-based practitioners and university faculty who were seeking opportunities to work collaboratively on topics of mutual interest. Our dean pledged her support to our plan and promised to help us. She suggested that we apply for grant funding. In the winter and spring of 1991, we spent many hours articulating our vision and describing the center we wanted to establish. We became familiar with various models of school–university collaboration and determined there was a need to provide an umbrella-like environment for school- and university-based educators to come together and work as equal partners. We brainstormed and designed such an organization and thus began the Center for Collaborative Research (CeCoR). Our vision was that this center would support the collaborative work of its participating school–university partners and would provide any help needed along the way. Such help would include support in planning and implementing the project, as well as with data collection, analysis, and interpretation. Because we believe that the results of each project should benefit all educators, we proposed that the partners share their findings with other educators by presenting the results formally and informally, through an oral presentation or in print.

In this chapter, we share our experiences, insights, and recommendations based on our roles as co-directors of CeCoR during the six years of the center's existence (1992 to 1998). This is also the story of our own collaboration and partnership over the last ten years. Unlike many of the other collaborations depicted in this book, we are both university faculty, rather than school–university partners. Therefore, there was never any real or perceived power hierarchy in our relationship. Our interests and goals were probably more similar than is the case in many school–university partnerships. Nonetheless, we feel that our credibility as educators who have promoted partnerships has significantly increased because the two of us have had this opportunity to experience and model collaboration. Firsthand experience has allowed us to better understand, plan, and anticipate process issues in the collaboration before and during its undertaking. It has also allowed us to better reflect and document the nature of collaboration.

In many ways, our collaborative relationship has resembled other school–university partnerships. We started as acquaintances and became best friends. We encouraged and supported each other, letting our personal and professional lives intermingle and intertwine. Each of us, through collaborating with the other, has become a more informed, more complete person. Neither could have carried out the CeCoR project alone, but together we could do it, despite the difficulties along the way. We compensated for each other's weaknesses and periodic downturns. When one faltered, the other rallied; when one felt disappointment, the other one persevered and encouraged. We continue as collaborators in the true sense of the word, as is evidenced by the publication of this book.

We begin this chapter with a brief overview of the Center for Collaborative Research and describe the context and the environment in which we collaborated. We then share the lessons and insights about collaboration gained as a result of our own experience as collaborators and the experience of the partners who collaborated under the umbrella of the center. We hope our story, written from the perspective of our model of collaboration, will add to the growing body of knowledge about school–university collaborations and the factors that contribute to their success and failure.

The Center for Collaborative Research

Underlying Philosophy

The philosophy undergirding our model is in congruence with the work of Cole and Knowles (1993) who discussed a model of partnerships between classroom teachers and university researchers. In their model, each partner contributes particular and important expertise; the relationship between the partners is multifaceted and does not follow a hierarchy of power. The Center for Collaborative Research provided a supportive environment in which university faculty and school-based practitioners came together to explore research questions of common interest. This model grew out of our strong conviction and desire to open the door of the research community to the voice of the school-based practitioner. We support the belief that the voice of the school-based practitioners should be added to the body of knowledge of the field. We promote the idea that there should be a forum for teachers' voices to be heard, and we support a strong emphasis on the dissemination of the findings of the joint research. Consequently, one of the components of the model we envisioned was the idea that the research partners would, in some way, share the findings of their research by publishing their findings or by presenting them to their school colleagues or at local, regional, or national conferences.

Cochran-Smith and Lytle (1993) pointed out that any truly collaborative endeavor must benefit all participants. The Center for Collaborative Research provided an environment for collaborative experience that empowers teachers through these professional growth opportunities. The university faculty, in turn, have seen their own research enriched by this opportunity; they have become participant observers in the classroom culture in a more open and authentic way. We believe our model provides many opportunities to bridge the gap that often exists between university faculty and school-based practitioners. This model also provides opportunity for all partners to honor and appreciate the work of the other.

In addition, the goals of CeCoR were compatible from the beginning with the mission of National College of Education at National-Louis University, where we both are faculty members. Our college values the balancing of traditional scholarly inquiry with knowledge and study of current practice. Our institution has a long tradition of working with schools, respecting practitioner knowledge, and honoring classroom life. Our college of education acknowledges, respects, and rewards the scholarly work of faculty members involved with the application of theory into practice who are interested in collaborating with classroom teachers.

The Process

The first step each year was to recruit school-based and university-based participants. Before or at the beginning of the school year, invitations were sent to local school administrators, to selected groups of teachers, and to other school-based practitioners describing the center and its activities. Interested practitioners completed a form indicating their interest and the area or topic they wished to explore. The application forms, signed by the practitioners' supervising administrator to indicate their approval and support, were returned to the center's co-directors, Marianne and Ruth.

While the center identified the school-based participants, we, as the co-directors, requested information from our colleagues asking if they were interested in being involved in a collaborative research project around school-based issues with a school-based practitioner. After receiving responses from both groups, we began the process of matching partners. We told the school-based practitioners to expect a call from their potential partners. All partners were told that they had the right to withdraw or seek other partners if they did not wish to work with the first suggested partner. Once a team was created, the center encouraged partners to meet and to begin clarifying their research focus.

Following the formation of the teams, the school-based practitioners participated in and received credit for a graduate level, tuition-free course, presented in a series of sessions throughout the year. Topics in this course included reviewing different paradigms of research, methods of data collection and analysis, the research design and planning process, and the role and process of reviewing literature and electronic data bases.

Next, school and university partners attended a session that focused on the nature of collaboration and the skills needed for a successful collaboration. This session also provided an opportunity for all teams to meet together for the first time. During this meeting, members of each team described the question they were considering for investigation and their initial ideas, thoughts, and plans. Members of the other teams and the co-directors provided feedback and suggestions to all participants. Teams were asked to articulate their ideas and write a detailed and formal study plan to be shared with the others and to guide them throughout the research.

Each team continued to meet during the year and implement its project following its own planned time line. Individual teams made their own meeting arrangements and times for school visits. All the teams came together several times between January and June for sharing sessions to report on progress and to seek and provide feedback. At the end of the year, the teams came together again for a final session to share, reflect, and evaluate the project and the process.

During the six years that the center operated, we were (and remain) full-time faculty in the College of Education. We work in separate departments, and each served as chair of our respective department while co-directing the center. Our role as the co-directors was in addition to our full-time responsibilities in the college. Although this created a consistent pressure on our time, we made every attempt to fulfill our duties and provide the necessary support and guidance to the participating teams. Our responsibilities as co-directors included (a) administering and coordinating the center's activities; (b) recruiting and matching practitioners and faculty; (c) coteaching the graduate course connected to the center; (d) facilitating sharing sessions throughout the year; (e) maintaining ongoing contact with the teams; (f) advising and providing resources, such as library computer search and transcription of audio tapes; (g) searching for future external funding; and (h) encouraging and facilitating the dissemination process.

CeCoR partners investigated a variety of topics. Examples include the use of manipulatives in the first grade, creating bridges between inner-city and suburban elementary-age students, emerging literacy in kindergarten, and literature circles in the middle school.

Frustrations

Funding

Funding remained an issue throughout the years that CeCoR operated. Even though we made several attempts to obtain external funding, we were unsuccessful. Nonetheless, our college did provide some resources to develop and maintain the center's programs. These funds have been used to pay tuition for graduate credit (Dean's Grants) for the school-based partners, for travel expenses for the university partners, for stipends for university partners, and for other minimal costs, such as supplies and transcription of audio tapes. Despite insufficient resources, most teams completed their work, and enthusiasm for the process remained high from beginning to end.

During the first year, we spent many hours writing grant proposals in the hope that our efforts would bring needed funds to the center. Because of the insufficient guidance and support from the university grant office at the time, we never did succeed in finding the right places to submit those proposals.

Time Constraints

All those who participated in CeCoR's activities—the co-directors, the school-based partners, and the university-based partners—reported feeling pressured by too many obligations and responsibilities. This is, of course, related to the lack of proper financial resources. For all CeCoR participants, the work associated with the research projects was an add-on to ongoing, full-time positions. As co-directors, we had to put aside plans because of time constraints and constantly juggle our schedule to find time to devote to the center's activities and our responsibilities. For example, we discussed many times our desire to visit the school-based partners and introduce ourselves to their administrators and colleagues but were unable to actually do it. Because of our various responsibilities at the university and the other research studies in which we were involved, neither of us had the opportunity to visit schools and develop a dialogue with teachers. Additionally, because of our sometimes-conflicting schedules, we found it difficult to find time to meet regularly or to spend more time in schools to recruit new practitioner partners. In spite of time constraints, co-directing CeCoR afforded us direct and continuous access to classroom teachers. Helping the participants to plan and carry out their projects was a rewarding experience, and it has increased our feeling of making a real and authentic contribution to the practice of education.

Recruiting Partners

In the first year of CeCoR's operation, we sent recruitment letters to superintendents and principals in all the school districts in the neighboring counties. This required extensive effort and substantial clerical assistance, and we were unable to duplicate that effort in the following years. In addition, we felt that the number of responses from those "cold solicitation letters" did not justify the expense and effort. In subsequent years, we targeted certain individuals and schools where teachers might be interested in participating in such partnerships. Nominations by our faculty colleagues were also helpful in identifying potentially interested practitioners. One major frustration we experienced most years was the difficulty in matching school-based and university-based partners. At times, we had too many practitioners and not enough faculty, whereas at other times the situation was reversed. In some cases, we had a number of school and university educators interested in this type of collaborative research, but the areas they wanted to investigate were not compatible, and we could not match them. This incompatibility caused the number of teams to be inconsistent each year, fluctuating between two to seven. With only two teams, the added layer of multiple teams supporting each other was not as strong as it could have been. Also, having so few groups decreased somewhat the motivation of the participants.

We had always hoped that the school-based partners would return to the center later, as senior partners of a school colleague who shared a school-based concern with them. This never happened and was a disappointment to us as co-directors.

Successes

Publications and Presentations

We asked all the teams to summarize their findings after completing their studies. We encouraged the partners to share their results with colleagues within and outside their own institutions. The results of several projects were presented at local, regional, and national conferences, such as those of the Mid-Western Educational Research Association and the American Educational Research Association. Several reports were also published in professional journals. One team's project resulted in a book designed to support practitioners using multimedia in their classrooms.

Professional Development

To improve the work of CeCoR and the experiences provided to the researcher–partners, we included a wrap-up session at the end of each year and asked faculty and school-based participants to complete a form with a series of open-ended questions. In addition, written surveys were sent to school-based participants to elicit their opinions and feedback. Those who indicated their willingness were later interviewed by phone.

For the University Partners

In informal conversations, as well as in wrap-up sessions held at the end of each year, the university partners shared their thoughts and reflections about the value this partnership had held for them. They indicated that they were glad for the opportunity to work collaboratively with school practitioners and to keep current with the practice of education. Some were pleased to take theoretical areas of interest and expand their research by applying ideas into the school settings with their partners. For others, many of them former K–12 teachers, it was rewarding to spend time in classrooms interacting with students.

For many university partners, participation in CeCoR offered an opportunity to learn, or to be reminded of, daily life in the schools, with its own pressures and instant decision making. They were given the chance to see teacher knowledge in action. This firsthand experience enriched their own teaching—and therefore the teaching of their in-service and preservice students as well.

For the School Practitioners

One major goal of CeCoR was to improve the school participants' perception of the relationship between theory and practice and of the role of research in education. In general, their responses indicated that the participants had improved their attitudes toward research; many indicated they would be interested in conducting other classroom research. Despite this positive response, the practitioners did not return to join the center with another partner at a later time (Ravid & Handler, 1994, 1996).

Another major goal of the center was to provide an environment and experience that would empower teachers, leading them to consider assuming more leadership roles in their own settings. The responses indicated that the respondents felt more confident as teachers and researchers as a result of participating in the center's activities and conducting the research project with a university partner. Although the majority of the respondents felt their administrators and colleagues valued and appreciated them, this was not always the case. Some felt that their administrators were not interested in their work and that their colleagues were not supportive. Other researchers have observed the necessity of such support from one's administration and colleagues, and this theme also appears in many chapters throughout this book.

Sharing the results of the research project was an important factor that has contributed to an increase in the perception of the participants about their own professional growth. In several instances, the projects resulted in papers presented in conferences or published in professional journals. In other cases, the practitioners were asked to present their findings to their colleagues or to write about their experiences in the school's newsletter.

One of the basic premises of the center was that the school-based and the university-based colleagues are considered equal partners. This, of course, does not mean that they both have to do the same things or benefit in the same way from their experience. Our findings indicated that this goal was fully met. An overwhelming majority of the practitioners who responded to the survey stated that they believed they had a role equal to that of their university partner and that the university partner treated the school practitioner as an equal. Elements that contribute to successful partnerships were identified by the respondents and include the following: commitment on the part of both partners; meetings that were perceived as sharing sessions; and ongoing, regularly scheduled meetings. School-based practitioners added two more reasons why they felt valued: The university partners did not look as them as "just a classroom teacher" and were perceived by the practitioners as truly interested and supportive of the school-based partner. Several practitioners commented that their university partners have expanded their knowledge base and provided reading and research resources.

Our research findings confirmed that teachers who participate in research with a university faculty improved their attitudes toward and views of the value of research in general and study of classroom practice specifically. These teachers also acknowledged their role in adding to the body of knowledge that inform practice in their profession. In addition, the experience in CeCoR has contributed to their professional self-concept through recognition from colleagues and administrators.

For the Co-Directors

During the center's first year, Marianne served as both a co-director and as one of the university partners. Although this was an extension of an ongoing collaboration, working within the center provided the needed structure for Marianne and her partner to formalize their goals and the environments in which they collected their data. That partnership resulted in the publication of a book on the uses of hypermedia in classrooms. Some years later Marianne again acted in both roles. This time she collaborated with two of the teachers who wanted to examine electronic note taking in their fifth-grade classrooms. The center again gave the support needed during that first year by helping them recognize the need to clarify, question, and revise their project. Based on the first year's work, Marianne and her partners began data collection the following school year. For the next two years, their partnership extended beyond CeCoR, and they presented their results at the National Educational Computing Conference in San

Diego. These opportunities to spend additional time in classrooms and work with teachers added to Marianne's understanding of the graduate students with whom she works. She was able to observe the pressures that exist in classroom teaching environments as teachers learn to use the technology tools she introduces to her classes.

For Ruth, who has not been in the role of a university partner in a CeCoR team, the professional development gains were different from those Marianne enjoyed. For the past twenty years, Ruth has taught numerous research and assessment courses at National-Louis University. As part of her research courses, Ruth guides her students through small-scale research studies, which are required in all the research courses she teaches. Therefore, she has accumulated much experience in guiding preservice and in-service graduate students through the process. In most courses, the projects are planned, carried out, and completed within ten weeks (our university follows the quarter system). At the end of the course, research projects are evaluated and graded. Working with the teams at CeCoR was different because more time was allocated for carrying the projects, and Ruth's role was not that of a teacher, but that of a mentor and advisor. In addition, all school-based partners at CeCoR conducted their studies in their own practice, unlike preservice students who do not have their own classrooms. Together with Marianne, Ruth served as the teams' guide and mentor; the projects were authentic and meant much more to the participants and their students.

Factors Contributing to the Success and Failure of Partnerships

In an attempt to help others who may consider initiating or improving school–university collaborations, we have analyzed the various partnerships that took place under the auspices of CeCoR. Based on our experience, the following is a discussion of factors that we believe have contributed to the success or failure of partnerships. Although our discussion is based on the partnerships we observed at CeCoR, many of the same factors can be generalized to similar partnerships.

Our Own Successful Collaboration

Ruth's background and expertise lie in the quantitative paradigm and in her more traditional approaches to research. Marianne, on the other hand, focuses her interest around the qualitative paradigms. Ruth is interested in assessment and program evaluation. Marianne's interest is in the application of technology and the role of the classroom teacher in helping students use technology tools in a meaningful way within the learning environment. Together we complement each other in our skills and expertise. Working together closely for more than ten years has allowed both of us to grow, learn new skills, and develop a better understanding of our respective fields.

Our personalities and styles are also different. Compromises, flexibility, and acceptance were necessary for both of us to understand each other and to work collaboratively without judging or trying to change the other person.

In other ways, the two of us are similar. We both tend to put things off, but not until the last minute. We each trust the other and are comfortable dividing assignments. We let the other partner take control of areas at which she excels. We aren't afraid of losing control, nor do we feel the need to be involved in everything.

Successful Partnerships with CeCoR Teams

Our experience has indicated that successful partnerships include most, or all, of the following characteristics:

- Shared educational philosophy
- Strong commitment to the project
- Mutual respect for the knowledge base each partner brought to the project
- A commitment to following through on the implementation of the project
- Regular and ongoing communication
- Investment of time on an ongoing basis
- For the practitioner: being respected and considered an equal by the university partner
- Mutual ownership and commitment to all phases of the project

Unsuccessful Partnerships

At different times, partnership teams were perceived as unsuccessful in meeting the goals they had set for themselves. At others times, the partners themselves recognized that something was lacking in the collaborative relationship. They may have completed the research project, but they had never built a true collaborative relationship. Those unsuccessful partnerships tended to have many of the following characteristics:

- Lack of shared vision
- Lack of a shared focus; this may be a problem even when both partners are committed to the project
- Power struggle among partners
- Irregular, inconsistent communication among partners
- Inability to work *with* each other; working *parallel* to each other instead
- Lack of recognition and support in respective educational context
- Conflict of schedule; difficulty in finding time to meet
- Each partner perceives the other as not fulfilling his or her role and not "carrying his or her weight"
- Lack of a clear agreement on a division of labor

Final Thoughts

As is true with the other authors in this book, we, too, have moved through all the stages of collaboration. As with many of these authors, ours has been a multiyear process, and the project and process have changed as we have moved through the years together. Most of the authors had one experience that was quite different from our collaboration, however. For the most part, they had the ability to watch the process in which they were involved develop from the original seed. We, on the other hand started each year with a group of new seeds—different faculty members, different practitioners, different issues to be addressed. This provided a somewhat different flavor to our partnership.

Our collaboration continued when, as editors of this book, we read through the chapter proposals and realized there were common experiences between our authors and ourselves. We, too, found the issue of time important. We, too, found it took time to build a relationship of openness and trust. We, too, found the importance of having a shared vision to guide and sustain us. We also found the importance of honoring and valuing the knowledge that each of us brought to the partnership, for we are very different in our style of work as well as in the way we approach the field of research. As several authors discovered, what started as partnership for a specific purpose developed into a meaningful friendship along the way. Many times, it was a struggle, but happily this was not true for each of us at the same time; there was always one of us to keep things moving. Would we do it again with all that we know today? You bet we would!

References

Coles, A. L., & Knowles, J. G. (1993). Teacher development partnership research: A focus on methods and issues. *American Educational Research Journal, 30,* 473–495.

Cochran-Smith, M., & Lytle, S. L. (1993). *Inside outside: Teacher research and knowledge.* New York: Teachers College Press.

Ravid, R., & Handler, M. (1994, April). *The many faces of school/university collaboration: Looking at the Center for Collaborative Research.* A Symposium Presentation at the annual meeting of the American Educational Research Association, New Orleans.

Ravid, R., & Handler, M. (1996, April). *School-based practitioners' perceptions of their experience in the Center for Collaborative Research.* Paper presented at the annual meeting of the American Educational Research Association, New York.

About the Contributors

About the Editors

Ruth Ravid (rravid@nl.edu) is a professor at National-Louis University's college of education and has taught courses in research, statistics, and assessment. Ravid served as the department chair of Foundations and Research for the last eight years. She has been active for many years in the American Educational Research Association Special Interest Group, School-University Collaborative Research. Ravid is the author of *Practical Statistics for Educators* (2nd ed., 2000), as well as *Workbook to Accompany Practical Statistics for Educators* (2nd ed., 2000; with E. Oyer), published by University Press of America. Ravid has a PhD and an MA in education from Northwestern University, a BA in psychology from Northeastern University, and a BA in Judaic Studies from Spertus College in Chicago.

Marianne Handler (mhandler@nl.edu) is a professor in the Technology in Education Program at National-Louis University. Handler served as the chair of Technology in Education Department for six years. She is coauthor of *Hypermedia for Student Authors: A Guide for Teachers* (2nd ed., 1998; with Ann Dana) published by Libraries Unlimited. Handler has an MEd and an EdD from National-Louis University. With Sandra Turner she developed *The Data Collector,* a HyperCard stack, for analyzing qualitative data. Her research interests lie in the area of the integration of technology into learning environments. She has served on the Board of Directors of the International Society for Technology in Education (ISTE). She has been recognized as an Apple Distinguished Educator.

About the Contributors

(in alphabetical order)

Nancy Bacharach (nbacha@stcloudstate.edu) is a professor in the Department of Teacher Development at St. Cloud State University in St. Cloud, Minnesota. She received her PhD from Texas A & M University and taught at Syracuse University for three years before going to St. Cloud. Nancy was a member of the steering committee that initiated professional development schools in St. Cloud and has been a faculty liaison for the professional development school for the last two years. Her research interests include collaboration, teacher preparation, and literacy.

William E. Bickel (bickel+@pitt.edu) currently is a professor of Administrative Policy Studies in the School of Education and a Senior Scientist at the Learning Research and Development Center, University of Pittsburgh. His research interests include evaluation methodology and research on evaluation utilization in various organizational and policy contexts and educational reform policy studies. Professor Bickel currently directs an evaluation partnership with the Heinz Endowments for its regional educational initiatives focused on comprehensive, school-based reform; preservice education policy and practice; and technology dissemination in urban school systems. He is past director of an institutional partnership between the University of Pittsburgh and the Lilly Endowment (1990–1997).

Barbara Bober (barbara.bober@det.nsw.edu.au) has been a teacher and educator in the New South Wales high school system for twenty-seven years. She is currently principal at Beverly Hills Girls High School, a metropolitan school in the southwestern area of Sydney, Australia. She was leading teacher at East Hills Girls Technology High School from 1990 to 1997, where much of her research was conducted. Here in collaboration with her university colleague, Les Vozzo, she developed a school-based model for teacher professional development. Barbara has copresented a number of workshops with Les on the issue of school-based professional development at national and international conferences; Bober and Vozzo have also cowritten articles for publication. Bober is currently a member of the Inter School Leadership Group, which works with aspiring leaders in a special leadership preparation program for the New South Wales Department of Education and Training.

Arlene Borthwick (aborthwick@nl.edu) is program coordinator and assistant professor, Technology in Education, at National-Louis University. Between the years 1987 and 1998, she served in roles as a coordinator, project director, external partner representative, and faculty member involved in continuing education and grant-related school–university programs at Kent State University, The University of Tulsa, and Northeastern Illinois University. Several of these programs focused on the implementation of new technologies in the K–12 setting. Borthwick's research interests include effective school–university collaboration, staff development, action research, and school reform. Borthwick received her PhD from Kent State University in 1994.

Donna Cronin (cronin@nh.ultranet.com) holds a bachelor's degree in mathematics from Northeastern University and a master's degree in secondary education from the University of New Hampshire, where she is currently a doctoral candidate. She received the 1990 Presidential Distinguished Teacher Award in Mathematics and was the 1996 recipient of the Presidential Award for Excellence in Mathematics and Science Teaching in the area of Secondary Mathematics. Cronin is a member of the National Council of Teachers of Mathematics, the Council of Presidential of Awardees in Mathematics, and the Association for Supervision and Curriculum Development. Cronin has been a mathematics educator for twenty-eight years, twenty-three of which have been at the middle school level. She has a strong commitment to providing preservice and in-service professional development opportunities for mathematics educators.

Ruth Freedman (rfreedman@nl.edu) is an associate professor in the Elementary Education Program at National-Louis University. She has been on the faculty at NLU for the past eleven years. During her first eight years at NLU, she was a classroom teacher in the second and third grade in the University's Baker Demonstration School and now works with preservice teachers. She has achieved national certification through the National Board for Professional Teaching Standards. Her professional interests include children's peer relationships and their development, literature-based reading instruction, and work with preservice teachers. Freedman and her coauthor, Diane Salmon, are currently working on a curriculum text about the Relational Literacy Curriculum.

Jonathan Fribley (jonathan.fribley@stcloud.k12.mn.us) is an early childhood specialist in the St. Cloud School District where he is working with the Dad's Project. Fribley is also currently serving as a consultant for the state department of Children, Families and Learning. He served as the Site Coordinator at Lincoln Elementary School as they entered into a partnership with St. Cloud State University. His interests lie in the areas of literacy, developmentally appropriate teaching practices, and authentic assessment.

Pamela Gates-Duffield (pamela.sue.gates-duffield@cmich.edu) is associate professor in the Department of English Language and Literature at Central Michigan University. She was involved in creating four professional development school links where she served as university coordinator for several years. Her teaching and publications are in the areas of literacy, children's literature, and professional development schools.

Robin Hasslen (rhasslen@stcloudsstate.edu) is an associate professor in the Department of Child and Family Studies at St. Cloud State University, where she has been since 1988. She received her PhD at the University of Minnesota. Her research interests lie in the areas of professional development, multiage classroom structures, and infant development. She has worked with school–university partnerships and other collaborative ventures.

John Kornfeld (john.kornfeld@sonoma.edu) is an associate professor in the School of Education at Sonoma State University in Rohnert Park, California. Before completing his PhD at Indiana University in 1996, he taught for sixteen years in elementary, middle, and high schools. His research interests include curriculum theory, teacher education, and school–university collaboration. He particularly enjoys research that takes him into the classroom and that requires ongoing conversation with students, teachers, and future teachers.

Clay Lafleur (claymar@home.com) is the curriculum and assessment officer for the Simcoe County District School Board in Ontario, Canada. For the past three years he was the manager of the Assessment Policy Unit in the Curriculum and Assessment Policy Branch of the Ontario Ministry of Education. Prior positions included head of evaluation and research services with the Educational Research Institute of British Columbia and research officer with the South Australian Education Department. Lafleur's current interests focus on issues related to organizations, educational change, inquiry, and school improvement. Recent publications and presentations have dealt not only with these interests, but also with topics such as time perspectives of educators, curriculum and assessment reform, policy development, participatory evaluation, values, organizational improvement, qualitative research methods, and practitioner action research.

Georgia Leyden (gjleyden@sonic.net) has taught first grade for sixteen years at Guerneville School in Sonoma County, California. She earned an master's degree in education from Sonoma State University, where she currently teaches a graduate course in elementary reading. She has conducted a variety of action research projects on inquiry learning and writers' workshop in her classroom, and she has served as teacher leader for the California Reading and Literature Project's Summer Institute. She is currently working on an action research project on democracy in the classroom.

Marylin Leinenbach (esleinen@BEFAC.INDSTATE.EDU) graduated from St. Mary-of-the-Woods College, Terre Haute, Indiana, with a bachelor's degree in mathematics. She has taught in middle schools for twenty-eight years. Leinenbach was a finalist for the Presidential Award for Excellence in Teaching Science and Mathematics (1996). In 1998, she was Disney's American Teacher Award Mathematics Honoree. In 1999, she received an honorary doctorate of science from Rose-Hulman Institute of Technology. In 2000, she became a National Board Certified Teacher. She is currently studying at Indiana State University for a PhD in curriculum, instruction, media and technology (CIMT).

Yvonne Lozano (ylozano@whc.net) is associate superintendent for curriculum and instruction in the Gadsden Independent School District. She is responsible for designing and ensuring implementation of the district professional development plan for all teachers and administrators in the district. In her service as associate superintendent over the past three years, Lozano has focused on providing systematic long-term training for teachers, administrators, and parents. She has led the district to begin use of student achievement data as a form of program assessment and a means to inform the community of school district progress. Lozano also directs the Gadsden Mathematics Initiative and the La Clave project, system-wide efforts to build expertise in standards-based mathematics instruction and technology integration for Gadsden administrators, teachers, students, and parents as an attempt to increase student achievement.

Jack MacFadden (jtmacfadden@home.com) is an elementary school teacher. He is a graduate of the University of Toronto and holds a master's degree from Brock University. Jack began his school-based research in the late 1970s and has worked in collaboration with Clay Lafleur since 1984. Jack was the first teacher president of the Ontario Educational Research Council and will soon become the president of the Ontario History and Social Science Teachers Association. Jack believes that putting the child at the center of learning promotes quality education and encourages an excellent learning environment for all students.

Rosemary McNelis (hattrup+@pitt.edu) is an independent research consultant with more than twelve years of experience in the field of educational evaluation. She received her EdD and master's degrees from the University of Pittsburgh's Department of Administrative and Policy Studies with a focus on Planning, Policy, and Evaluation. She holds a bachelor's degree in English literature and creative writing from Saint Mary's College, Notre Dame, Indiana. As an evaluation consultant, Rosemary has documented and evaluated several educational initiatives including the National Humanities Center's Teacher Leadership for Professional Development Initiative. McNelis formerly served as a research assistant at the University of Pittsburgh's Learning Research and Development Center where her work focused on evaluation research in a variety of settings.

Ann Cox Parham (johnny_parham@hotmail.com) is retired from the New York City Board of Education and is currently a clinical supervisor at Pace University, New York City. She is a graduate of Spelman College in Atlanta, Georgia. She received a master of arts degree from Teachers College, Columbia University, in New York City. Her teaching career includes teaching elementary grades and working with school-based innovative programs involving parents, schools, and communities.

Lil Perre (d4210pn1@ozemail.com.au) is principal of Mount Pritchard East Public School in Sydney, Australia. She taught children from kindergarten to year six for thirty-two years and is in her twelfth year as principal. Her goal as an educator and leader is for literacy and numeracy to be taught in a systematic and explicit way, and her role is to provide the resources to make that happen.

Cathy K. Pine (pineck@mrl.ucsb.edu) is an evaluator for the Educational Outreach Program of the Materials Research Laboratory (MRL) at the University of California, Santa Barbara. She is currently documenting an MRL-sponsored professional development initiative, funded by the National Science Foundation. This initiative supports science teachers in creating standards-based lessons that incorporate innovative uses of current information technologies and strengthen student English language literacy through scientific investigation. In addition to providing research and evaluation assistance to clients in business and academia, Pine has held positions as a computer specialist, mathematics teacher, and teacher trainer in both public and private school settings.

Cathleen Rafferty (cdr11@humboldt.edu) is professor of education and the director of the new Center for Educational Renewal at Humboldt State University in Arcata, California. Educated at Southern Illinois University, Carbondale, Rafferty earned bachelor's and master's degrees in education before teaching remedial reading in Illinois and developmental reading and social studies at a middle school in Gunnison, Colorado. While living in Colorado, Rafferty received a Ph.D. in curriculum and instruction at the University of Colorado, Boulder. Before her move to California, Rafferty was a teacher educator and worked at Eastern Illinois University, Central Michigan University, and Indiana State University. While in Michigan, she completed a postdoctoral fellowship at Michigan State University which focused on professional development schools. She later joined the faculty at Indiana State University, where she was actively involved as a liaison to a middle-level professional development school for eight years. Her special interests include school–university collaboration, the impact of technology on literacy and learning, and performance-based teacher education.

Judith Robb (jkull@christa.unh.edu) is associate professor of education at the University of New Hampshire, Durham, and director of teacher education at the university's urban campus in Manchester. She has a master's degree in science education from the University of South Florida and a doctorate in curriculum and instruction from the University of Rochester. She has served as co-principal investigator for a number of grants from the National Science Foundation and the U.S. Department of Education in support of this work. She is a regular contributor to the American Association of Colleges for Teacher Education, the American Educational Research Association, and the National Educational Computing Conference. Robb is past president of the Northeaster Educational Research Association and current vice president of the National Educational Computing Association.

Judy C. Rotto (j_rotto@yahoo.com) is a primary teacher in the St. Cloud Public Schools, where she has taught children in grades K–3 for twenty-eight years. Judy has served as an adjunct faculty member at St. Cloud State University and recently worked as a Site Coordinator for Learning Connections, a professional development school project uniting St. Cloud State University, St. Cloud Public Schools, and the community. Currently she is teaching second grade at Talahi School, a professional development school located near the SCSU campus.

Diane E. Salmon (dsalmon@nl.edu) is an associate professor of educational psychology and the program director for the School Psychology Program at National-Louis University. She has been on the faculty there for the past eleven years. Her professional interests include children's thinking and cognitive development and children's peer relationships and their relational development. Before her position at National-Louis University, Diane worked as a school psychologist in the public schools.

Richard R. Schramm (rschramm@ga.unc.edu) is the director of education programs at the National Humanities Center in Research Triangle Park, North Carolina. On his way to a Ph.D. in English from the University of North Carolina at Chapel Hill, he taught high school and served as a social worker. Before joining the staff of the Humanities Center in 1984, he taught American literature and designed public programs in the humanities for four years at UNC–CH. He designed and administers the center's Teacher Leadership for Professional Development Program and TeacherServe, the center's on-line curriculum enrichment service for high school teachers. He also organizes the center's summer programs for high school and college faculty.

Catherine Sinclair (c.sinclair@uws.edu.au) is a senior lecturer (associate professor) at the University of Western Sydney and practicum coordinator for the elementary undergraduate teacher education program within the Faculty of Education and Languages. Her teaching and research interests include teaching and learning, the practicum experience, professional development and mentoring, and school–university partnerships.

Judith Slater (slaterj@fiu.edu) is an associate professor of curriculum and instruction at Florida International University, Miami. She is the author of *Anatomy of a Collaboration* (1996) and the coauthor of *Acts of Alignment: Of Women in Math and Science and All of Us Who Search for Balance* (2000). She has published numerous articles on curriculum theory, evaluation, and essays and commentary on educational policy issues.

Adrienne "Andi" Sosin (asosin@ccny.cuny.edu) is associate professor at Pace University's School of Education in New York City and was the director of student teaching from 1989 to 1999. She earned a bachelor of arts in history and education from the State University of New York at Stony Brook, a master of science in reading from Queens College at the City University of New York, and a master of science in industrial relations from the Lubin Graduate School of Business, Pace University. She earned a doctorate in education from Teachers College, Columbia University, specializing in college teaching and academic leadership. She has taught in the New York City public schools and in colleges in New York and New Jersey, and was a corporate assistant vice president for training.

Carol Stark (cstark@birchrun.k12.mi.us) is assistant superintendent for the Birch Run Area Schools. She has been a high school and community college business teacher, vocational director, assistant principal at the high school level, and middle school principal. Stark was instrumental in the decision of the middle school staff to establish the professional development partnership with Central Michigan University.

Susan Steffel (susan.steffel@cmich.edu) is an associate professor of English at Central Michigan University in Mt. Pleasant, where she has taught young adult literature and English education courses for the past ten years. Previously, Susan taught secondary English for eighteen years at Maple Valley Jr.-Sr. High School in Vermontville, Michigan. She also taught young adult literature and secondary methods courses at Michigan State University where she earned her PhD in English. In 1998, she was named CMU's Towle Professor for her collaborative work in the schools. Susan is active professionally at both the state and national levels and currently serves on the executive board of Michigan Council of Teachers of English.

Chuck Steltenkamp (cstelt@hotmail.com) teaches English at Troy High School in Troy, Michigan. He also teaches writing at Oakland Community College. He has taught for eighteen years and holds a PhD in English from Michigan State University. Steltenkamp previously collaborated with Susan Steffel for an article on student e-mail dialogue that appeared in the *Language Arts Journal of Michigan*. He has also written on coaching for *Scholastic Coach* magazine.

Karin M. Wiburg (kwiburg@nmsu.edu) is an associate professor and coordinator of the Learning Technologies program in the College of Education at New Mexico State University. Her research interest is the design, implementation, and evaluation of technology-integrated learning environments in K–12 and higher education. She has published widely in the field and supervises multiple university–public school collaborative projects. She has worked for more than twenty-five years as a teacher and administrator both in K–12 schools and in higher education.

Les Vozzo (L.Vozzo@uws.edu.au) is a lecturer in secondary education at the University of Western Sydney, Australia. He has held this position for five years after working as a science teacher for twenty years in schools in New South Wales. Vozzo has been a strong advocate for teachers to undertake practitioner research and develop school–university partnerships. As a high school teacher, Vozzo focused on improving the way students approached their learning and at the same time investigated what he could do to improve his own teaching practice. Vozzo has been able to use his classroom research in the professional development of teachers and the training of preservice teachers.

Index

from *Teacher Ideas Press*

CELEBRATING THE EARTH: Stories, Experiences, Activities
Norma J. Livo

Invite young readers to observe, explore, and appreciate the natural world through engaging activities. Livo shows you how to use folk stories, personal narrative, and a variety of learning projects to teach students about amphibians, reptiles, mammals, constellations, plants, and other natural phenomena. Designed to build a Naturalist Intelligence in young learners, these stories and activities are packed with scientific information. **All Levels.**
xvii, 174p. 8½x11 paper ISBN 1-56308-776-6

FAMOUS PROBLEMS AND THEIR MATHEMATICIANS
Art Johnson

Why did ordering an omelet cost one mathematician his life? The answer to this and other questions are found in this exciting new resource that shows your students how 60 mathematicians discovered mathematical solutions through everyday situations. These lessons are easily incorporated into the curriculum as an introduction to a math concept, a homework piece, or an extra challenge. Teacher notes and suggestions for the classroom are followed by extension problems and additional background material. **Grades 5–12.**
xvi, 179p. 8½x11 paper ISBN 1-56308-446-5

SCIENCE AND MATH BOOKMARK BOOK: 300 Fascinating, Fact-Filled Bookmarks
Kendall Haven and Roni Berg

Use these 300 reproducible bookmarks of fascinating facts, concepts, trivia, inventions, and discoveries to spark student learning. They cover all major disciplines of math and physical, earth, and life sciences—ready to copy, cut out, and give to your students. **Grades 4 and up.**
xii, 115p. 8½x11 paper ISBN 1-56308-675-1

WRITE RIGHT! Creative Writing Using Storytelling Techniques
Kendall Haven

Haven's breakthrough approach to creative writing uses storytelling techniques to enhance the creative writing process. This practical guide offers you directions for 38 writing exercises that will show students how to create powerful and dynamic fiction. All the steps are included, from finding inspiration and creating believable characters to the final edit. Activities are coded by levels, but most can be adapted to various grades. **All Levels.**
Xv, 213p. 8½x11 paper ISBN 1-56308-677-8

VISUAL MESSAGES: Integrating Imagery into Instruction
2d Edition
David M. Considine and Gail E. Haley

The authors provide effective media literacy strategies, activities, and resources that help students learn the critical-viewing skills necessary in our media-dominated world. Various media and types of programs are addressed, including motion pictures, television news, and advertising. Activities are coded by grade level and curriculum area. **Grades K–12.**
xxiii, 371p. 8½x11 paper ISBN 1-56308-575-5

For a free catalog or to place an order, please contact:
Teacher Ideas Press
Dept. B051 • P.O. Box 6633 • Englewood, CO • 80155-6633
800-237-6124 • www.lu.com/tip • Fax: 303-220-8843